The River

A Play

Charles Mander

A SAMUEL FRENCH ACTING EDITION

FOUNDED 1830

SAMUELFRENCH-LONDON.CO.UK
SAMUELFRENCH.COM

Copyright © 1979 by Charles Mander
All Rights Reserved

THE RIVER is fully protected under the copyright laws of the British Commonwealth, including Canada, the United States of America, and all other countries of the Copyright Union. All rights, including professional and amateur stage productions, recitation, lecturing, public reading, motion picture, radio broadcasting, television and the rights of translation into foreign languages are strictly reserved.

ISBN 978-0-573-02509-9

www.samuelfrench-london.co.uk

www.samuelfrench.com

FOR AMATEUR PRODUCTION ENQUIRIES

UNITED KINGDOM AND WORLD
EXCLUDING NORTH AMERICA
plays@SamuelFrench-London.co.uk
020 7255 4302/01

Each title is subject to availability from Samuel French,

depending upon country of performance.

CAUTION: Professional and amateur producers are hereby warned that *THE RIVER* is subject to a licensing fee. Publication of this play does not imply availability for performance. Both amateurs and professionals considering a production are strongly advised to apply to the appropriate agent before starting rehearsals, advertising, or booking a theatre. A licensing fee must be paid whether the title is presented for charity or gain and whether or not admission is charged.

The professional rights in this play are controlled by Samuel French Ltd, 52 Fitzroy Street, London, W1T 5JR.

No one shall make any changes in this title for the purpose of production. No part of this book may be reproduced, stored in a retrieval system, or transmitted in any form, by any means, now known or yet to be invented, including mechanical, electronic, photocopying, recording, videotaping, or otherwise, without the prior written permission of the publisher. No one shall upload this title, or part of this title, to any social media websites.

The right of Charles Mander to be identified as author of this work has been asserted by him in accordance with Section 77 of the Copyright, Designs and Patents Act 1988

THE RIVER

This play was specially commissioned for the Plymouth Theatre Company and was first presented at the Plymouth Arts Centre on 23rd November 1978 with the following cast:

Bert Thorne   Barry Woolgar

Richard   Cecil Humphreys

Tina, Richard's sister   Kathi Gordon

The play directed by Simon Dunmore
Setting by John Bell

The action takes place on part of the sea wall on the tidal estuary of a river in Somerset

Time: the present. An early morning in summer

SETTING

A ramshackle hut, a flimsy erection of corrugated iron and driftwood with a door and no windows, stands to the right of the stage. The door is partly open and bears the legend BEWARE OF DOG, handwritten in red paint. Below and to the left of the hut is a small, fragile, flat-bottomed fishing boat, known as a Flattener. The boat is pointed fore and aft, roughly constructed and lies upside down against the weather. It does not have to be very big or functional, but strong enough to be used as a seat from time to time.

This part of the sea wall is the base, and often the living quarters of a solitary salmon and eel fisherman. A once thriving occupation on the river, now virtually extinct. It is not a beautiful place and the river that sweeps on huge tides, unseen through the audience, is not beautiful either. It is a lonely, desolate, untidy jumble of fishing gear and flotsam, salmon traps made of willow, hand nets and cork floats mingle with discarded oil drums, plastic containers and all sorts of rubbish thrown up by the river. Some of the flotsam has been put to good use, oil drums serve as seats for instance, an old plank across two containers a useful bench against the hut. Human occupation has created some semblance of order, but on the whole, the fight against pollution on this part of the river has not been entirely successful.

But in spite of all this, there is an air of grandeur, a feeling of distance, a man could stay here all day and not meet another human being.

The scenery does not have to be substantial. The hut can be no more than a façade with a functional door, the boat little more than a suggestion. The play, however, would benefit from the use of rostrums to create the elevation and uneven structure of the river bank and sea wall and a cyclorama for a sense of space.

THE RIVER

The time is early morning on a summer day. The weather is fair

The stage is empty except for a boy's foot, a dirty canvas training boot and a bit of tattered blue jean protruding from the half open door of the hut. Gulls scream distantly a man whistles away off-stage and calls his dog

Man   Sandy? . . . *(He whistles again)* Sandy?

The foot disappears

(Coming closer) Sandy? . . . I'm telling you! . . . *(He whistles again)* Y'ere, boy . . . y'ere. . . . Damn thee eyes!

A weatherbeaten man in his fifties with a greying beard and ruddy complexion enters. He is scruffy and neglected looking, in old serge trousers, waders, a torn fisherman's jersey and an ancient yachting cap. He carries a pair of binoculars slung round his neck and is not in the best of moods. His name is Bert Thorne and he is probably the last of a generation of river fishermen. He goes to the edge of the bank and yells once more

Bert   Will thee come back y'ere. . . . Bloody pie-eyed mongrel! . . . Sandy! . . . Sandy! . . . *(Muttering)* Damn and blast it! *(He sits on an oil drum and peers across the river with his glasses. After a moment. Over his shoulder)* Come on out. *(He gets no response)* You heard! . . . Come on out!

A boy of about seventeen crawls out of the hut. He is an attractive, sensitive, rather immature lad, with the eyes of a dreamer. He has a slightly apologetic appearance that disguises the obstinacy and arrogance of adolescence. He is rumpled and exhausted, with the remains of a bruise on his cheek. His name is Richard. He wears faded, muddy jeans and a T shirt

Richard   *(hovering apologetically)* How did you know I was here?
Bert   *(still occupied with his glasses)* I'm not daft.
Richard   *(uncertainly)* How are things then? . . . *(Bert says nothing)* . . . *(Trying again)* You going on the river?
Bert   No.
Richard   Why's that then?
Bert   I 'aint got me dog.
Richard   Oh. . . . *(After a moment)* Run off has he?

Bert	Likely.
Richard	Where's he to?
Bert	Dunno ... didn't ask him.
Richard	*(after a while)* That's what I done.
Bert	*(without interest)* Eh?
Richard	Run off.
Bert	Oh ah.
Richard	Had a row with me dad.
Bert	*(thoughtfully)* Dog's randy ... dips his wick.
Richard	I been on the river all night.
Bert	*(putting his glasses down and getting up)* Can't work with a randy dog. *(He looks at Richard for the first time)* You'll be hungered.
Richard	*(brightening)* Could do with a bite.
Bert	That figures. *(He goes into the hut)* ....
Richard	*(following him and speaking with more confidence)* Had a row with me dad.
Bert	I heard you ... the first time. *(He emerges from the hut carrying an old canvas bag)*
Richard	Says I'm to go down the factory .. but I 'aint. *(Fiercely)* Not never I 'aint. ... Never! *(Pause)* I got better things to do.
Bert	*(offering the boy a hunk of bread and cheese)* 'Ere. ... You 'aint getting no more. 'Tis me breakfast.
Richard	Ta. *(He lays into the sandwich. After some moments with his mouth full)* Plashtic Bucketsh!
Bert	Eh?
Richard	*(swallowing energetically)* I shaid ...
Bert	Don't speak with thee mouth full. *(He takes a huge bite himself)* Didn't thee mum ever tell 'ee that?
Richard	I said.... *(Completing the operation)* I said ... plastic buckets!.. That's what I said.
Bert	Oh, ah. *(He picks his teeth)*
Richard	And if he thinks ... if he thinks, I'm going down that grotty factory to make plastic buckets for the rest of me life.... He can piss in the wind!
Bert	Aw shut thee gob. *(He munches in gloomy silence)*
Richard	That's work for morons, that is.... I 'aint going and that's a fact.

Bert does not reply. He is still munching morosely

I run off ... been on the river all night. *(Angrily)* Do you know *(He points to his bruise)* No I 'aint going down the factory ... not never! Never! NEVER!

Gulls clamour in the distance. Bert picks up his glasses

THE RIVER 7

Bert *(scanning the river)* Them gulls is on to summat. Where's that bloody dog to? ... *(He sweeps his glasses round, then returns and peers in the direction of the gulls)* Booger it! 'Tis a salmon by there ... stranded. *(Shouting)* Sandy? ... SANDY! Where be to? *(Giving up)* What's he want to go running after bitches for, at his age?

Richard Going across?

Bert No.

Richard Them gulls'll have that salmon.

Bert Likely.

Richard You could go across in the boat.

Bert No.

Richard Why not?

Bert I 'aint got me dog.

Richard I'd help ... be yer mate.

Bert *(laughing)* You?

Richard Yes, me! *(He scowls at Bert)* Why not? I been here often enough. ... Know the river. ...

Bert Dog's edicated.

Richard *(indignantly)* So am I. ... *(Boastfully)* Got an O level in history.

Bert What's that got to do with fish?

Richard *(casting round)* Well ... I mean ... er. ...

Bert Won't catch no fish with O levels ... for sure.

Richard *(triumphantly)* What about karate then?

Bert Eh?

Richard Karate. *(He makes a pass)* I bet that dog can't do karate.

Bert What's he want that for?

Richard Chopping the fish. *(He leaps about)* Ha! Hoy!

Bert *(watching him with a grin)* Daft little booger. Always was a daft little booger. *(He goes back to searching the river with his glasses)* One of they collie bitches over to Strethun, I wouldn't be surprised. Randy as a toad.

Richard *(subsiding)* I should've chopped him ... used me karate ... give him summat to think about. ... *(He fingers his bruise)* Bastard!

Bert Shut thee gob ... yatter ... yatter. ...

Richard *(indignantly)* Well, 'tis my life 'aint it? ... mine! Not his. Go down the factory, he says ... get off yer backside ... do some honest work for once. And then he smashes me with the back of his hand, like I was ... like I was. ...

Bert My old man smashed plenty of folk ... always at it he was. Didn't mean nowt. Put Johnny Lamb the milkman into hospital two days 'afore he snuffed it. Mind you there were a reason for that ... aye. ... *(He chuckles)* There were a reason.

Richard An animal ... that's what he is ... an animal.

Bert	Powerful skittler however . . . spares, floppers, he were a good skittler.
Richard	Why should I do what he wants? Just 'cause he can't do nowt better himself? Day after day . . . going down that factory, turning out plastic buckets. . . .
Bert	'Course he didn't have no book learning. . . . No O levels . . . couldn't hardly write his name. But he were a damned good skittler. . . .
Richard	That's a living hell down there, a salt mine. Jesus . . . plastic buckets!
Bert	Bide quiet. . . . I'm thinking. . . .
Richard	I bet you could walk to Bristol on the plastic buckets, what my dad's turned out. And what's he got from them, eh? Nowt . . . bloody nowt!
Bert	Got a roof over his head.
Richard	Aye, a council roof . . . so what?
Bert	Got a car.
Richard	Oh yea . . . and a tele and a washing machine and a packet of flaming Fairy Liquid to go with it. If that's what life's about, then you can stuff it. I got better things to do.
Bert	Such as?
Richard	Working the river . . . like you.
Bert	Daft Booger . . . you'd not do that. *(He gets up and goes into the hut)*
Richard	*(gazing into the river)* I will . . . I will . . . I'll work the river.
	Bert returns with some salmon traps and starts to work on them
	Like you . . . like your Dad . . . and my Grandad . . . and all our folk 'afore us, like they done for more'n a thousand years. . . .
Bert	I hate that river.
Richard	Like in olden times . . . when King Arthur was around . . . and Sir Lancelot . . . and Sir Galahad . . . and all them knights. . . .
Bert	Treacherous, she is . . . I hate her.
Richard	*(dreaming)* And as I walked along the bank of the river, I saw a great stone, and it floated on top of the water. . . .
Bert	*(scowling at the river)* Bitch! Whore!
Richard	And into this stone was thrust a sword.
Bert	I hate that river! . . . *(He spits)*
Richard	King Arthur walked on these banks . . . must have . . . he's buried to Glastonbury . . . and Sir Galahad. . . . My heart is as the strength of ten, sang Sir Galahad gladly, because my heart is pure.
Bert	Killed my old man, she did. Sucked him up and spat him out twelve mile in the Channel. . . .

THE RIVER

Richard *(coming out of his reverie)* And do you know why he was pure of heart?
Bert Who?
Richard Sir Galahad. 'Cause he didn't have to go down no factory turning out plastic buckets and muck . . . *(he picks up a container)* . . . like this. Spewing out crap, wasting his life. And that's why I shan't never go down there . . . not never . . . *(He hurls the container off stage)* . . . NEVER!
Bert You've been off with they fairies again.
Richard What?
Bert They fairies—what you always on about—King Galahad—Sir Whatsisname—fairies.
Richard They 'aint fairies. How many times do I have to tell you?
Bert Fairies.
Richard They was real, they lived in these parts. Knights they was . . . on horses.
Bert *(enjoying himself)* Never.
Richard They fished the river, same as you.
Bert Not on horse they didn't.
Richard 'Course not! You thick or summat?
Bert Horses 'aint no bloody good for fishing. That's what thee needs . . . *(He points to the Flattener)* . . . a Flattener . . . and maybe a dog. Thee's got a screw missing son, that's for sure.
Richard I 'aint never! How can I have a screw missing? I've got an O level!
Bert Gor booger!! . . . 'Twas peaceful 'yere 'afore thee came. Go on home.
Richard I 'aint going home . . . not ever!
Bert Bide quiet then.
Richard *(muttering)* Always at you . . . always in your hair. When are you going to do this? . . . When are you going to do that? Go down the factory. . . . Get off your arse . . . layabout! . . . Yobo! . . . Drop out! *(He jumps up)* Sod 'em! I 'aint never going home! I'm staying.
Bert Not 'yere thee 'aint.
Richard Why not?
Bert No fish.
Richard There's plenty of fish.
Bert Who says?
Richard I says.
Bert Oh, ah . . . an expert.
Richard Yes.
Bert On account of the O level, I daresay.
Richard Watch it! . . . I've got karate!

Bert	God save us!... I did forget!

> *Richard scowls at Bert for a moment. Then his mood changes*

Richard	Reckon I'll live here... on the bank. Sleep in the hut like you. We could work together. Make a great team, with my brains and your brawn. And when you've gone, I could take over, carry on the tradition.
Bert	Cheeky little booger!
Richard	Well, you'll not last forever... got to face facts.
Bert	*(chuckling)* Oh aye.
Richard	You 'aint got nobody, no progeny, no relatives. Except old Mrs Underwood up to Rose Cottage, and I can't see her fishing the river. Not with her bad feet.
Bert	I don't want nobody. I've got me dog.
Richard	He's on the way out for starters.
Bert	He bloody 'aint! Got plenty of vigour, go and ask they collie bitches.
Richard	*(hectoring)* Tottering he is... old and mangey. Oh, I know he's edicated, can swim the river and piss on the bad fish. But he's clapped out... half dead....
Bert	*(wagging his finger)* Lay off me dog, boy! That's the best fishing dog in the County.
Richard	'Tis the only fishing dog in the County.
Bert	And there's plenty of life in him, plenty. He's just randy... that's his nature... can't help being randy... we're all randy.
Richard	*(giving Bert a funny look)* Aye... that's what they say... down the village.
Bert	What's that got to do with it?
Richard	Nowt.... *(With arrogance)* Well, I'm not like that.... I'm pure of heart.
Bert	You're three sheets to the wind!
Richard	*(after a moment—slyly)* Supposing summat's happened to that dog?
Bert	He's all right, he's just....
Richard	*(quickly)* Supposing he's dead?... Supposing the milk lorry's had him, or the combine, or Birket's mower....
Bert	*(getting to his feet in some agitation)* He's all right I tell thee... nowt's happened to he....
Richard	He could be legless... chopped up by Birket's mower... a bleeding mass....
Bert	Shut thee gob!
Richard	You'd be knackered without that dog.... You'd have to turn to me, 'cause I'm your only mate. The only one you got left. The only one that knows the river. You'd be knackered!

Bert	Shut up! Or I'll fetch thee one!
Richard	I bet he's dead. I bet he won't piss on no more salmon, won't swim no more rivers....
Bert	I'm telling thee!...
Richard	Face facts! You know what they say about you down the village?
Bert	Don't 'ee go too far boy! Don't 'ee go too far!
Richard	*(rushing into disaster)* Loopy they call you, soft in the head. There's some would put you away... shoot that old dog and put you away in a nut house... they say you're evil, jump out at old ladies and such, and boys too, they say you have it off with sheep when there's....

Bert sends him sprawling with a blow from the back of his hand

	(Clutching his face) Not you?... Not you too? *(He buries his face in his hands)*
Bert	Shouldn't say.... 'Tis dirt... dirt....
Richard	You didn't have to....
Bert	*(anguished)* I did son.... I did... 'cause I 'aint got words. Nobody teached I, how to hurt with words.
Richard	*(writhing extravagantly)* Animal... animal... same as me dad.
Bert	Aye... aye.... *(He shakes his head in misery, then goes to the bank and calls his dog)* Sandy?... Sandy?... Where be to boy? ... come back 'yere... come back... come back....
Richard	*(getting to his feet and sensing Bert's distress)* Don't matter... don't matter if you did smash me.... I'm used to it.
Bert	Go home son... please go home.
Richard	But I love you, Mr. Thorne... always have done... since I were a nipper.
Bert	*(shaking his head)* Get on home... leave I be.
Richard	I don't mind you hitting me... if it makes you feel better.... I don't mind... honest.

Bert stares out at the river

	'Twas only village talk.... 'Taint what I think.
Bert	Village talk... muck! *(Calling)* Sandy?... where be to? Come back to I....
Richard	'Tis all muck down the village, 'cause they 'aint pure of heart. There's not many what's pure of heart these days. Not like in olden times, before them bloody factories came along, polluting things and such. A man could love, in them days... like... Sir Galahad, he loved King Arthur, and it wasn't muck. And if a man was real pure of heart, he could see wonderous things, like stones floating on water....
Bert	*(bleakly)* Stones don't float... they sink.

Richard	Not in them days. Anything could happen in them days. And if a man were real pure like Sir Galahad, he could see a sword in that stone, and pull it out, and strike down evil . . . like . . . like . . . bloody plastics factories. . . .
Bert	Daft booger.
Richard	Reckon I might do that . . . if I see the stone floating along. I'd grab that sword . . . damn right I would. *(He sits dreaming for a moment or two)* He'll come back.
Bert	Reckon?
Richard	Aye . . . reckon.
Bert	'Course he will.
Richard	'Course.

They sit in silence for a time

Richard	But if he don't . . . what are you going to do?

Bert does not reply

	Now, if I was to be your mate. . . .
Bert	No.
Richard	Why not? . . . I'm as good as that old dog. I can piss on fish just as easy as him. I could swim the river too . . . easy. . . . 'Cause I'm tough. . . . *(He goes over to Bert and presents his arm and shoulder)* . . . Feel that . . . muscles like cannonballs.
Bert	*(uneasily)* Get off of I.
Richard	Feel 'em.
Bert	*(moving away)* NO!
Richard	*(grinning slyly)* What's the matter, Mr. Thorne?

Bert says nothing, only stares at the river with loathing

	(teasingly) Don't you want to feel my muscles?
Bert	*(swinging on him and speaking urgently)* Never try to swim that river . . . do thee hear . . . never!
Richard	Why not?
Bert	'Cause she'll have thee. Kill thee as easy as that! *(He snaps his fingers)*
Richard	Dog swims it.
Bert	Different . . . dog knows.
Richard	Can he swim on his back?
Bert	Eh?
Richard	Can he do butterfly? . . . Has he got a life-saving certificate? 'Cause I have.
Bert	Don't make no difference. She'll take thee . . . taken plenty 'afore . . . good strong swimmers . . . makes no difference to the river.
Richard	You scared of the river?
Bert	Oh aye . . . real scared.

THE RIVER

Richard That's 'cause you 'aint pure of heart. If you was pure of heart, she wouldn't scare you. . . . She don't scare me.

Bert *(looking at him—puzzled)* I don't reckon thee, boy. Gor booger it, there's time when I do think thee's soft in the head. Not in this 'ere world, up with they fairies. Goddamm it! Why do 'ee want to come by 'ere for in the first place? 'Tis. . . . *(He looks around)* 'Tis Godforsaken.

Richard Godforsaken? . . . How can you say that? . . . 'Tis paradise.

Bert Well, it may be your idea of paradise. . . . 'Taint mine. I don't see no paradise by 'ere. I don't see nowt but mud and muck. There 'aint hardly nowt can live up 'yere . . . nowt. . . . 'Cause of that there river, she's filthy and murderous and there's nowt can live in her. 'Taint paradise son . . . not up 'yere . . . 'tis desolation.

Richard Don't talk like that. . . .

Bert I hate that river . . . taken my whole life she has. Killed my old man and my brother Geoff, along with him, Flattener and all, just sucked 'em down. There's thirty foot in them tides, she'll turn a coaster when she has the mood. Twenty-five year ago she burst through this 'yere wall and took half the village . . . and now 'tis more than likely, she's taken my dog. *(He stares at the river with loathing)*

Richard You're blind . . . blind! Can't see the truth of this river. . . . You're no better than the others.

Bert There's nowt' yere for thee boy. Only a daft, fisherman, who 'aint got the sense to clear out, and that there river, and filth and muck and desolation. Why do 'ee come? . . . Why do 'ee come by 'ere. . . . 'Taint natural.

Richard Blind . . . that's what you are . . . they have eyes and they see not.

Bert There'll be no more fishing when I'm gone, that's for sure. River's dying . . . there's nowt can live in her. She's dying and there 'aint nothing up y'ere for the likes of thee.

Richard *(wildly)* She 'aint dying! She 'aint! She's being murdered, murdered to death by that bloody factory! 'Tis our river . . . ours . . . and those bastards up there are killing her! Christ! *(He rushes down to the bank)* If only I could get my hands on that bloody sword!

Bert There 'aint no sword. Get down, get out of the clouds.

Richard You don't understand . . . you're ignorant!

Bert *(laughing)* I am that. For if I weren't, I'd have gone off with the others . . . down the factory . . . got myself a place to live . . . a family . . . kids . . . maybe a car. *(Bitterly)* There 'aint no sword, and there 'aint no stone floating on the water. 'Tis all dreams.

Richard *(turning on him)* You traitor . . . you filthy traitor. I loved you . . . like King Arthur you was to me, a light shining in the wilderness . . . God, you're pathetic . . . no better than them . . . full of evil faith . . . and . . . and poor belief. . . .

Bert   Dreams . . dreams . . . put your feet on the earth boy . . . grow up.
Richard   *(furiously)* Jump in the bloody river!

Richard stalks out in a fury

Bert   *(calling anxiously after him)* Where be to?
Richard   *(off)* Get stuffed!
Bert   Don't do nothing daft! . . . Do you hear I? . . . don't do nothing daft! *(Getting no response)* Damn and blast it! *(He goes back to his traps. After a moment he gets up and goes to the river's edge—calls)* Sandy? . . . Sandy? . . . 'Yere, boy . . . 'yere.

Richard rushes in and makes for the hut

Richard   *(scrambling into the hut)* I'm not here. . . .
Bert   What?
Richard   If she asks where I am. I'm not here. . . . I'm dead . . . or summat. . . .
Bert   Who?
Richard   Our Tina . . . she's coming up the wall. . . . What's she playing at? . . . Stupid cow.
Tina   *(off)* Hoy . . . I saw yer.
Richard   Oh God! I'm not here. . . *(He hides in the hut)* I've drownded myself!
Bert   *(shrugging)* Daft booger.

He goes back to his work and after a moment or two Tina enters. She is not the sort of girl one is likely to meet on the river at seven o'clock in the morning. Or indeed at any time. She is an office girl, with an office pallor and apart from an outsized pair of gumboots she is dressed for the office. She is Richard's sister, about eighteen years of age with pallid, rather self-conscious, good looks and sexuality. She is not at her best, being livid and worn out by the long walk. She approaches Bert with some trepidation, well aware of his reputation in the village and half hoping that he might do something outrageous.

Tina   *(feigning surprise)* Oh? . . er . . . Hi.
Bert   Fine day.
Tina   Pardon?
Bert   'Tis a fine day . . . no good for fishing, however.
Tina   Oh. *(She giggles nervously)*

Bert winks at her and gestures towards the hut.

Tina   *(springing back—alarmed)* What?
Bert   *(winking and gesturing—then speaking loudly)* Reckon I'll go behind the hedge.
Tina   Oh . . . er. . . .

THE RIVER 15

Bert   What goes in must come out. . . . *(He starts to go. Then stops)* You seen a dog?

Tina   Pardon?

Bert   Kind of collie-dog with cross eyes.

Tina   *(nervously)* Er . . . no.

Bert   Run off he has . . . 'cause he's randy. *(He winks again and gestures towards the hut)* . . . morning.

> *He strolls out*
> *Tina watches him go, with her mouth open. Then her rage returns and she clumps over to the hut*

Tina   Come out you little shit! *(She gets no answer)* Are you coming out, Richard? . . . or do I have to pull you out by your ears?

Richard   *(emerging)* What you doing up here, Tina?

Tina   God! I could kill you! I could wring your bloody neck! What you bloody well playing at?

Richard   *(picking up a salmon trap and inspecting it casually)* Nowt . . none of your business.

Tina   *(furiously)* You know what you done? You have any idea what's been happening since you buggered off?

Richard   Nope . . . and I don't care.

Tina   You don't care? . . . God! You're a right little shit! They've gone spare! Mum's been climbing up the wall! Dad's been feeding her Valium like Maltesers. Up and down, in and out of the toilet, all bloody night—banging the door. Not had a wink of sleep . . . and I need eight hours. God! I could murder you! God, my feet are killing me. *(She collapses on to a drum and takes her boots off)* God!

Richard   *(examining the trap with studied indifference)* I 'aint going back.

Tina   *(massaging her feet)* Oh, be your age.

Richard   I am being my age. I 'aint going back, so you can piss off!

Tina   *(bridling)* Don't you talk to me like that! 'Aint you got no sense of responsibility?

Richard   I'm leading my own life from now on. I'm staying here.

Tina   *(nodding off stage)* With him?

Richard   Why not?

Tina   *(narrowing her eyes)* What you been up to?

Richard   None of your business.

Tina   *(in a loud whisper)* You know he's a freak?

Richard   Crap. . . .

Tina   He is! You should see the way he looked at me. . . . *(She shivers pleasantly)*

Richard   He don't fancy you, Tina. . . . He's got more sense. *(He looks away across the river glumly)* Dog's the only thing what he fancies.

Tina   Among other things.... *(She makes a face)* ... From what I hear. So you'd best watch your back.

Richard   Village talk ... muck!

Tina   *(putting her boots on)* Coming then?

Richard   No.

Tina   *(indignantly)* Look, shit-face! I been sent up here at God knows what hour in the morning, without any breakfast, and damn-all sleep to bring you back. Mum and Dad are climbing up the wall. Don't you understand?

Richard   I 'aint going back. I 'aint going down that sodding factory.

Tina   Where else can you go, with what you got? ... One O level ... in History.... *(She laughs)* ... I mean nobody's going to take you on because of your scintillating personality are they? ... You're going down that factory and that's that!

Richard   *(obstinately)* I bloody 'aint. I'm not going.

Tina   Okay ... if you want to be a freak.... *(She nods off)* ... Like him.

Richard   *(shouting)* He's not a freak!

Tina   Keep your voice down, for God's sake.... He'll hear.

Richard   He's my mate.

Tina   Oh yea?.... *(She grins knowingly. She looks at her watch)* God! Look at the time. If I'm late for work ... I'll kill you. *(She gets up)* You coming or not?

Richard   I'm staying.

Tina   Don't be thick.

Richard   I tell you, I'm staying. Now piss off!

Tina   They'll have the police on you.

Richard   So what!

Tina   He's a freak, you know. A nutter. They'll have the police on you, and him too ... more than likely.

Richard   You'll be late for work, Tina.

Tina   *(indignantly)* God you're a selfish little prick! Don't you never think of nobody but yourself?

Richard   No ... 'cause nobody thinks of me!

Tina   Oh ... you poor sod. What you think they sent me up here for? To pick mushrooms or summat? Grow up!

Richard   Leave me alone.

Tina   What's so wrong with the factory? Tell me that? What's so wrong with it?

Richard   You wouldn't understand ... you're one of them.

Tina   *(dangerously)* One of what?

Richard   *(vaguely)* Them.... Look, hadn't you better get on down there?

Tina   What am I going to tell Mum and Dad?

Richard   I don't know ... tell 'em I've gone to Glastonbury ... joined the hippies ... that I've gone mad on magic mushrooms and thrown

	myself into the tumultuous river . . . make summat up . . . you're good at that. Only leave me alone—I've work to do.
Tina	Work? . . . Work? . . . You call this . . . work?
Richard	Aye . . . work . . . 'cause that's what we was made for. Tilling the soil . . . fishing the river . . . going free. Not wasting our lives down some bloody factory . . . banging a typewriter and having it off with the chargehand in the tea break.
Tina	You mind what you're saying, Richard! . . . you mind your tongue.
Richard	Well, it's true, 'aint it?
Tina	*(furiously)* If I had the time. . . . If I had. . . .
Richard	But you 'aint . . . 'cause you got to go off at nine o'clock with all them other zombies and lay your eggs in bloody rows like battery hens. Cluck. . . . Cluck . . . bloody cluck . . . cluck. . . .
Tina	Do you know what I'd do if I were them? . . .
Richard	Cluck . . . cluck. . . . .
Tina	I'd exterminate you. . . . I'd put you down!
Richard	*(infuriatingly)* Keep your voice down, Tina . . . he'll hear you. Cluck . . . cluck. . . .
Tina	*(lowering her voice)* There's too many of your sort about. Freaking out. Living off handouts. Sponging off the workers. You're a loafing little shit! That's what you are. . . . Yes. . . . *(She clumps off)* I'd put you down. . . .
Richard	Cluck . . . cluck. . . .
Tina	And don't you bloody cluck at me! You'll be clucking on the other side of your face when Dad hears about this. . . . Cheerio. . . .

Tina goes

Richard	*(shouting after her)* Get stuffed . . . sex mad cow!
Tina	*(off)* Freak!

Richard kicks the ground petulantly. Bert returns

Richard	*(still fuming)* Cow!

Bert looks at him, but says nothing

	What she want to come up here for? . . . Stupid cow.
Bert	Got more sense than what thee has. . . .
Richard	You was listening then?
Bert	Likely.
Richard	More'n likely!
Bert	No sense . . . should've gone with her.
Richard	*(suddenly turning on him—angrily)* Do I stink or summat?
Bert	Eh?
Richard	Why do you keep trying to see me off?
Bert	Just talking sense.
Richard	Christ, you're as bad as they are. Why should I go with that cow?

	Don't owe her nowt . . . don't owe none of them nowt. Didn't ask to be born.
Bert	Neither did I, son, but I'm 'yere.
Richard	Three pints of scrumpy and a quick screw, that's how I come into the world. A bloody inconvenience. . . .
Bert	Ah, shut thee gob!
Richard	That's all you can say, isn't it? . . . "Shut thee gob!" . . . "Go on home!" You're like a bloody parrot, you are!

He sits down and starts to take off his boots

Bert	Hoy! What's on?
Richard	None of your business.
Bert	*(getting angry)* I asked civil . . . now answer civil!
Richard	*(ripping off his shirt)* Going to smash me again are you? . . . Take your hand to me? . . . You don't give a shit what I do! You're no better than the others . . . don't give a shit! *(He starts to remove his trousers)* Fancy me do you? . . . Like this?
Bert	*(shouting)* Get they things back on. . . .
Richard	Or do you fancy our Tina? . . . Hell, I bet you seen more through them glasses than just fish. . . .
Bert	Get they things on, boy! 'Afore I. . . .
Richard	'Afore you what, Mr. Thorne? . . . 'afore you what?
Bert	*(clenching his fists)* Get they clothes on! What's got into thee?
Richard	Just going for a swim, Mr. Thorne . . . nowt wrong with that.
Bert	Thee bloody 'aint!
Richard	Oh yes I am . . . I'm going to swim that river. See what's left of that salmon.
Bert	*(getting in front of Richard)* Oh no, son . . . that thee 'aint.
Richard	I'm not scared. River don't scare me. If that dog can swim her . . . so can I. *(He dodges round Bert and makes for the bank)*
Bert	Come back 'yere—daft bugger . . . she'll kill 'ee. . . . She'll suck 'ee down!
Richard	No . . . she'll not do that . . . 'cause I'm pure of heart. . . .
Bert	*(shouting at Richard—very agitatedly)* What's got into thee? . . . Bloody little vool! Come back 'yere!
Richard	*(taking up a diving position—fantasizing)* And I saw a great stone, and she was floating on the water and I have the strength of ten because my heart is pure and I 'aint scared.
Bert	*(hurling himself after Richard)* Stop it! . . . Stop it! . . . Wake up! Wake up you daft vool. . . . For Christ sakes wake up!

Bert grabs Richard as he is about to dive and brings him to the ground

Richard	*(thrashing about furiously)* Let go of me! Let go! . . . What do you care? . . . What do you bloody well care?

THE RIVER

Bert	I care, boy.... I do!... Now bide quiet!
Richard	*(yelling and fighting)* No you don't! You don't! Give more thought to that bloody dog than you do to me! Let go!
Bert	*(forcing him down)* Thee 'aint going in that river... If'n I do have to knock thee bloody head off!
Richard	Lay off will yer!... What does it matter if I drown myself? Who'd bloody care.... I don't mean nowt to nobody.... I'm just a dirty thought ... shat out to make plastic buckets!... A bloody inconvenience... what does it matter?... *(He subsides—exhausted from his efforts)* ... What does it matter?... What does it matter?
Bert	*(standing over him, and throwing down his clothes)* Put 'em back on!... 'Taint seemly!
Richard	*(making one last defiant gesture)* Freak!... Kinky old freak!

Bert raises his fists

All right! All right!... Don't do yourself an injury. *(He starts to get dressed)*

Bert	More like it.... That's sense. *(Watching Richard closely)* Now then.... What's the game?
Richard	No game.... 'Taint no game.
Bert	Oh ah....
Richard	*(sullenly)* You wouldn't understand.
Bert	*(with some anger)* Now listen 'yere! I 'aint daft! I know what thee has in mind and I don't like it, 'cause I do care for thee, boy.
Richard	That's a joke!
Bert	No. 'Taint. 'Taint no joke. *(He moves away, full of frustration at the inadequacy of his vocabulary)* ... Blast it!
Richard	'Tis a joke ... but it 'aint funny.
Bert	*(turning)* Now harken to I....
Richard	Why should I? Why should....
Bert	*(his voice powerful with ferocity)* Harken! I did say!...

Richard subsides

Now, I'm a lonely man and I 'aint got words. But I care for thee, boy, always have done, since 'ee first come up 'yere as a nipper, with thee head full of fancies, and fairy tales, and daft ways and such. Made I laugh thee did ... and that's powerful good for a man. Thee and that old dog ... just about all I do have for myself ... after ... more'n fifty year ... and that's the truth.

Richard	Reckon?
Bert	Aye ... reckon.
Richard	Then why see me off? Why treat me like I was shit ... if you care for me?
Bert	I don't never do that son ... never.... Thee'll not say I do that.
Richard	Then why can't I be your mate?

Bert	Things change . . . they change . . . and 'taint no good pretending they don't.
Richard	*(dogmatically)* I 'aint going down that factory.
Bert	That factory. . . . *(He laughs)* I'll tell 'ee summat . . . you'll maybe not reckon it . . . for thee's too full of shouting and yelling and cussing to listen to sense. But I'll tell 'ee. When I were your age . . . maybe a bit younger, that there factory were just starting up. Making bricks, she was. 'Twere like the second coming in these 'yere parts. Good money . . . regular work. Never had that 'afore see . . . not by 'ere. That's where I did want to bide . . . and all they young folk. . . . There's many would've selled their souls for a job up there. . . . *(He nods towards the factory)*
Richard	Never! Never!
Bert	Oh aye! . . . A man could eat regular up there, have shoes on his feet and maybe a cycle. That were living . . . that were life . . . that's where I did want to bide.
Richard	Then why didn't you? . . . If you loved the bloody place so much . . . why didn't you bide there?
Bert	'Cause of my old man. He wouldn't have it see. He'd fished the river and his dad afore he, and his dad afore that, and way back. Never done nowt else, there weren't nowt else. So I had to fish the river too, 'cause he said so, and I did never have the guts to stand against him. *(He sits, shaking his head)* Funny 'aint it? . . . 'Cause with thee. . . . 'Tis arse about tit.
Richard	Well, 'tis better up here, than down a bloody factory.
Bert	Reckon?
Richard	Well, of course it is. . . . Christ, I know.
Bert	Do 'ee?
Richard	For sure.
Bert	Ah . . . same as 'ee know, 'ee can swim that river, eh?
Richard	'Course.
Bert	*(getting up)* I'll show 'ee summat. *(He goes down to the river's edge and looks upstream)* Aye, that'll do . . . see it? *(He points out across the river)*
Richard	What?
Bert	That there . . . see her? . . . that there galvanised oil drum, coming by on the tide. . . .
Richard	Oh aye . . . what's so bloody strange about that? . . . Ten a penny they are.
Bert	You just watch her . . . over to Black Rock . . . go on watch her.
Richard	'Aint you got nothing better to do?
Bert	Watch her, I said.
Richard	Well, okay . . . I am.
Bert	Don't 'ee take your eyes off her.

They watch her carefully for a moment

THE RIVER

Richard I don't know what you're trying to prove, I reckon you've gone soft in the head. I mean. . . .
Bert *(triumphantly)* There!
Richard Jesus! . . . *(He whistles)*
Bert Down current . . . 'tis the tide . . . that's a whirlpool. You'll not see that drum, 'afore Steart Island, three mile off.
Richard What about the dog then?
Bert Edicated . . . he don't swim when the tide's like that.
Richard *(moving to the Flattener and sitting)* Maybe . . . maybe. . . . Maybe, I'll get on one of they coasters up to Dunball. Sign on . . . sail to foregn parts . . . like . . . like Barry Island . . . or Swansea. . . . Make my fortune . . . go down a coal mine . . . better than the plastics factory, I mean anything's better than that . . . even a coal mine or is it?
Bert That old dog's been gone a sight too long . . . a sight too long.
Richard Surely . . . there must be . . . I mean . . . I mean. . . .
Bert Sandy? . . . Sandy? . . . where be to? . . . Come on home, boy . . . come on home. Saandy! . . . Saandy! . . . Saandy!
Richard *(suddenly leaping up with excitement)* 'Tis there! 'Tis there!
Bert *(startled)* Gor booger I. . . . Can't 'ee keep quiet for two minutes?
Richard 'Tis the sword! . . . The sword . . . there . . . thrust into a stone, floating on the water. Can't you see her? Flashing in the sunlight . . . by there . . . by there. . . .
Bert Calm down will 'ee . . . mad booger I . . .
Richard Can't you see her? . . . Can't you see her flashing on the water?
Bert I can't see nowt . . . bide quiet will 'ee!
Richard No, you wouldn't . . . you wouldn't. Folk like you don't see nothing . . . can't hardly see your feet. Give us them! *(He snatches the glasses from Bert)*
Bert Hoy!
Richard That sword's special . . . shining and sparkling and wonderous . . . she's special . . . just special . . . just . . . just. . . . *(He thrusts the glasses back at Bert and turns his back on the river)* Oh shit! . . . SHIT!
Bert Aye, there's plenty of that in the river. *(He peers through the glasses)*
Richard *(castigating himself)* Fool! Daft bloody fool! . . . Berk!
Bert Ah, I got her now. . . . Could've fooled I. . . . Would 'ee reckon it. *(He chuckles sympathetically)*
Richard Go on, laugh . . . laugh. . . . 'Tis only a bloody nit, would see summat wonderous in bloody rubbish.
Bert Oh. . . . I wouldn't say that, boy. 'Tis a packing case with tin foil . . . and with the sun on her, flashing like. . . . *(He re-adjusts his glasses)* Well, damn me eyes! . . . *(He takes out an old rag from his pocket and cleans the lenses, his face animated with suppressed excitement)*

Richard	I should've known. . . . Jesus Christ, I should've known. . . . 'Tis always the same. Whenever you look for summat wonderous, turns out muck . . . just muck! 'Tis always the same . . . sod it! Bloody sod it! *(He buries his head in his hands)*
Bert	By God! . . . *(He peers intently through his glasses)* 'Taint so. . . . No, by God, 'taint so. *(He puts his glasses down and moves purposefully to the hut)* Come on, boy . . . lend a hand. *(He disappears into the hut)*
Richard	Lend a hand? . . . what for?
Bert	The dog, boy . . . the dog . . . didn't thee see him?
Richard	No.
Bert	*(in the hut)* Well, he's there. *(He comes to the door and shouts across the river)* Stay there, Sandy, boy . . . don't 'ee try nothing daft now . . . w're coming for 'ee.
Richard	Where is he? . . . I never saw no dog . . . never saw him.
Bert	*(coming out of the hut, with his arms full of boots and gear)* No, thee wouldn't. 'Cause thee was too taken up looking for they swords and stones floating on the water and such. But he were there . . . right behind that old packing case, up to his belly in mud, with the tide about him. *(He laughs)* He'll not be so keen to dip his wick after this. *(Shouting)* Stay there you randy bastard! . . . We're coming after 'ee! *(To Richard)* Well? . . . going to lend a hand? . . . or sit on thee arse all day?
Richard	*(getting up slowly, casually)* Reckon I might . . . reckon you'll need me.
Bert	*(looking at him with a twinkle)* Aye . . . reckon.
Richard	Okay then . . . let's go. *(They start to go. But Richard stops and shouts at the dog)* Hoy, Sandy! . . . you clapped out old rat bag! Do you hear me? . . . Jump in the river . . . jump in the river and drown thee bloody self!
Bert	*(severely. Wagging his finger at Richard)* Hoy. . . . Now then! *(But Richard is grinning innocently and Bert's mood changes)* Naw! Got more sense . . . he'll not jump in the river . . . the dog'll not do that. . . . Dog's got more sense.

They look at each other for a moment or two grinning

Reckon?

Richard	*(still grinning)* Get lost!

Bert slaps him on the back and they hurry off

Bert	*(as he goes, shouting to the dog)* All right me old son . . . we're coming . . . we're coming. . . .

They go out and the play ends

www.ingramcontent.com/pod-product-compliance
Ingram Content Group UK Ltd.
Pitfield, Milton Keynes, MK11 3LW, UK
UKHW021849210426
5322IPUK00022B/556

Philosophy, Death and Education

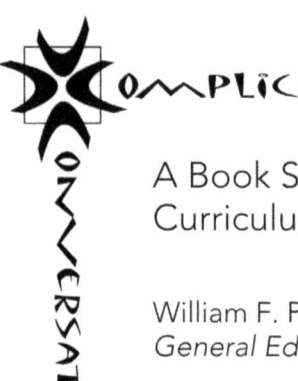

A Book Series of
Curriculum Studies

William F. Pinar
General Editor

Volume 58

The Complicated Conversation series is part of the Peter Lang Education list.
Every volume is peer reviewed and meets
the highest quality standards for content and production.

PETER LANG
New York • Berlin • Brussels • Lausanne • Oxford

Peter Roberts, R. Scott Webster & John Quay

Philosophy, Death and Education

PETER LANG
New York • Berlin • Brussels • Lausanne • Oxford

Library of Congress Cataloging-in-Publication Data

Names: Roberts, Peter, 1963- author. | Webster, R. Scott, 1963- author. | Quay, John, 1964- author.
Title: Philosophy, death and education / Peter Roberts, R. Scott Webster, John Quay.
Description: New York : Peter Lang, 2023. | Series: Complicated conversation; Vol. 58 | ISSN 1534-2816 | Includes bibliographical references
Identifiers: LCCN 2022058020 (print) | LCCN 2022058021 (ebook) | ISBN 9781636670973 (paperback) | ISBN 9781636670980 (ebook) | ISBN 9781636670997 (epub)
Subjects: LCSH: Education—Philosophy. | Thanatology. | Existentialism.
Classification: LCC LB14.7 .R623 2023 (print) | LCC LB14.7 (ebook) | DDC 370.1—dc23/eng/20230113
LC record available at https://lccn.loc.gov/2022058020
LC ebook record available at https://lccn.loc.gov/2022058021
DOI 10.3726/b20692

Bibliographic information published by **Die Deutsche Nationalbibliothek**.
Die Deutsche Nationalbibliothek lists this publication in the "Deutsche Nationalbibliografie"; detailed bibliographic data are available on the Internet at http://dnb.d-nb.de/.

© 2023 Peter Lang Publishing, Inc., New York
80 Broad Street, 5th floor, New York, NY 10004
www.peterlang.com

All rights reserved.
Reprint or reproduction, even partially, in all forms such as microfilm, xerography, microfiche, microcard, and offset strictly prohibited.

Table of Contents

Introduction: Death: An Educational Perspective — vii
    PETER ROBERTS, R. SCOTT WEBSTER & JOHN QUAY

Chapter One: Philosophy, Death and Education — 1
    PETER ROBERTS

Chapter Two: Dancing with Death — 21
    R. SCOTT WEBSTER

Chapter Three: Education, Attention and Transformation — 41
    PETER ROBERTS

Chapter Four: Immortality, Uncertainty and Education — 59
    PETER ROBERTS

Chapter Five: Educating the Horizon of Understanding — 75
    R. SCOTT WEBSTER

Chapter Six: Learning From the Death of Others — 99
    JOHN QUAY

Introduction

Death: An Educational Perspective

PETER ROBERTS, R. SCOTT WEBSTER & JOHN QUAY

Often regarded as one of life's few certainties, death is both instantly familiar to us and deeply mysterious. Every adult will have encountered death in some form, sometimes through the loss of a family member, sometimes less directly via friendships with others or the viewing of news items on television or the Internet. Yet, few take the time to examine death closely and to consider its significance in shaping and potentially educating human lives. This is, in part, because death can be a highly sensitive, 'charged' topic. Indeed, in the realms of human experience and thought, it is perhaps the most difficult subject of all. No reflective person can approach the question of death lightly. In existential terms, death holds us all to account: we cannot escape its clutches, yet we often spend our lives attempting to do just that. Death can be dignified but it can also be horrific. Death takes many forms, and attitudes towards it have varied greatly across different cultures and historical periods. Death generates its own distinctive rituals, reflecting the diverse pathways taken in understanding and responding to this one event that all lives have in common.

For centuries philosophers have wrestled with the meaning and significance of death, examining its ontological, epistemological, ethical, and aesthetic dimensions. The rich body of philosophical work associated with death stretches back more than 2000 years, in both the East and the West. Death has been a favorite theme too for novelists, playwrights, poets, and film-makers, and has featured prominently in the history of painting and sculpture. Death has been studied at length in a range of other academic fields, including Theology, Psychology, Sociology, and Anthropology. Educational theorists have, with some exceptions, been more reluctant to tackle this topic. The reasons for this relative lack of engagement are not clear. It may have something to do with the sensitivities to which we referred above. Or, perhaps it is believed that death is simply not relevant to the theory and/or practice of education and that little of value will come from work in this area. This book sets out to suggest otherwise. Drawing on insights from Kierkegaard, Tolstoy, Unamuno, Heidegger, Levinas, and Weil, among others, the book considers some of the key elements of death as an object of philosophical investigation and explores its educational implications.

It is important at the outset to distinguish the terrain being traversed here from two other areas of inquiry. First, there is an established body of work on 'death education' (Fonseca & Testoni, 2011; Wass, 2004), but this is predominantly concerned with something quite specific: the provision and evaluation of educational initiatives designed to assess and enhance understanding of death and dying. Research in this area has been undertaken in a number of institutions and professional contexts, including schools (Puolimatka & Solasaari, 2006), universities and colleges (Brabant & Kalich, 2008; Fowler, 2008; Mak, 2011, 2013; Wong, 2009, 2017), community rehabilitation centers (Leung et al., 2015), social work and human services (Cacciatore et al., 2015; McClatchey & King, 2015), nursing (Cui et al., 2011), and counselling (Servaty-Seib & Parikh, 2014). There is also a substantial literature on the 'philosophy of death' (Luper, 2009; see also, Cholbi, 2016; Scarre, 2007), but this has been mainly the preserve of those working in philosophy departments, not educationists. Scholarship in this domain has focused on whether death is 'bad' for us (Belshaw, 2000; Bradley, 2004, 2007; Brueckner & Fischer, 1986; Cyr, 2016; Draper, 1999; Feldman, 2013; Hetherington, 2013; Johansson, 2013; Nagel, 1970; Stoyles, 2011), on the nature and desirability of immortality (Fischer, 2005; Fischer & Mitchell-Yellin, 2014; Smuts, 2011), and on whether it is rational to feel fear or terror in the face of death (Bradley, 2015; Draper, 2004; Murphy, 1976), among other areas.

'Death education' has a strong practical and professional focus; the 'philosophy of death' draws primarily on the analytic philosophical tradition in its methods and aims. Other approaches to the question of death are possible. There is, in particular, a longstanding interest in death among existentialist thinkers, and it is in this tradition that we place most chapters of the present volume. Death, we argue, has a valuable educational role to play in allowing us to better understand the nature, meaning and significance of human existence. The book begins, in the first chapter, with an overview of ideas on death from antiquity to the present day. The chapters that follow build on the philosophical foundations established in Chapter 1 and offer fresh perspectives on contemporary themes, questions and debates in education. In keeping with the history of existentialist inquiry, we do not construct rigid boundaries between different genres of work, drawing on literature as well as philosophy and educational theory in developing our argument. We have also been influenced by Kierkegaard and other existentialists in our decision to retain author names for each chapter. This is a co-authored volume, not an edited collection, and this project has been conceived and developed jointly, over several years, in a spirit of collegiality, dialogue and friendship. The book has been designed to be read holistically, not in parts, and there are clear thematic links across chapters. At the same time, we wanted to uphold the existentialist principle of respecting the integrity and distinctiveness of each individual authorial voice. Both our similarities and our differences are important in shaping the ideas developed in the pages that follow. As one of the first book-length studies of death from an educational perspective, there are risks associated with the scholarly exploration undertaken here. But we believe these are risks worth taking. We hope the book will be of interest to anyone who has probed this most troubling of subjects and will open up new areas for educational inquiry.

Chapter 1 starts with the ancient idea of philosophy providing a preparation for death. Often traced back to Socrates, the notion of 'learning how to die' has been explored by a number of thinkers over the ages. Philosophy, as conceived and practiced by the ancient Greeks, was more than an intellectual exercise; it was a way of life. We frequently fear death but there is, as Socrates, Plato and Aristotle counselled, no need for this. Lucretius, following Epicurus, argued that death should be 'nothing' for us. Schopenhauer embraced a similar view, taking the position that if we did not concern ourselves with non-existence before birth, there is no need to do so when facing our non-existence after death. Some writers, such as Montaigne, have stressed the need to always be ready for death, such that when it comes, we will have left nothing undone and will fear neither what we leave behind nor what lies beyond our life on Earth. Death, and its links with uncertainty, despair, freedom, and responsibility in life, also figures prominently in the work of existentialists. The second part of the chapter introduces the work of several key contributors to this tradition, including Kierkegaard, Nietzsche, Heidegger, Unamuno, Sartre, Camus, and Beauvoir. The final section considers the educational implications arising from the preceding philosophical discussion, acknowledging insights already gained by other scholars while also signaling possibilities for further inquiry.

In Chapter 2 our interest in Kierkegaard is picked up again, specifically through his well-crafted pseudonymous author Johannes Climacus. We explore this character of Johannes and come to see him as living a life of skepticism and critical thinking, specifically in the form of doubt. This is understood to be central both for religious faith and for living an authentic – and educated – life which is essential for democracies. Understanding Johannes's character better assists in making sense of his provocation that "the thought of death is a good dancing partner" (Kierkegaard, 1985, p. 8). Here the 'weighty thought' of one's own death provides an opportunity to 'dance' in the form of existential dialectics. This focus upon authentic thinking is provokingly contrasted with the sort of doublethink conceptualized in Orwell's novel *Nineteen Eighty Four* and characteristic of inauthentic life within authoritarian societies. Johannes's 'dancing' with the thought of death enables individuals to resist succumbing to the sort of cognitive dissonance which works against education and democracy.

Chapter 3 considers what it might mean to engage in an educative struggle with death. It takes as its central reference point Leo Tolstoy's famous story, "The Death of Ivan Ilyich" (Tolstoy, 2009). "The Death of Ivan Ilyich" depicts the life of a man who, when suddenly faced with the prospect of his own death, is at first unable to comprehend the reality of his situation. He is angry, fearful and disgusted. As he gradually comes to terms with his mortality, he undergoes a harrowing, but ultimately liberating, process of decreation. Drawing on ideas from the French philosopher and pedagogue Simone Weil (1997, 2001), it is argued that Ivan's experience is consistent with the passage from 'gravity', through the void of intense suffering, toward a state of grace. Educational transformation, this story suggests, is often difficult, uneven and incomplete. From Tolstoy, and from Weil, we can learn that right up to the moment of our death, there is always more work to do.

Miguel de Unamuno, the main focus for Chapter 4, was obsessed with death. Unamuno (1972) identified what he saw as tragic tension in the human condition between our desire for immortality and the doubt cast on this idea by our capacity for critical reason. He saw consciousness as a 'disease' with which we must learn to live. For Unamuno, death was a source of anguish but also of hope. The uncertainties created by death can sustain us; they can give our lives meaning and significance. The quest for immortality, Unamuno shows, is always there for us as human beings, even if we do not recognize its presence or influence over us. We seek to 'live on', in one way or another, and education can reinforce this impulse. Education does not allow us to forget; it seeks to preserve something of us, and the ideas we develop, while also playing its part in undermining structures of belief that might hitherto have nourished us. Unamuno's educational purpose, as a writer, was to 'wake up' his readers; he wanted to create lives of restless longing. He was aware that the restlessness he fostered might lead to suffering, to inner turmoil, but he felt this was preferable to being 'asleep'. To suffer, he pointed out, was still to live, and for Unamuno, this was always preferable to the prospect of nothingness. The chapter situates these ideas in the context of Unamuno's broader ontology and epistemology and assesses his educational prescription from an ethical point of view.

In Chapter 5, we again continue with the importance of the ontological disposition of 'wakefulness' through the concept of death anxiety. The educational significance of this can be located in the exhortation given by existential philosophers to live an authentic life. A key characteristic of becoming authentic is being able to *choose* for oneself what is to be one's ultimate values and purpose for life, because it is through such choosing that one's authentic self is disclosed. However, such choosing also involves experiencing a sense of anxiety, and it is 'death anxiety' in particular which is considered in this chapter to be of most assistance. Being educational as well as existential, working through one's death anxiety can expand our 'horizon of meaning' as explained by Gadamer, from which we give sense and meaning to all of our experiences. By including insights from Dewey and Vygotsky we explore how this horizon can itself be challenged and *re*formed, allowing individuals to experience educative growth.

Like Chapters 2 and 5, Chapter 6 highlights the philosophical interrelatedness of death and authenticity, but this time in the phenomenological and methodological sense striven for by Heidegger. The ontological import of Heidegger's authenticity and inauthenticity is not lost on Levinas, who critiques Heidegger's phenomenological interpretation of death. For Levinas, it is the death of others, rather than one's own, which has the highest priority philosophically. Chapter 6 therefore begins by identifying the challenge to education of categorial murder (Bauman, 2004), wherein killing is justified via ontological categorization. The question is asked, 'Can education work against categorial murder?' In responding to this question, we provide a detailed account of the well-known philosophical challenge made by Levinas to the phenomenological ontology of Heidegger (see for example Bax, 2017; Cohen, 2006; Taminiaux, 1997, 2008). We draw on the differing phenomenological interpretations of death described by Heidegger and Levinas, to then consider the consequences for education, for teaching and learning. These consequences include those described by philosophers of education who have brought Levinas's philosophical account into educational discourse, including Biesta (2003, 2008) and Todd (2003, 2008). However, in this chapter we reach a broader conclusion which ties teaching and learning to both ethics and ontology, by emphasizing interconnections between infinity and totality. Education is not just about truth within a totality; it must embrace the limitless possibilities that the other brings via the face to face relation. In this way, education is about the good beyond being; and there is hope, then, that education can work against categorial murder. This is what can be learned from the death of others.

Together, these chapters are intended to demonstrate the importance of death as a theme for educational inquiry and to show how the philosophical examination of death can contribute to the practices of teaching and learning. Education is a constant of life, and death is the certain uncertainty that characterizes life. In this way, death is implicated in any philosophical account of education. We should stress that the philosophical terrain covered in this volume constitutes just one part of a much bigger picture; there are many other theoretical perspectives that might be brought to bear on questions relating to death and education. This book appears in a series with a focus on complicated conversations, and few subjects lend themselves more readily to consideration in this light than death. Death has always been a complex and contested topic, and we believe there is much that can be gained by fostering further dialogue in this area among educationists. As we have prepared the book, we have recognized and respected our differences, on matters of theoretical detail, in our styles of writing, and in the ways we have responded to practical ethical dilemmas in daily life. Death, as a philosophical problem and an ever-present social reality, can repel but it can also attract, drawing us closer together in seeking to unravel some of its mysteries. Death can provide the stimulus for deep reflection on why and how we educate. It can help us to see ourselves in a new light, and in so doing, allow us to better appreciate what others, who must also face this certain uncertainty, have to offer.

REFERENCES

Bauman, Z. (2004). Categorial murder, or: How to remember the Holocaust. In R. Lentin (Ed.), *Re-presenting the Shoah for the 21st century* (pp. 25–39). Berghahn Books.
Bax, C. (2017). Otherwise than being-with: Levinas on Heidegger and community. *Human Studies, 40*, 381–400.
Belshaw, C. (2000). Death, pain and time. *Philosophical Studies, 97*(3), 317–341.
Biesta, G. (2003). Learning from Levinas: A response. *Studies in Philosophy and Education, 22*, 61–68.
Biesta, G. (2008). Pedagogy with empty hands: Levinas, education, and the question of being human. In D. Egéa-Kuehne (Ed.), *Levinas and education: At the intersection of faith and reason* (pp. 198–210). Routledge.
Brabant, S., & Kalich, D. (2008). Who enrolls in College death education courses? A longitudinal study. *Omega, 58*(1), 1–18.
Bradley, B. (2004). When is death bad for the one who dies? *Noûs, 38*(1), 1–28.
Bradley, B. (2007). How bad is death? *Canadian Journal of Philosophy, 37*(1), 111–127.
Bradley, B. (2015). Existential terror. *Journal of Ethics, 19*, 409–418.
Brueckner, A. L., & Fischer, J. M. (1986). Why is death bad? *Philosophical Studies, 50*, 213–221.
Cacciatore, J., Thieleman, K., Killian, M., & Tavasolli, K. (2015). Braving human suffering: Death education and its relationship to empathy and mindfulness. *Social Work Education, 34*(1), 91–109.
Cholbi, M. (Ed.). (2016). *Immortality and the philosophy of death*. Rowman & Littlefield.
Cohen, R. A. (2006). Levinas: Thinking least about death – contra Heidegger. *International Journal for Philosophy of Religion, 60*, 21–39.
Cui, J. et al. (2011). What do nurses want to learn from death education? A survey of their needs. *Oncology Nursing Forum, 38*(6), 402–408.
Cyr, T. W. (2016). A puzzle about death's badness: Can death be bad for the paradise-bound? *International Journal of the Philosophy of Religion, 80*, 145–162.
Draper, K. (1999). Disappointment, sadness, and death. *The Philosophical Review, 108*(3), 387–414.

Draper, K. (2004). Epicurean equanimity towards death. *Philosophy and Phenomenological Research*, 69(1), 92–114.

Feldman, F. (2013). Brueckner and Fischer on the evil of death. *Philosophical Studies*, 162, 309–317.

Fischer, J. M. (2005). Free will, death, and immortality: The role of narrative. *Philosophical Papers*, 34(3), 379–403.

Fischer, J. M., & Mitchell-Yellin, B. (2014). Immortality and boredom. *Journal of Ethics*, 18, 353–372.

Fonseca, L. M., & Testoni, I. (2011). The emergence of thanatology and current practice in death education. *Omega*, 64(2), 157–169.

Fowler, K. L. (2008). 'The wholeness of things': Infusing diversity and social justice into death education. *Omega*, 57(1), 53–91.

Hetherington, S. (2013). Where is the harm in dying prematurely? An Epicurean answer. *Journal of Ethics*, 17, 79–97.

Johansson, J. (2013). Past and future non-existence. *Journal of Ethics*, 17, 51–64.

Kierkegaard, S. (1985). *Philosophical fragments* (H. V. Hong & E. H. Hong, Trans). Princeton University Press.

Leung, P. P. et al. (2015). The effects of a positive death education group on psycho-spiritual outcomes for Chinese with chronic illness: A quasi-experimental study. *Illness, Crisis & Loss*, 23(1), 5–19.

Luper, S. (2009). *The philosophy of death*. Cambridge University Press.

Mak, M. H. J. (2011). Quality insights of university students on dying, death, and death education – A preliminary study in Hong Kong. *Omega*, 62(4), 387–405.

Mak, M. H. J. (2013). Quality insights of university teachers on dying, death, and death education. *Omega*, 66(2), 173–194.

McClatchey, I. S., & King, S. (2015). The impact of death education on fear of death and death anxiety among human services students. *Omega: Journal of Death and Dying*, 71(4), 343–361.

Murphy, J. G. (1976). Rationality and the fear of death. *The Monist*, 59(2), 187–203.

Nagel, T. (1970). Death. *Noûs*, 4(1), 73–80.

Puolimatka, T., & Solasaari, U. (2006). Education for death. *Educational Philosophy and Theory*, 38, 201–214.

Scarre, G. (2007). *Death*. Acumen.

Servaty-Seib, H. L., & Parikh, S. J. T. (2014). Using service-learning to integrate death education into counselor preparation. *Death Studies*, 38, 194–202.

Smuts, A. (2011). Immortality and significance. Philosophy and Literature, 35(1), 134–149.

Stoyles, B. J. (2011). Challenging the Epicureans: Death and two kinds of well-being. *The Philosophical Forum*, 42(1), 1–19.

Taminiaux, J. (1997). The early Levinas's reply to Heidegger's fundamental ontology. *Philosophy & Social Criticism*, 23(6), 29–49.

Taminiaux, J. (2008). Levinas and Heidegger: A post-Heideggerian approach to phenomenological issues. *Journal of Chinese Philosophy*, 35, 31–46.

Todd, S. (2003). Levinas and education: The question of implication. *Studies in Philosophy and Education*, 22, 1–4.

Todd, S. (2008). Welcoming and difficult learning: Reading Levinas with education. In D. Egéa-Kuehne (Ed.), *Levinas and education: At the intersection of faith and reason* (pp. 170–185). Routledge.

Tolstoy, L. (2009). *The death of Ivan Ilyich and other stories* (R. Pevear & L. Volokhonsky, Trans.). Vintage.
Unamuno, M. de (1972). *The tragic sense of life in men and nations* (A. Kerrigan, Trans.). Princeton University Press.
Wass, H. (2004). A perspective on the current state of death education. *Death Studies, 28*, 289–308.
Weil, S. (1997). *Gravity and grace* (A. Wills, Trans.). Bison Books.
Weil, S. (2001). *Waiting for God* (E. Craufurd, Trans.). Perennial Classics.
Wong, W. (2009). The growth of death awareness through death education among university students in Hong Kong. *Omega, 59*(2), 113–128.
Wong, W. (2017). The concept of death and the growth of death awareness among university students in Hong Kong: A study of the efficacy of death education programmes in Hong Kong universities. *Omega: Journal of Death and Dying, 74*(3), 304–328.

CHAPTER ONE

Philosophy, Death and Education*

PETER ROBERTS

Death is sometimes treated as a highly 'sensitive' topic; as a subject best avoided. "Modern Western culture," Arcilla (1997) observes, "has increasingly distanced itself from death" (p. 449). Yet, history is replete with examples of individuals who have rubbed against the grain and talked openly about death – both in the abstract and in relation to their own anticipated demise. Death is of interest both for what we know about it (in observing and living with others who die) and for what we do not know about it ("What will happen to me after I die?"). Death seems, on the face of it, to lend itself well to both philosophical and educational inquiry. For, if, as Socrates claimed, philosophy prepares us for death, this suggests an educational process ("*How* does it prepare us?") that warrants careful investigation. It is, however, not just philosophy that prepares us for death but also death that prepares us for philosophy. Our understanding of death can exert a powerful but often unnoticed influence over our ontological and epistemological views, our ethical commitments, and our educational endeavors.

Death, as Pinar (2011) puts it, "provides a focus for living" (p. 5). Death can prompt us to ask: Why are we here? What is our purpose? How can we give our

---

* The original version of Chapter 1 was published as Roberts, P. (2017). Philosophy, death, and education. In G.W. Noblit (Ed.), *Oxford Research Encyclopedia of Education* (pp. 1–19). Oxford University Press. https://doi.org/10.1093/acrefore/9780190264093.013.1271. Small parts of the Introduction also draw on this chapter. With the permission of Oxford University Press.

lives meaning and significance? Death can help us in setting priorities; in deciding what really matters, given the limited time available to us. Beginning with the ancient Greeks, the first part of this chapter introduces the notion of 'learning how to die', linking this with the concept of philosophy as a way of life. This is followed, in the second section, by an examination of existentialist approaches to the question of death. Attention will be paid to the work of Kierkegaard, Nietzsche, Unamuno, Heidegger, Sartre, Beauvior, and Camus. Several of these thinkers also feature in later chapters. The idea of fearing death, considered in the first part, is extended in the second section with reference to the existentialist themes of consciousness and subjectivity, angst and despair, and freedom and responsibility. The final part builds on both of the preceding sections, teasing out in more explicit detail some of the possibilities for philosophical work in education on death, with special attention to the social nature of teaching and learning.

LEARNING HOW TO DIE: PHILOSOPHY AS A WAY OF LIFE

Death has featured as a subject for reflection from the beginning of recorded Western history. From its representation in ancient cave paintings and early forms of sculpture to its appearance as a dominant theme in the epic Homeric poems, *The Iliad* and *The Odyssey* (Homer, 1992, 2003), death has, in subsequent centuries, cast its shadow over Western art and culture. The question of what happens to us when we die has been a key concern in most traditions of religious thought. Across the ages, death has been present as a concrete reality to be faced, directly or indirectly, by individuals and families negotiating their way in the world. Human beings have always had to deal with death, in one way or another, sometimes with fear, shock, grief, or anger, at other times with quiet acceptance or a sense of relief. But what might it mean to make death the subject of philosophical investigation? In the West, it is the figure of Socrates as depicted in Plato's dialogues to whom we most frequently turn in seeking a starting point for inquiry. In the *Phaedo*, Socrates claims that philosophy is a preparation for death. If we truly love wisdom, Socrates maintains, we will want, as far as possible, to free our souls from our bodies. We will not be afraid of dying, for in death this separation finds its ultimate fulfilment (Plato, 2003, pp. 128–130). Socrates is of interest not just for his views on death but also for the example he provided in the manner of his own death. Accused by the Athenian authorities of impiety and corrupting the minds of the young, he was put to death in 399 BCE. By all accounts, he remained calm and composed right up to the last moment of his life, reinforcing, throughout his trial, the central tenets of his philosophy and the value of his mode of life. He could, it has often been noted, have saved himself, yet he did not do so, maintaining his commitment to the rule of law and retaining his philosophical principles until the end.

Socrates is, along with Hypatia, Thomas More, Giordano Bruno, and Simone Weil, among others, an example of a philosopher who was willing to "die for an idea" (Bradatan, 2015, p. 5). Whatever the differences between these thinkers in their circumstances, responsibilities and worldviews, all shared a commitment to the idea of philosophy as a something practiced, something not merely studied but *lived* (p. 5). This conception of philosophy, as a "way of life," with "spiritual exercises," is evident in the work of the Stoics and the Epicureans as well as the writings of Plato and Aristotle (Hadot, 1995). From the Middle Ages to modern times, this orientation to the nature and purpose of philosophical work has largely been ignored; philosophy has become nothing more than "philosophical discourse" (p. 269; see also Neiman, 1997, pp. 457–458). There have been some notable exceptions to this discursive turn – Kierkegaard, Nietzsche and Wittgenstein were all admired by Hadot – but the dominant tendency has been to separate philosophy from the concerns of the "concrete, living, and perceiving subject" (Hadot, 1995, p. 273); to restrict philosophical activity to a kind of "technical jargon reserved for specialists" (p. 272). Rather than focusing on ever increasing layers of abstraction, philosophy as a way of life has as its central focus the existing individual (Kierkegaard, 2009). But if we are concerned with the problem of existence, we are also concerned with the problem of non-existence. In considering what it means to live, or to be, we cannot, if our inquiry is comprehensive, avoid questions relating to what it means to die. As Bradatan points out, "[w]hat philosophy as an art of living boils down to is, paradoxically, learning how to face death – an art of dying" (2015, p. 5).

Approaches to the question of death have often circled around the idea of fear. Should we be afraid of death? Our answer to this question will often depend on what we understand death to be. Among the ancients, Lucretius (1999) is perhaps the best known exponent of the thesis that death should hold no fear for us. Death, Lucretius says, should be "nothing" to us (p. 92). "Look back upon ages of time past," the long periods of time before we were born, and we will see that they have "been nothing to us, nothing at all" (pp. 96–97). This is the mirror that Nature holds up for us: the image of what death will be for us – nothing horrible, nothing sad (p. 97). If we are mortal in mind, body and spirit, death for the individual is the end of life. After death, there is, for each us, nothing, just as before our birth there was, for each of us, nothing. For Lucretius, as for his mentor Epicurus, "fearing what it will be like to exist after we die is as silly as revulsion at the thought of what it *was* like to not exist before we were born" (Luper, 2009, p. 63). As Epicurus puts it, "so long as we exist, death is not with us; but when death comes, we do not exist" (in Enright, 1987, p. 8). A similar view was adopted, many centuries later, by Schopenhauer: "it is irrefutably certain that non-existence after death cannot be different from non-existence before birth, and is therefore no more deplorable than that is" (Schopenhauer, 1966, vol. 2, p. 466). For Lucretius, not only is there no need for fear in the face of the nothingness of non-existence; death might even be considered something to be welcomed. Death releases us from our cares and relieves us from the pain we experience in life. There is no need to grieve, for in death we find the rest of a permanent sleep (Lucretius, 1999, p. 95).

Just as our understanding of death bears on how we live our lives – including whether we live in fear of death – so too does our understanding of life, and particularly what constitutes a *good* life, bear on our approach to death. Plato's (1974) concept of the Good rests on the metaphysical foundations of his theory of Forms. For Plato, all specific, particular acts of goodness participate in something higher: the Form of the Good. Forms are ideals; they are timeless and universal. Plato conceives of the soul as immortal. He calls "anything that harms or destroys a thing evil, and anything that preserves and benefits it good" (p. 441). The soul has its own particular fault – moral wickedness – but even this cannot destroy it. Indeed, there is, as Plato sees it, no evil, either the soul's own or another's, that can weaken or annihilate the soul. The soul must therefore "exist for ever" (p. 443). For Plato, goodness is to be valued not just for the rewards it brings in life but for those it furnishes after death. Pursing justice, with wisdom, will bring happiness in this life and the next (pp. 453, 455). Aristotle (1976), like his teacher Plato, believed a good life is a happy life. He also accepted, with Plato, that the rational person would be happy. But where for Plato, specific acts of goodness must be understood in relation to the greater goodness that is the Form of the Good, for Aristotle goodness lies in the application of practical reason in everyday human activity. "The quality of a life," Aristotle argues, "is determined by its activities" (p. 84). This will be evident in the virtues we exhibit; virtuous activities make us happy. Happiness is "an activity of the soul in accordance with perfect virtue" (p. 87). The happy person will remain happy throughout life, and die in this same state (pp. 83–84). Happiness is "an *end* in every way utterly final and complete" (p. 84).

Spinoza (1969) shares with Socrates and Plato a faith in the power of reason to set us free, and argues that if we are directed by reason we will be led not by the fear of death but by a desire for what is good. Wisdom for Spinoza should be a "meditation not of death but of life" (p. 187). Reflection on death should be avoided, "since the fear of death diminishes a person's power to live and her ability to act according to her genuine interests" (Puolimatka & Solasaari, 2006, p. 204). Others have responded to the fear of death in quite the opposite way. Montaigne (1991), for example, acknowledges the hold that death has over us – the fear it creates – but suggests that our best response is to "stand firm" and "fight" death (p. 96). Death, Montaigne observes, follows us all and cannot be avoided; no one can escape from its clutches. Faced with this reality, what should we do? We should, Montaigne counsels, "begin depriving death of its greatest advantage over us" (p. 96). We need to rid death of its alien character; its strangeness. "Let us frequent it, let us get used to it; let us have nothing more often in mind than death. At every instant let us evoke it in our imagination under all its aspects" (p. 96). Montaigne continues: "We do not know where death awaits us: so let us wait for it everywhere. To practice death is to practice freedom. A man who has learned how to die has unlearned how to be a slave" (p. 96). We must, Montaigne argues, always "have our boots on" (p. 98); we should, in our daily activities, be constantly ready for death, as we do not know when it will approach us. As far as practically possible, we must never put off until tomorrow what can be done today. Nature can come to our aid with a sudden death, allowing us no time to be fearful. Illness too, with the pain and suffering it entails, can make the prospect of death seem less unpalatable. Nature is also kind to us in making the process of aging a gradual affair; were we to be thrust into old age without warning, we might find the change unbearable. The length of our life should not concern us, for when considered in relation to all that exists in Nature, all human lives are short (pp. 100–103).

For Montaigne, life and death are intimately related. Death is a part of us, from the moment we are born. We are "*in* death" while we are "*in* life" (p. 103). After life, we are dead, but during life we are *dying* (p. 103). Life's continual task, Montaigne claims, "is to build your death" (p. 103). There is little point in spending our lives in anguish over the one thing that will free us from all anguish: death (p. 102). Taking up the Socratic challenge, but in a more expansive fashion, Montaigne speaks of strengthening our souls to better prepare ourselves for death. We must "educate and train" our souls to be unafraid of the encounter with death that awaits us all (p. 101). Death, Montaigne contends, should be less feared than nothingness (p. 105). Death should not concern us in life because alive, we *are*; neither should death concern us in death, for in death we *are no more* (p. 105). More frightening than death itself, Montaigne believes, are the forms of expression often associated with death: "those terrifying grimaces and preparations with which we surround it" (p. 107). Weeping and wailing, doctors and ministers, beds kept in darkness: all of these can make death seem horrifying where it need not be so (p. 107). Preparing ourselves for death means *letting go* of everything, having, as it were, said as many of our goodbyes as we can already, and "regretting nothing except life itself" (p. 98). We should be "ready to leave" at anytime, anywhere (p. 98). This may be on the battlefield or in a hospital but it may also be in the middle of the most mundane activities of daily life. "I want Death to find me planting my cabbages," Montaigne says in a famous phrase, "neither worrying about it nor the unfinished gardening" (p. 99).

EXISTING AND DYING: CONSCIOUSNESS, FEAR AND FREEDOM

Thus, for Montaigne, as for Socrates, 'learning how to die' involves developing a form of readiness that is built on an overcoming of our fear of death. For Socrates, the path to readiness is explicitly philosophical; for Montaigne, readiness emerges through everyday reflection and practice. Our fear of death diminishes, Montaigne believes, when we come to see that death is part of life, part of us, part of our very being. But what of situations where, for an existing individual (to use the Kierkegaardian terminology), this fear cannot be overcome? Can we still conceive of death as having educative value in such circumstances? One thinker who is instructive in considering this possibility is Miguel de Unamuno. Unamuno was obsessed with the question of death. In his philosophical and theological writings and in his literary work (Unamuno, 1972, 1996, 2000), he explores fundamental problems relating to reason, faith and emotion. He finds, contrary to the position adopted by Socrates and Montaigne, that reason and reflection lead not to a stronger sense of acceptance and readiness in dealing with death but to greater distress and uncertainty. Unamuno argues that there is an irreconcilable, tragic tension between our longing for eternal life and the dictates of the critical, inquiring mind. As human beings, we have been endowed with a consciousness that allows us to grasp the ideas of temporality and finitude. We have a distinctive awareness of death, not just as an abstract subject but as something we as individuals will each have to face. Yet, we are also endowed with wants and feelings. Reason tells us that the idea of immortality is an absurdity, yet this does nothing to dampen our desire to go on living. Trying to make faith and reason compatible with each other by providing 'proofs' for life after death is, from Unamuno's point of view, a fruitless task. Philosophy cannot prepare us adequately for death; it can at best deepen our understanding of the suffering we experience in living with the "disease" that is consciousness (Unamuno, 1972).

Unamuno's work raises other intriguing questions. For Epicurus, Lucretius and Schopenhauer, the idea of non-existence provided a philosophical antidote to the fear of death; for Unamuno, the prospect of nothingness was horrific. Being released from the cares of the world, from the pain of living, was no consolation for Unamuno if what followed from life was nothingness. Unamuno wanted to live on, even if this was in a state of despair. To suffer, as he saw it, was still to live. Living on, as the imperfect, distinctive individual that he was, was more important to Unamuno than anything else (Roberts & Saeverot, 2018). Questions about the existence or non-existence of God were, it might be said, of interest to Unamuno only insofar as they related to questions about immortality. And in Unamuno's philosophy, the question of death is really a question of life. Death haunts all of Unamuno's work precisely because it provides a threat to the life he so desperately wanted to continue to embrace. It is easy to dismiss Unamuno's unusually intense desire for immortality as an idiosyncratic, irrational, impossible dream. But the uncompromising nature of his appeal prompts us to delve deeper in thinking about life and death. We might ask: Why, if at all, would or should we want to live? The Stoic philosopher Seneca (2007) claimed that nothing was so deceptive, and nothing so treacherous, as the life of a human being; no one "would have accepted it as a present, if it were not given to us in a state of ignorance" (p. 78). "Accordingly," Seneca suggests, "if the greatest fortune is not to be born, the next best … is to die after a short life and be restored to one's original state" (p. 78). The question of whether we should want to live *at all* is, of course, not the same as the question of whether we should want to *live on*, having lived. Montaigne (1991) felt that eternal life would not be a blessing but a curse. This idea has also been explored in literature by, for example, Simone de Beauvoir (1992), who in *All Men are Mortal* depicts the boredom, frustration, sense of purposelessness, and despair experienced by a man who cannot die.

Existentialist thinkers, both before and after Unamuno, have made the relation between death and life central to their inquiries. Kierkegaard (2009) regards the question of immortality as a deeply personal matter. His principal concern is not with abstract reflection and 'objective' truth; his focus is, as noted earlier, on the existing individual and on the "subjective truth" that is pursued through looking inwards. For Kierkegaard, subjectivity *is* truth, or at least the truth that is most worthy of our attention. Immortality has long been regarded as a topic of interest but it has frequently been treated merely as an object for abstract investigation – as a "learned question" (p. 145). Against this approach, and anticipating the stance that would later be taken by Unamuno, Kierkegaard argues that the question of immortality is "a question of inwardness, which the subject by becoming subjective must put to himself" (p. 145). "Objectively," Kierkegaard continues, "the question cannot be answered at all, for it is not one that can be put objectively, since immortality is precisely the intensification and highest development of the developed subjectivity" (p. 145). It is not possible to 'prove', systematically, that immortality exists. Attempts to do so are, as Kierkegaard sees it, a waste of time and effort. From a systematic standpoint (Kierkegaard has Hegel's 'system' in mind here), the "whole question is nonsense" (p. 146). Kierkegaard adopts a somewhat different perspective: the 'proof' of immortality lies not in rational argument, or in 'objective' knowledge, but in the *interest* itself. Immortality is "subjectivity's most passionate interest" (p. 146). Objectively, it is irrelevant; subjectively, for the existing individual, it matters more than anything else.

Developing an appropriately receptive attitude toward the possibility of immortality, for oneself, is more important than finding definitive, 'objective' answers to one's questions. For Kierkegaard, "a person who passionately strives after the highest good advances to a qualitatively higher form of existence" (Puolimatka & Solasaari, 2006, p. 206). Asking about immortality, wondering about it, pondering it: these inner activities are themselves forms of action for the existing individual. More than this, though, the individual might consider how to conduct him- or herself to express his or her immortality. Whether the individual *actually* expresses his or her immortality is not the point; for the time being, the task of asking, of inquiring, is sufficient. "For the time being" in this context may be for a lifetime, which is, after all, but a brief moment when considered in relation to eternity (Kierkegaard, 2009, p. 148). It is the process of searching that is significant here. The importance of this task becomes all the clearer when we reflect on how little time we have. An awareness of the limits of a human lifetime can "sharpen the distinction between the essential and the trivial and emphasize the urgency of discovering the right rank ordering of values" (Puolimatka & Solasaari, 2006, p. 206). A "bold commitment" is needed; indifference inhibits our ability to advance in our understanding of our ourselves and the good (p. 206). An existing individual "cannot simply observe life as an outsider; she has to commit herself and take the risk of commitment in order to be able to apply the test of reality" (p. 206). It is *passionate* interest and commitment with which Kierkegaard is concerned, even if this places him at odds with the spirit of his times. Passion is, for Kierkegaard, "the very height of existence"; in passion, "the existing subject is infinitized in the eternity of imagination, and yet is also most definitely himself" (Kierkegaard, 2009, p. 166).

While Nietzsche differed from Kierkegaard in many respects, he shared a similar view of philosophy not as a dry, abstract, purely theoretical affair but as a passionate mode of life. In *Thus Spoke Zarathustra*, Nietzsche instructs us to "Die at the right time" (1976, p. 183). "Everybody considers dying important," he notes, "but as yet death is no festival. As yet men have not learned how one hallows the most beautiful festivals" (p. 183). He implies that if we have not lived at the right time, we cannot die at the right time; in such cases, it would have been better to never have been born. If we "consummate" our lives, we can die "victoriously" (p. 183). Next best is to "die fighting and to squander a great soul" (p. 184). Nietzsche wants a "free" death: one, he says, that "comes to me because *I* want it" (p. 184). If we have a "goal and an heir," we will want death at the right time for them (p. 184). If we want fame, good timing is even more important. A quick death is, as Nietzsche sees it, preferable to the slow, patient death usually prescribed. With maturity, our approach to death changes: "in the man there is more of the child than in the youth, and less melancholy: he knows better how to die and to live" (p. 185). Knowing how to die and to live means being "[f]ree to die and free in death, able to say a holy No when the time for Yes has passed" (p. 185). Nietzsche says of his own death (through the voice of Zarathustra), "I want to die myself that you, my friends, may love the earth more for my sake;

and to earth I want to return that I may find rest in her who gave birth to me" (pp. 185–186).

Heidegger, in his magnum opus *Being and Time*, argues that we cannot consider what comes after death without a full ontological understanding of death itself. We sometimes talk about the experience of death, but this presupposes a concept of death. Psychologies of dying are less about dying itself and more about the life of the dying person (Heidegger, 1996, p. 230). If death is seen as the end of Da-sein – of "being-in-the-world" – there remains the question of whether after death "another being is still possible, either higher or lower, whether Da-sein 'lives on' or even, 'outliving itself', is 'immortal'" (p. 230). Heidegger speaks of the end being "imminent" for Da-sein. Death is, Heidegger holds, "the possibility of the absolute impossibility of Da-sein"; death reveals itself as "the *ownmost nonrelational possibility not to be bypassed* … [;] it is an *eminent imminence*" (p. 232). This position is contrary to our common perceptions of death. We encounter death as a familiar event in the everyday world. Through its very familiarity, death remains inconspicuous and we talk about it only fleetingly. Our attitude toward death is frequently of the kind, "One also dies at the end, but for now one is not involved" (p. 234). In saying "one dies," the suggestion is that death shows up from somewhere, but in not yet being objectively present to the person making the utterance, it poses no threat. "One dies" thus fosters the view that death strikes the "they"; "dying" becomes an event that belongs to "no one in particular" (p. 234).

We seek to show concern and provide comfort to those who are dying, but this, Heidegger points out, is as much a matter of trying to bring comfort to ourselves as it is of comforting the one dying. By endeavoring to bring the dying person back to Da-sein, death is tranquillized (p. 234). Thinking about death is regarded as a sign of fear or insecurity; the expectation is that one will remain calm, indifferent to the reality of one's death (p. 234). Death is seen as a certainty, but there is uncertainty about what this certainty means. From a Heideggerian perspective, we can say that in "this enduring present moment, we are 'ahead' … of ourselves; what we are doing is future oriented" (Quay, 2015, p. 11). An existential approach to the question of death construes Da-sein, being-in-the-world, as "always already *toward* its end, that is, … constantly coming to grips with its own death" (Heidegger, 1996, p. 239). There is "angst" in the face of death, but angst in this context is not the same as fear. Angst arises from the fact that in being-in-the-world, we are already "thrown" into the possibility of being-toward-its end (pp. 232–233). It is this throwness that distinguishes an existential concept of dying from ideas of "pure disappearance" or the "experience" of death (p. 233). Being-toward-death belongs, in a primordial and essential sense, to Da-sein, even if Da-sein flees from it or covers over it (p. 233).

Camus (1991), in *The Myth of Sisyphus*, fashioned the question of death into the starting point for all philosophical inquiry: "There is but one truly serious philosophical problem, and that is suicide. Judging whether life is or is not worth living amounts to answering the fundamental question of philosophy" (p. 3). Camus observes that while some people die because they conclude that life is *not* worth living, others die "for the ideas or illusions that give them a reason for living" (p. 4). Camus pays homage to Kierkegaard but does not share his Christian faith. For Camus, then, a key question is how life can be made meaningful in the absence of a God or the possibility of eternal life. Suicide may have a confessional element – an admission that life is too difficult – but it can also be a form of political protest (p. 5). At a deeper level, the question of suicide is intimately related to the sense of absurdity and alienation we experience when the illusions that might have provided comfort in the past are removed. Faced with an absurd world, suicide is one answer but hope is another. We may judge this world to be absurd but retain hope for another – in this life or beyond – that will be better (cf. Roberts & Freeman-Moir, 2013). In taking the path of suicide, we opt for death, but in doing so, we enter a domain that is unknown: "in reality, there is no experience of death" (p. 15). We may see other deaths, but these are merely substitutes for the real thing, and they never quite convince us (p. 15). We are certain we exist but we can never be certain of the knowledge that tells us about our existence. The Socratic command "Know thyself" can at most help us to form an "approximate" view of ourselves; this dictum also has more than a hint of nostalgia and ignorance (p. 19). The world is not "reasonable" (p. 21), and no amount of logic can fully explain, or explain away, the existential problems we face.

Despite the failures of reason and religion in providing adequate answers to the riddles of life, hope does not have to be extinguished. Camus notes with interest that not one existentialist thinker advocates escape as the preferred option: "Through an odd reasoning, starting out from the absurd over the ruins of reason, in a closed universe limited to the human, they deify what crushes them and find reason to hope in what impoverishes them" (p. 32). Some, such as Jaspers, find hope in our very inability to understand. Others, such as Chestov, make God a source of hope not because it is rational to do so but precisely because the idea of God does *not* correspond to conventional categories for reasoning; we turn to God to attain the impossible (pp. 32–34). Kierkegaard, terrified by the Christianity of his childhood, returns in his later work to embrace what had hitherto been a source of despair. Kierkegaard's answer is to take a 'leap' of faith. Kierkegaard disrupts the equilibrium between "the irrational of the world and the insurgent nostalgia of the absurd" (p. 38). Aware that this world fails us in attempting to explain our existence in purely rational terms, Kierkegaard makes a deliberate choice to embrace the irrational in another form. For Kierkegaard the mature Christian, death is not the end; it "implies infinitely more hope than life implies for us, even when that life is overflowing with health and vigor" (cited in Camus, 1991, p. 39). For Camus himself, the absurd is "sin without God," and the answer is "living in that state of the absurd" (p. 40). This means that, rather than giving in to falsehoods as a source of consolation, we must be prepared to accept despair as a part of human existence (p. 41). For Camus, there is no "love of life" without "despair of life" (Camus, 1968, p. 56). Camus turns the problem of suicide, and its relation to the meaning of life, on its head: "It was previously a question of finding out whether or not life had to have a meaning to be lived. It now becomes clear, on the contrary, that it will be lived all the better if it has no meaning" (p. 53). Living, as Camus sees it, is "keeping the absurd alive" through contemplation and metaphysical revolt (p. 54). This is "not aspiration, for it is devoid of hope" (p. 54). The revolt Camus has in mind is "the certainty of a crushing fate, without the resignation that ought to accompany it" (p. 54).

Sartre (2007), like Camus, rejects the Christian path forged by Kierkegaard, espousing an existentialist ethic that centers on human beings and the choices they make. Sartre's existentialist humanism starts from the position that as human beings, we are always "outside" ourselves. It is by projecting and losing ourselves, beyond ourselves, that we realize ourselves. Pursuing transcendent goals allows us to exist. There is no world beyond this one; the "only universe that exists is the human one – the universe of human subjectivity" (p. 52). Where for Kierkegaard subjectivity is inwardness, for Sartre transcendence is to be found in pursuing goals outside ourselves – "in the form of liberation, or of some special achievement" (p. 53). Human beings are, as it were, "abandoned," and must make their own way in the world. Far from being a recipe for despair, Sartre sees this orientation to the human condition as "optimistic" (p. 54). According to Sartre, the real problem is not whether God exists, for even if the existence of God could be proven, there would still be a need for "man to rediscover himself and to comprehend that nothing can save him from himself" (p. 53). This is an ethic not of quietism or resignation but of *action*. "Man," Sartre says, "is nothing but a series of enterprises … [;] he is the sum, organization and aggregate of the relations that constitute such enterprises" (p. 38). This approach to existentialism emphasizes responsibility and commitment. Virtues are not given but created and exemplified by human decisions and actions: "the coward makes himself cowardly and the hero makes himself heroic; there is always the possibility that one day the coward may no longer be cowardly and the hero may cease to be a hero" (p. 39).

There is, for Sartre, no universal human 'nature' or 'essence'; we can speak of a human 'condition', but this is always in the making (pp. 42–43). Thus, human beings, faced with the reality of nothing beyond death, nothing beyond this world, must exercise *freedom* in the existence they carve out for themselves. We have no God to guide us, but we are not alone. Seeking freedom for oneself is, at one and the same time, a matter of willing it for others too (p. 49). Beauvoir (1948) takes this line of argument further: "Freedom is the source from which all significations and all values spring. It is the original condition of all justification of existence" (p. 24). In seeking to give life meaning and significance, we will want freedom "absolutely and above everything else" (p. 24). We do not 'create' the world; we *disclose* it through the resistance posed by the world to us (p. 28). Our original state is one of "ambiguity," but this does not, for Beauvoir, serve as an impediment to action. There is, Beauvoir claims, "hardly a sadder virtue than resignation" (p. 28). Existing is risky and uncertain, but this is where freedom resides. "My freedom," Beauvoir says, "must not seek to trap being but to disclose it. The disclosure is the transition from being to existence" (p. 30). Freedom, Beauvoir adds, "can always save itself, for it is realized as a disclosure of existence through its very failures, and it can again confirm itself by a death freely chosen" (p. 32). People may be wary of existentialism, Beauvoir argues, because it appears to be so "gloomy"; we are often uncomfortable with the sense of "danger" it poses. Yet, "it is because there are real dangers, real failures and real earthly damnation that words like victory, wisdom, or joy have meaning" (p. 34).

TEACHING, RESPONSIBILITY AND IMMORTALITY: SHAPING OTHER LIVES

Thus far, the focus of the discussion has been mainly on death as an 'individual' question. We have considered a range of views on what it means to die, and on how we as individual human beings might face the prospect of our own death. The question of immortality, it has been noted, is often regarded as a deeply personal matter: as something we need to 'figure out' on our own. But there are other ways of thinking about death and the concept of 'living on'. As Samuel Scheffler (2013) has argued, we do not need to believe in the idea of an afterlife in the traditional sense – that is, in the notion of living on as conscious beings beyond our biological deaths – in order to take seriously the question of another form of afterlife: the anticipated reality that *others* will continue to live, on Earth, after we have died. The existence of an afterlife in that sense, Scheffler shows, can bear significantly on how we think about our own deaths, what we come to value, and how we grapple with limits of time in our lives (pp. 15–16). This observation has important implications for education, and particularly for how we understand the nature and purpose of teaching. For teaching is very much a *social* process, involving a relationship between two or more people. In teaching, we hope to pass on something to others – not just knowledge, but something, perhaps, of 'ourselves'. As teachers, we consider the consequences of our actions for the students with whom we work, aware that our influence will play its part in shaping their lives – lives that will usually go on after we have died. We teach because we want to make a worthwhile difference in those lives. In attempting to leave a 'positive imprint' on students' hearts and minds (Ciaccio, 2000, p. 48), we also hope that they too will, in turn, leave their mark on others.

David Blacker argues that "immortality remains an important animating ideal for teaching and learning" (1998, p. 8). He identifies two broad approaches to the question of immortality in the ancient world, both of which begin with Socrates, and both of which remain relevant in considering contemporary pedagogical contexts: the first is "the other-regarding paideia of the sophists that seeks immortality in human affairs"; the second is "a relatively disembodied Platonism that looks toward mindful communion with eternal ideas" (p. 8). The former has a practical focus on the educated *person*, whereas the latter is more concerned with the pursuit of truth through reason and reflection (pp. 11–13). In the first approach, teaching is vital; in the second, it is more a means to the end of entering the world of Forms (p. 11). Both approaches are evident in the way we discuss educational experiences today. The Platonic vision comes to life when, for example, someone is struck with a sense of wonder at the beauty of a mathematical proof. Education can be seen as a process of advancing knowledge, with each discovery contributing to this ancient quest (p. 16). Pushing the boundaries of knowledge in this way brings us closer to the immortal, timeless, universal Forms. The Sophists' pathway also remains significant, connecting, as noted above, with a central motivation for many teachers: the desire to make a difference in other lives. Teaching is not just concerned with the advancement of knowledge or the pursuit of truth but also with the development of relationships and the passing on of something valuable from one person to the next. Immortality in this context has to do with the idea of 'living on' in the lives of those with whom we come into contact as teachers.

Blacker argues for a balance between both approaches. The desire to leave a mark on others, to 'live on' through them, can, if it is not coupled with a respect for the value of reason and knowledge, become self-centered and manipulative. Equally unhelpful is the possibility, in our quest to know, of becoming oblivious to others. Scientists and other researchers need to consider the human consequences of their endeavors (pp. 22–24). Knowing that something is the case is not enough; we also need to keep in mind other questions: With whom we seek to know? For what reasons? With what possible outcomes? The idea of seeking the truth remains a noble goal, but it is a goal we cannot pursue alone: dialogue with others who are similarly committed to knowledge is necessary (p. 25). Dialogue is not a contest, with winners and losers, but a shared enterprise where both the teacher and the learner are "irrevocably human, but somehow also more than human" (p. 26). "Teacher and student care for one another," Blacker maintains, "by *taking care* to allow the arising of the subject matter itself – the logos – that is to be disclosed in their interaction" (p. 26). The immortality of education resides in the fact that while both the teacher and the learner participate in the process, something that is more than the two of them – knowledge, the logos – survives (p. 27). Teachers are immortal not just in the sense of remaining a part of students' lives, influencing how they think and feel and act, but also in the sense of becoming interwoven with what is known. Education, Blacker contends, "is neither 'mine' nor 'yours', but both of us may *become* it" (p. 27). A teacher needs to be prepared to "vanish into wisdom for the sake of wisdom's pupil, as the pupil searches for his past and for his future"; the teacher must die, Blacker concludes, in order to live (p. 27).

Immortality can be conceived in other ways that are significant from an educational point of view. Arendt (1998), in discussing the ancient Greeks, notes that "the task and potential greatness of mortals lie in their ability to produce things – works and deeds and words – which would deserve to be and, at least to a degree, are at home in everlastingness" (p. 19). Producing something to leave behind in this manner allows human beings, as mortals, to "find their place in a cosmos where everything is immortal except themselves" (p. 19). The eternal can be distinguished from the immortal by the fact that where the former lies "outside the realm of human affairs" (p. 20), the latter "means endurance in time, deathless life on this earth and in this world as it was given" (p. 18). Arendt speculates that the embrace of the eternal by philosophers such as Plato may have been prompted by doubt about the possibility of the *polis* attaining immortality. Perhaps, Arendt wonders, "the shock of this discovery was so overwhelming that they [the philosophers] could not but look down upon all striving for immortality as vanity and vainglory, … placing themselves thereby into open opposition to the ancient city-state and the religion which inspired it" (p. 21). Regardless of whether this is what motivated the ancients, there is an important sense in which achieving immortality in the sense described by Arendt can be seen as an educational task. To produce something that endures after we are gone requires learning, and with that, teaching in some form. Blacker's (1998) focus is on how teaching can leave its mark on the student, and on how both the teacher and the student have a responsibility to their subject matter – to what is investigated and known. But teachers also play a crucial role in shaping what the world, the *polis*, becomes. "Teachers" here need not be limited to those employed in educational institutions such as schools and universities but could also include the full range of influential figures – parents, friends, workmates, and so on – who might be encountered in a human life. The prospect of death, and the awareness that time is limited, can prompt us to seek out ways to 'make the world a better place', in a manner that will be evident after we have gone. In this way, we might speak of 'living on' through not only those whom we teach but also through the systems, structures, and cultural practices we help to create in our time on earth.

There are also other ethical considerations that are relevant in pondering how death should be understood, approached and engaged in educational environments. Socrates conceived of philosophy as a form of preparation for death, and Montaigne stressed the importance of being 'ready' for death. We have seen that different thinkers have, over the ages, felt more ready for, or more comfortable with, death than others. In contemporary Western culture, it is not uncommon to be in 'denial' over death; to want to avoid thinking about it altogether (Becker, 1997). This is not the same as saying, with Lucretius, that death is (or should be) 'nothing' to us; death, for many people, is simply too difficult, too sensitive to be approached. If we cannot escape from it, the next best thing is to minimize the time we spend focusing on it; we seek to amuse ourselves, distract ourselves, lose ourselves in other activities. Seeking to disrupt this denial is no light matter. When dealing with teaching situations, a strong sense of responsibility toward those being taught is needed if death is to be addressed with appropriate sensitivity and care. Underlying much of the work on 'death education' is the premise that enhancing awareness of death, reflecting on it, and discussing it are all worthwhile activities. Engaging in programs of death education will, it is hoped, reduce anxiety over death and thus improve the lives of participants. But when working with children in particular, there are important prior ethical considerations. In some circumstances, any benefits that arise from raising the question of death may be outweighed by the possible harm that might be done in doing so. As Puolimatka and Solasaari (2006) point out, in teaching situations attention needs to be paid to the developmental maturity of those with whom one is working. There is no easy 'solution' to such dilemmas: "On the one hand, children have a right to know fundamental facts about their own existence. On the other hand, a full acquaintance with the facts about human mortality is psychologically agonizing" (p. 211).

There are dangers too in treating death as if it is just another topic to be covered in an already crowded curriculum. The idea of study serving as a process of deepening our understanding of ourselves can end up being reduced to 'learning', via instruction, for assessment purposes (Pinar, 2006, p. 116). This can diminish the significance of death for an existing individual, as Kierkegaard might have noted, but it can also denude death of its broader historical importance. In particular, if death is somehow separated from us, either by its abstraction or by its reduction to the status of an assessable subject in an education program, it can become all the more difficult to appreciate how horrific many deaths have been – horrific that is in the manner of the death, or the scale of the atrocities committed, or the depth of the grief felt by friends and family. It is possible to treat death in the abstract as 'nothing', as Epicurus and Lucretius believed we should, but in our lived relationships with others, particularly those to whom we are closest, it can be *everything*. Experiencing the death of a child, spouse, parent, or close friend can change a life dramatically, and forever. Taking death seriously as a subject for educational investigation, both in written work and in classroom practice, arguably requires more of us as teachers, learners and scholars than almost anything else we might encounter in our educational lives. Teaching can be conceived as an "immortality project" in the sense that it is "a form of compensation to help resolve a certain kind of existential terror" (van Kessel & Burke, 2018, p. 1). Terror can take many different forms, almost all of which can in some way be associated with death. With this point in mind, where we begin our investigation can become a matter of no small significance. For Levinas, whose parents and brothers were killed by the Nazis, the starting point in considering death is *murder* (Wang, 2008, p. 146). Death, for Levinas, cannot be grasped; it does not fall within our usual horizons for understanding. It is imminent and menacing, threatening from beyond while remaining invisible and mysterious (Levinas, 1969, pp. 233–235). Death, Levinas says, "takes me without leaving me the chance I have in a struggle, for in reciprocal struggle I grasp what takes hold of me. In death I am exposed to absolute violence, to murder in the night" (p. 233).

From a somewhat different perspective, we might also speak of death in relation to examples of symbolic violence. Death can serve as a metaphor for acts of destruction that leave an imprint not just on the human body but on the Earth and on concepts, relationships, and fields of inquiry. We might consider, for example, the violence done to the arts and humanities in contemporary higher education – their marginalization in policy and institutional practice – as a form of death. More could be said also about the 'death of the professor' (Lyotard, 1984) in a world where knowledge is treated as a commodity and technology is seen as a replacement for university teachers. Simone Weil (1997) argues that if we love the truth, we need to endure, through a painful process of decreation, 'the void'; truth, she suggests, is "on the side of death" (p. 56). The 'death' of truth can also be witnessed, in a rather different light, as the disregard for evidence, facts and rigor that is the hallmark of the so-called 'post-truth' age. With rapid changes in medicine and technology, 'death' is itself being redefined. Education as a form of preparation for death can now be seen as a process that might extend for decades longer than previously anticipated. Indeed, now and in the future, with the blurring of boundaries between the 'human' and the 'non-human', and with developments such as cloning, it will become increasingly challenging to determine *who* or *what* is 'dying' (cf. Brown, 2008).

Reference has already been made to the idea of teachers 'dying', both for the sake of their students and for the advancement of knowledge. This could be taken further to include investigation of other forms of sacrifice made by those committed to education. Education can be seen as a bridge between life and death: a sacrificial process of coming to recognize our own incompleteness as human beings (Roberts, 2012). There is also a sense of loss, a death that must be accepted, in the act of committing to critical reflection as an ideal. As Unamuno (1972) recognized, the reflective consciousness with which we have been endowed is a two-edged sword. It can open us up to the riches of philosophy and literature and lead to extraordinary scientific and technological discoveries. But it can also lead to great suffering. Education can be joyous and uplifting; yet it can also be a source of utter despair (Roberts, 2016). Education is 'dangerous', not merely as a process that can be politically subversive (and, in some cases, lead to literal deaths), but also as an endeavor that calls into question – threatens to annihilate – some of the assumptions, values and ideals we hold most dear.

CONCLUSION

Educational priorities vary over time. Different approaches to teaching come in and out of vogue. The ideals we espouse, the structures we build, the technologies we harness, and the languages we employ to describe our educational activities all change as the years go by. But some fundamental questions remain important regardless of the particulars of a given time and place. In education, we are, or should be, ultimately concerned with the question of why we exist (Webster, 2009, p. ix). The question of existence is, as this chapter has shown, intimately related to the question of death. Philosophers of education can contribute to the ongoing conversation on death in a number of ways. They can consider what is meant by 'death', how 'death' relates to 'life', what role death plays in our formation as human beings, how death is relevant to conceptions and practices of teaching and learning, and how death influences pedagogical decisions and actions. This is by no means an exhaustive statement of possibilities. Given space constraints, the focus in this chapter has been limited to Western perspectives on death. There is, of course, a good deal more that can be said about death from a range of Eastern philosophical and religious perspectives. There are, in addition, important insights on death that can be gained from the teachings and practices of indigenous cultures. The focus here has been mainly on non-fiction philosophical and educational texts, but in addressing the theme of death philosophers of education need not limit themselves to such sources. Death is explored in countless novels, plays, and films, all of which can be helpful in addressing philosophical and educational questions. With an abundance of potentially worthwhile avenues for further investigation, the theme of death is likely to receive increasing attention in the international philosophy of education community in the years ahead.

REFERENCES

Arcilla, R. V. (1997). Education of the undead? In S. Laird (Ed.), *Philosophy of Education 1997* (pp. 449–451). Philosophy of Education Society.
Arendt, H. (1998). *The human condition* (2nd ed.). University of Chicago Press.
Aristotle (1976), *Ethics* (The Nicomachean Ethics), revised edition (J.A.K. Thomson, Trans.). Penguin.
Beauvoir, S. de (1948). *The ethics of ambiguity* (B. Frechtman, Trans.). Citadel Press.
Beauvoir, S. de (1992). *All men are mortal* (L.M. Friedman, Trans.). W.W. Norton.
Becker, E. (1997). *The denial of death*. Free Press.
Blacker, D. (1998). Education as immortality: Toward the rehabilitation of an ideal. *Religious Education, 93*, 8–28.
Bradatan, C. (2015). *Dying for ideas: The dangerous lives of the philosophers*. Bloomsbury.
Brown, G. (2008). *The living end: The future of death, aging and immortality*. Macmillan.
Camus, A. (1968). Love of life. In A. Camus, *Lyrical and critical essays* (E.C. Kennedy, Trans.). Vintage Books.
Camus, A. (1991). *The myth of Sisyphus and other essays* (J. O'Brien, Trans.). Vintage International.
Ciaccio, J. (2000). A teacher's chance for immortality. *Education Digest*, February, 44–48.
Enright, D. J. (Ed.). (1987). *The Oxford book of death*. Oxford University Press.
Hadot, P. (1995). *Philosophy as a way of life*. (M. Chase, Trans.). Blackwell.
Heidegger, M. (1996). *Being and time* (J. Stambaugh, Trans.). State University of New York Press.
Homer (1991). *The Odyssey* (D.C.H. Rieu, Trans.). Penguin.
Homer (2003). *The Iliad* (E.V. Rieu, Trans.). Penguin.
Kierkegaard, S. (2009). *Concluding unscientific postscript* (A. Hannay, Trans.). Cambridge University Press.
Levinas, E. (1969). *Totality and infinity* (A. Lingis, Trans.). Duquesne University Press.
Lucretius (1999). *On the nature of the universe* (R. Melville, Trans.). Oxford University Press.
Luper, S. (2009). *The philosophy of death*. Cambridge University Press.
Lyotard, J.-F. (1984). The postmodern condition: A report on knowledge (G. Bennington & B. Massumi, Trans.). University of Minnesota Press.
Montaigne, M. de (1991). *The complete essays* (M.A. Screech, Trans.). Penguin.
Neiman, A.M. (1997). Teaching and eternal life: The love of learning and desire for God. In S. Laird (Ed.), *Philosophy of Education 1997* (pp. 456–460). Philosophy of Education Society.
Nietzsche, F. (1976). *Thus spoke Zarathustra*. In W. Kaufmann (Ed.), *The Portable Nietzsche* (pp. 103–439). Penguin.
Pinar, W. F. (2006). *Synoptic text today and other essays: Curriculum development after the reconceptualization*. Peter Lang.
Pinar, W. F. (2011). *The character of curriculum studies: Bildung, currere, and the recurring question of the subject*. Palgrave Macmillan.
Plato (1974). *The Republic* (H.D.P. Lee, Trans.). Penguin.
Plato (2003). *The last days of Socrates* (H. Tredennick & H. Tarrant, Trans.). Penguin.
Puolimatka, T., & Solasaari, U. (2006). Education for death. *Educational Philosophy and Theory, 38*, 201–214.
Quay, J. (2015). *Understanding life in school: From academic classroom to outdoor education*. Palgrave Macmillan.

Roberts, P. (2012). *From West to East and back again: An educational reading of Hermann Hesse's later work*. Sense Publishers.
Roberts, P. (2016). *Happiness, hope and despair: Rethinking the role of education*. Peter Lang.
Roberts, P., & Freeman-Moir, J. (2013). *Better worlds: Education, art, and utopia*. Lexington Books.
Roberts, P., & Saeverot, H. (2018). *Education and the limits of reason: Reading Dostoevsky, Tolstoy and Nabokov*. Routledge.
Sartre, J-P. (2007). *Existentialism is a humanism* (C. Macomber, Trans.; J. Kulka, Ed.). Yale University Press.
Scheffler, S. (2013). *Death and the afterlife* (N. Kolodny, Ed.). Oxford University Press.
Schopenhauer, A. (1966). *The world as will and representation*, vol. II (E.F. Payne, Trans.). Dover.
Seneca (2007). *Dialogues and essays* (J. Davie, Trans.). Oxford University Press.
Smuts, A. (2011). Immortality and significance. *Philosophy and Literature*, *35*(1), 134–149.
Spinoza, B. de (1969). *Ethics* (A. Boyle, Trans.). Heron Books.
Unamuno, M. de (1972). *The tragic sense of life in men and nations* (A. Kerrigan, Trans.). Princeton University Press.
Unamuno, M. de (1996). *Abel Sanchez and other stories* (A. Kerrigan, Trans.). Regnery Publishing.
Unamuno, M. de (2000). *Mist: A tragicomic novel* (W. Fite, Trans.). University of Illinois Press.
van Kessel, C., & Burke, K. (2018). Teaching as an immortality project: Positing weakness in response to terror. *Journal of Philosophy of Education*, *52*(2), 216–229.
Wang, T. (2008). The concepts of death in Heidegger and Levinas. *Journal of Chinese Philosophy*, *35*(1), 143–154.
Webster, S. (2009). *Educating for meaningful lives through existential spirituality*. Sense Publishers.
Weil, S. (1997). *Gravity and grace* (A. Wills, Trans.). Bison Books.

CHAPTER TWO

Dancing with Death

R. SCOTT WEBSTER

Writing through his pseudonymous author Johannes Climacus, Kierkegaard (1985, p. 8) suggests that "the thought of death is a good dancing partner." In this chapter insights are sought which can be gleaned from this statement by exploring both the character of this pseudonymous author and Kierkegaard's overall educative philosophy including the implications that these have for both education and democracy. Education, along with philosophy, originated as the quest for a good life. Such a goal might be better understood as a meaningful life rather than a *happy* life because the focus of this latter approach can be superficial. For Kierkegaard, the educational project of becoming a self which is meaningful, purposeful, worthwhile and *good*, is understood as something which is *achieved* through actively valuing, choosing and devoting ourselves, rather than as something which is passively inherited or essentialized such as one's name, age, gender or ethnicity.

Kierkegaard suggested that there are three modes of living or existing. His lowest stage is described as the aesthetic and involves pleasure seeking where individuals pursue experiences and items which they believe will make them happy. This stage focusses upon acquisition and satisfaction rather than upon personal change and growth. His second stage is the ethical and pertains to the universal applicability of ethical responsibility. In order to attain the good life within this stage one must comply to the publically accepted ways of conduct. Consequently one learns to live according to the standards and purposes set by society or 'the crowd'. The third and highest stage is described as the religious which may require one to go beyond the ethical. Kierkegaard's best known example of this is presented through his pseudonym Johannes de Silentio, who describes the story about how Abraham was willing to sacrifice his son Isaac. Using the second stage of the ethical he concludes that "Abraham was a murderer" and should anyone attempt to do likewise he is likely to be criticized along the lines, "You despicable man, you scum of society, what devil has so possessed you that you would want to murder your son" (Kierkegaard, 1983, p. 28). However, through the religious stage he understands that this event should importantly be understood differently as a willing sacrifice rather than as murder. This is because "The great thing was that he [Abraham] loved God in such a way that he was willing to offer him the best" (p. 28).

From an educational perspective this third stage offers a significant insight into what it might mean to *be* an educated person. It is important to investigate this because it would appear that Kierkegaard's reference to Johannes' *dancing* might indicate that Kierkegaard could be appealing to the aesthetic stage, which is not the case. Understanding how the thought of one's death as a dancing partner can have educational value requires us to inquire beyond the aesthetic and the ethical, where dancing, as embracing doubt and thinking, is made possible through existential dialectics. It is something that only the individual person can do for herself because only she can live her own life and die her own death.

A LIFE OF DOUBT AS NECESSARY FOR DEMOCRACY

In the preface to his book *Philosophical Fragments*, Kierkegaard's (1985, p. 8) pseudonymous author, Johannes Climacus, states that "the thought of death is a good dancing partner." To explore this idea it is considered worthwhile to first understand some of the character of this pseudonym Johannas himself which Kierkegaard created. This will add more insight into how the thought of death might be better understood as a good dancing partner. Indeed Kierkegaard (1998, p. 288) actually recommended this approach when studying his works through stating "I have expressly urged once and for all that anyone who wants to quote something from the pseudonyms will not attribute the quotation to me". Kierkegaard wrote many books using a variety of pseudonymous authors and editors such as Johannes de Silentio, Vigilius Haufniensusand, Hilarius Bookbinder as well as Johannes Climacus, and he gave to each of them a particular character to which he requested that his readers respect as the authors of the words rather than he himself.

By respecting this request of Kierkegaard, this section will now turn to Johannes himself in order to better understand this character and what *he* might mean through this metaphor of dancing with death. Kierkegaard (2001), who identifies himself as the author of another novel titled *Johannes Climacus, Or: A Life of Doubt*, introduces us to Johannes. One of the main dispositions Johannes has, is that he is one who is continually confronted with experiencing doubt. An initial reflection on this by educators may conclude that this is nothing profound because since the postmodern turn uncertainty has been a constant. It can be appreciated that doubt is also essential for scientific thinking which has emerged as a predominant characteristic of the modern era which has developed since the time of Kierkegaard. What has assisted to catapult Western societies forward to modernity is scientific thinking which is intrinsic to the actual scientific knowledge which has been produced. By drawing upon Popper's hypothetical deductive approach, scientific thinking can be understood as involving actively doubting a hypothesis. This active doubting is sometimes identified as dissenting from the status quo or consensus of the views of particular scientific communities and is understood to be essential if scientific understandings are to progress. However, Westphal (1996, p. 68) astutely makes the observation that being "Brought up on John Dewey and Ludwig Wittgenstein and Heidegger, we have abandoned the quest for certainty" and so reading Climacus's life of doubt "sounds like congratulations to us. 'I knew that,' we say, not noticing how close our scepticism is to cynicism and nihilism." Therefore, Westphal is suggesting there is a great deal more for us to glean from this life of doubt so that people should be well protected against nihilism by having greater clarity for a life full of meaning and purpose. This is the theme which shall be developed throughout in this chapter.

For Kierkegaard the role of doubt has great importance for all his writings which deal with faith, where he argued that Christian faith must embrace the experience of uncertainty and doubt if it is to be authentic. He also goes to great length to explain why doubt is essential for thinking, and in particular, philosophical thinking. In addition to doubt being essential for faith, along with being essential for thinking, philosophy and a scientific attitude, it is also essential for democracy. Authoritarian regimes require their citizens *not* to engage in doubt because this can lead to critical thinking. Instead citizens are told to trust their government and mainstream media, to be compliant, readily obedient and follow expectations and roles assigned to them so that they behave in accordance with what they uncritically believe to be is 'the right thing to do'. They accept that their government and its agencies are fundamentally good and care for them and so they accept them as the 'one stop shop' where citizens can confidently consume information they can trust. The internet on the other hand, is not controlled by responsible authorities and therefore must be regarded as full of misinformation and disinformation and therefore the public are encouraged to give their support to government attempts to regulate and censor the content. Consequently, Windholz (2020) observes that the Australian State and Federal governments are typical of many in the West which have become autocratic technocracies since the Covid-19 pandemic. Without reference to argument or a rigorous examination of evidence, citizens in authoritarian cultures uncritically believe and therefore obey what their authorities dictate to them. This is famously portrayed by Winston who is the main character in Orwell's book *Nineteen Eighty Four*. While beginning to doubt and question the norms of society, Winston nevertheless came to be threatened and seduced into believing that his Big Brother government actually cares for the well-being of the masses, and in doing so he gave up doubting and thinking in exchange for happiness and security.

In contrast to Big Brother-like governments, democratic societies are characterized by the public actively exercising a disposition of skepticism, holding their governments to account by demanding transparency. This is often achieved through the people themselves and their representatives participating and deliberating in efforts to pursue the public good. Such active and critical engagements can also be understood as being served by an attitude of doubt which assists in the critical engagement of civil life by all citizens. Hence this is why such an active approach to political life is described by Mouffe (2013) as agonistic rather than as adversarial. Clearly, the common element of doubt must be present for all sorts of thinking and especially for both science and democracy as has been recognized by Dewey (1989), who consequently championed the value of doubt for education. Hence, Johannes's doubt to which Kierkegaard draws our attention, is significantly important for educators in democracies to consider.

In the introduction of the novel *Johannes Climacus* this young man Johannes is described as a serious thinker and who has little interest "to be captivated by a woman's beauty" as might be typical of the other young men of his age (Kierkegaard, 2001, p. 15). Instead he devotes himself to the pursuit and practice of thinking. Interestingly, as a young child he was forbidden by his father to leave the house and explore the world outside. Instead his father supplemented the young lad's desire to venture to the outside world by allowing Johannes to "take his hand and go for a walk up and down the room" inside the house, where his father would gladly allow Johannes the complete freedom to imagine that he could walk anywhere he pleased such as through the city streets, beyond the city gates or to the beach. During such walks up and down the room, his father enthusiastically and vividly described the sights, sounds and smells of the journey to his son in a dramatically descriptive fashion (pp. 17–18).

While the reader might baulk at this overly-protective father figure and the inadequacy of his supplementary imaginative activities which denied Johannes first-hand experiences with the real world beyond the house, Kierkegaard (2001, p. 19) provokingly then adds that "While the life in his paternal home thus contributed to the development of his imagination… the education he received in school was in harmony with this." Here Kierkegaard confronts teachers with the nature of schooling as it is often experienced by so many students. School classrooms, similarly to the lounge room to which Johannes was restricted by his father, also tend to deny students first-hand access to the 'real world' and instead deliver pupils the curricular approved knowledge of the world as abstract and second-hand through teachers and texts which if *good*, provide descriptions of the world in a vivid and lively fashion.

Both of these experiences of attending school and Johannes walking around the room holding his father's hand, might provide very detailed and accurate descriptions of the world. These descriptions could be understood as *knowledge*, which if retained by pupils can be assessed through examinations. However, this abstract knowledge is significantly different to actual *existence*. In the novel Johannes reflects upon Descartes who offered doubt as a method upon which he was able to advance knowledge. Such a philosophical approach leads to abstract, objective and theoretical knowledge as a product but which is distinctively different to existential understandings which explore personal, moral and religious concerns relating to one's existence and its ultimate meaning. This contrast between these two sorts of knowing is accentuated further in the novel where Kierkegaard (2001, p. 59) writes;

> If one could teach a child of two a mathematical thesis, it would be essentially just as true in the mouth of a child as in the mouth of Pythagoras. But if one were to teach a child of two to say 'I believe in the existence of God', or 'Know thyself', nobody would take him seriously.

Here Kierkegaard makes plain that thinking about and proclaiming understandings which relate to 'objective' knowledge, such as the relation that the three sides of a right-angle triangle have to each other as per the Pythagorean theorem, tend to be universal, existing independently from the *being* of the individual who holds them to be true – even if the individual is very young. However, such 'objective' understandings are significantly different to thinking about and attempting to formulate understandings which are existential in nature as these are inextricably related to the *being* of the individual who is doing the inquiring. As Dewey (1988, p. 196) summarizes, "knowledge of spiritual truth is always more than theoretical and intellectual. It was the product of activity as well as its cause. It has to be lived in order to be known." This latter dimension of spiritual truth, or insight and self-understanding, is the significant frame of reference when it comes to the dancing partner of the thought of one's death.

Drawing upon the wisdom of the day, and in particular the phrase *De omnibus dubitandum est* (everything must be doubted), the novel follows Johannes as he struggles with this imperative to doubt in order to think and to philosophize. The activity of doubting is understood to be absolutely necessary for thinking and by adopting it as a method in which rationality is rigorously applied it would appear that one can attain certain amounts of 'objective' knowledge such as mathematical insights as demonstrated by Descartes. However, this *system* of moving beyond doubt to certainty, while appearing to have great value for producing some kinds of knowledge, seems to be problematic in relation to one's own personal existence. This is because there seems to be very little certainty or objective knowledge available for resolving existential concerns. Any ultimate sense and meaning which can be given to one's life, tends to be applicable at death, which is *after* one's life has ended where there are no other possibilities available. Hence Kierkegaard saw a need to advance his idea of existential dialectics which is quite different to the sort of dialectics offered by Hegel because Kierkegaard recognized that there are no sources available which can provide absolute resolutions for the sort of existential angst which is experienced when grappling with an ultimate sense of meaning and purpose for one's personal life.

To frame this difference between theoretically 'objective' knowledge compared with understandings about existence in terms of dialectical thinking and learning, Kierkegaard references Hegel's system which involves the three aspects of the subjective, objective and the absolute. While this system indicates that an initiate is located at the subjective beginning where doubt and dialectical thinking are experienced in a first-hand manner, such a system offers resolutions to the dialectical activities due to an assumed unity of the absolute which underpins all of reality and to which an individual can eventually come to know and hence leave her doubting behind. This enables, for example, Johannes's father to provide all that Johannes needs to 'know' about the world through his detailed and animated descriptions being given to the young boy's questions and by-passing Johannes's requests to have first-hand experiences with the world. However, what Kierkegaard's Johannes seems to be stumbling upon is a slippage between the 'subjective beginning' of Hegel's system, which, while offering first-hand experiences of doubting and grappling with dialectical thinking in which one's very life and existence is involved, but on the other hand the arrival at objective and universal conclusions as knowledge of reality which can be acquired through receiving it second-hand, perhaps through an authority such as a parent or teacher. It is this transition from the very personal and subjective experiences of existential dialectics to objective but abstract knowledge that troubles young Johannes.

Writing from the perspective of Johannes, Kierkegaard (2001, p. 68) explains that "to acquire something without difficulty was a paradox to his adventurous soul." So while Pythagoras, along with Egyptian and Indian philosophers, seemed to commanded silence from their students, Johannes "was for another reason a little hesitant about the preparation prescribed for him because it did not seem to him to be sufficiently humble or modest" (p. 68). Therefore, rather than being given positive commands by a master, such as being told to walk behind, carry a pot, kneel, etc., by which "the disciple becomes an imperfect being, one who has his life in another person" even although there might be a "joy of obeying", Johannes recognizes that "by imposing something negative upon the disciple[i.e. doubting his teacher], the teacher emancipates the disciple from himself, makes him just as great as himself" and thereby makes Johannes realize that "I am delivered over to myself, I must do everything on my own responsibility" (p. 69). In order to be truly emancipated through education, Johannes, and every other student, must be able to have the first-hand experience of doing things by themselves without the comfort and security of any authority or certainty being offered by teachers or by knowledge from the Hegelian *system* of reality. Lacking such comforting guidance means embracing doubt, anxiety and adventure recognized by Johannes as being "like the one who rows a boat, [where] I turn my back on my destination" (p. 70).

This very same sentence of rowing towards a goal behind one's back is again repeated not by Kierkegaard (1985, p. 159) but by his pseudonym Johannes in *his* book *Philosophical Fragments*. Here it is stated to emphasize the responsibility that must be exercised by each individual who takes on the burden of doubt and therefore of thinking, in contrast to the 'joy', pleasure or security which comes through compliant believing and obedience. Johannes seems to be recognizing that the one who takes on this burden of doubt "elevates himself above the person from whom he learns, and thus there is no frame of mind less appreciated by a teacher in his pupil than doubt" (Kierkegaard, 1985, p. 158).

As young Johannes was living his life of doubting everything, Kierkegaard (2001, p. 16) likened him to someone who was carrying a tall stack of breakable things which caused him to walk unsteadily. This tall stack of breakable objects represents "all the conclusions he had arrived at" but were all nevertheless precarious due to being held together by logical inferences which lacked objective certainty. Interestingly Kierkegaard (2001, p. 17) describes this unsteady walk of Johannes as being "in a dance" as he made his way through the streets of the world where Johannes "remained a stranger." Later he explained that this was acknowledged by Johannes as trying to roll a heavy load up the side of a mountain, and through this analogy he was able to then make "a distinction between the difficulty of thinking and the weight of the thought" (p. 45). It is from this that 'dancing' can be appreciated as being very much like subjective grappling and thinking, while the thought of one's death is a significant example of a weighty thought.

One of the weightiest thoughts for Johannes, and indeed perhaps for many others, is the thought of one's own death and the possibilities associated with it. Questions such as, 'How did life first emerge in the universe?' 'Does life continue after death in some form?' and in particular, 'Might *my very own life* continue after death?' These are indeed weighty thoughts to contemplate. However, rather than feel overwhelmed by the weight of these, Johannes recognized that it is one's relation to them, that is, one's *thinking* which can in fact be quite like a dance – even although a clumsy one. Thinking, as existential dialectics, is the relation that one can have between oneself and a profound and weighty idea such as life, death and eternity. It is a characteristic of existential living in the present moment as one grapples with trying to give sense and meaning to current concerns. History, on the other hand, consists of knowledge which has been abstracted out from the context of its own presence and arranged logically to give sense and meaning retrospectively. Such meanings cannot be grappled with subjectively because they have been established as statements of objective fact. Similarly, if a future history could be revealed, it too would nullify the present subjective experiencing of existential dialectics and replace it with something 'objective' and certain. However, Kierkegaard's Johannes was able to grasp that life itself, characterized with its grappling and thinking in the present moment as existential dialectics, conferred that living itself can only ever be part of the present. It can never escape backwards to the safety of a certainty of historical meanings. Kierkegaard (2001, p. 53) reviewed what Epicurus had said, "for when I am, death is not, and when death is, I am not. Is there anything that might unite the two parts into a whole?" Rather than point in an obvious way to what might be able to unify these, he continued by pointing out that "Johannes did not ask such questions as these, but only asked about the single individual's relation to that thesis" (p. 53), and in doing so, pointed to the activity, or 'dance', of existential dialectics.

In light of our understanding of Johannes Climacus and his life of doubt, *his* writing can be explored with better clarity. He considers that his own conclusions of matters, what he refers to as 'opinions', are irrelevant. Johannes (Kierkegaard, 1985, p. 7) explains, "To have an opinion is to me both too much and too little, it presupposes a security and well-being in existence akin to having a wife and children in this mortal life" and instead he explains what is of most importance to him, namely "I have trained myself… to be able to dance lightly in the service of thought… renouncing domestic bliss and… joys that go with having an opinion." At the end of this section he concludes, "All I have is my life, which I promptly stake every time a difficulty appears. Then it is easy to dance for the thought of death is a good dancing partner, my dancing partner" (p. 8). Rather than being a dance partner for another person, here Johannes is indicating that one's *own* dance partner ought to be the thought of one's *own* death which is made possible when one stakes one's whole life. This shall now be examined as to why such dancing is so important for education.

DOUBLETHINK AND THE IMPORTANCE OF DOUBT

Drawing upon the importance that Johannes's doubt and his notion of dancing with the thought of one's death have for being educated, this section will now explore how they can protect one from becoming indoctrinated. Both education and indoctrination involve teaching and learning. Clearly then, only some types of teaching and learning can be regarded as having educative value while other sorts can be recognized to be miseducative as Dewey described, or even indoctrinatory. One criterion which can be used to help distinguish between education and indoctrination is the presence of doubt and thinking. Educators are generally familiar with the championing of thinking by Dewey (1985, p. 170) who concluded that "the important thing is that thinking is the method of an educative experience." In addition, he importantly warned that a "cold-storage ideal of knowledge… swamps thinking" (p. 165). This is very similar to Freire's (2000, p. 71) 'banking concept' of indoctrination which is characterized by knowledge of reality being presented as "motionless, static, compartmentalized, and predictable" typified through such direct instruction as "'Four times four is sixteen; the capital of Pará is Belém'." Knowledge is able to 'swamp thinking' and be 'banked' into the minds of students especially when it is accepted second-hand by perceived authorities. Perhaps it is not too much of an exaggeration to 'bank' into the minds of the compliant, that 2 + 2 = 5, as this was exactly suggested by Orwell (2016) in his *Nineteen Eighty Four*.

In this parody Orwell describes a society in which the citizens were manipulated by the propaganda (or soft subjugation) of the government, which was referred to as Big Brother. This novel offers important insights for education because Orwell himself (i.e. Eric Arthur Blair) had first-hand experience producing propaganda material for the BBC when he worked for them between 1941 and 1943 during the Second World War.

As described by Orwell (2016, p. 16), the three slogans of the ruling party of Big Brother were:

WAR IS PEACE
FREEDOM IS SLAVERY
IGNORANCE IS STRENGTH

These slogans were also mounted on the building of the Ministry of Truth, which symbolized the state/corporate-owned media. Importantly, they also represent examples of doublethink which is a form of cognitive dissonance, which is a key for accepting life under authoritarian governments. For doublethink, each statement contains conflicting concepts which do not align with the others but are nevertheless believed to be true by those who simply accept them as 'cold-storage' facts. Doublethink, according to Orwell (2016, p. 34), involves "…carefully constructed lies, to hold simultaneously two opinions which cancelled out, knowing them to be contradictory and believing in both of them… [for example] to believe that democracy was impossible and that the Party was the guardian of democracy…" If statements of doublethink are believed, then believers are accepting them being 'banked' into their minds without any critical questioning. Believing that 2 + 2 = 5 for example, is only possible if one does not think actually about the relation between each element of '2 + 2' on the one hand and the total '5' on the other. One just accepts it as a matter of credulity, and especially so when the force of consensus and fear of government punishment are applied. To differ is to dissent and our societies and institutions have little toleration for views which genuinely challenge the status quo.

It is of great concern that many similarities in our current society with Orwell's *Nineteen Eighty Four* can be observed. However, this is not a recent phenomenon which has emerged. A century ago Bertrand Russell (1922, pp. 41–2) observed that in his day "everything in newspapers is more or less untrue" and that "Credulity is a greater evil in the present day than it ever was before" and indeed operated as one "of the chief obstacles to intelligence." What was needed, he declared, was the element of doubt and the development of a scientific temper, one which enabled individuals to seriously question what was published by the media and by politicians. Such doubting can be employed toward various political slogans to seriously question and examine them. The conceptual relation is between life and death and how this helps students – and all people – to defend themselves against manipulation and propaganda.

Russell and Dewey were both well aware of the 'corporate age' of their time, or what is now referred to as rampant neoliberalism and monopoly capitalism, which operates as a highly influential network of elites who dominate world capital and control the mainstream media. Together these are often referred to as the military-industrial-academic complex (Giroux, 2015; Peters & Besley, 2021; Schostak & Goodson, 2020). This network literally controls much of the world, especially the West (Chomsky, 2016; Pilger, 2016), and they successfully indoctrinate the public through mass education and propaganda (Chomsky, 1989, 2001; Furlong, 2013; Gatto, 2010; Herman & Chomsky, 2002) and fear (Dodsworth, 2021) to consent to their various policies and practices. This is largely possible because through formal education the masses adopt a disposition of uncritical credulity rather than one of doubt and of a scientific and critically thoughtful temper. As Corske (2011, p. 93) observes, "an effective system of soft subjugation [i.e. propaganda] will cultivate naïve and trusting subjects, in order to capture their human energy." Importantly, what Corske and Chomsky (1989, p. 38) also both contend, is that it is "the educated elites who are the prime targets of propaganda" who have been indoctrinated the most, because they are the primary potential source for spreading dissenting views.

Even Dewey and his immediate circle of colleagues are included as one of Chomsky's (2001, p. 163) examples of the most educated who have been deceived by propaganda and yet were claiming 'self-adulation' with their own moral views. One of the key strategies of propagandists is to move people emotionally so that they come to assume they occupy the moral high-ground and they are the ones who 'are doing the right thing' as encouraged by what they are led to believe is their good and caring government which is reflective of Kierkegaard's second stage of ethical existence. On this Chomsky (1989, p. 13) quotes James Mill who made the observation "in the early days of the establishment of the system: to 'train the minds of the people to a virtuous attachment to their government'." Consequently it is the most educated amongst us who ought to be all the more attentive, reflective, and even doubtful, as to our being 'educated' rather than indoctrinated.

Orwell was significantly influenced by Burnham's 1941 book *The Managerial Revolution*. In this Burnham argued that the democratic societies of the West were being taken over by a new form of totalitarianism in the form of managerialism. In his own book *Nineteen Eighty Four*, Orwell portrayed his totalitarian society as being one that was tightly controlled managerially. He argued that this was made possible by subjecting the public to continual emotional stress. They were clearly very fearful of punishment, including being vaporized and literally written out of existence if they failed to comply with every expectation made on them by the State. The other strong emotion they were subjected to was hate, and this was supported by participating in a full-bodied hate session every day. Their hate could be directed against various sub-groups, individuals or causes that the government identified as being worthy targets. The public were also disconnected from history and so lacked perspective on how to judge current circumstances. Such a disconnection from history reflects the Marxist doctrine that was enthusiastically embraced by the Bolsheviks to totally remove historical cultural knowledge as much as possible, under their slogan that it was all bourgeoisie and needed to be rooted out, especially the Orthodox Church because this organization offered a set of criteria which offered guidance for moral conduct and a sense of ultimate values for adherents who staked their lives – and their deaths – upon their religious convictions. Consequently religion was understood as offering resistance to 'massaging' the minds of the masses emotively to 'do the right thing' as defined by the State, because converts tended to have a very strong sense of self that was integrated into a coherent and unified world view and one that they were willing to stake their lives upon – just like Johannes.

In his book *After Virtue*, MacIntyre (2007) recognizes that our societies in the West are currently dominated by bureaucratic managerialism and emotivism – just as predicted by Orwell and Burnham. He defines emotivism as "the doctrine that all evaluative judgements and more specifically all moral judgements are *nothing but* expressions of preference, expressions of attitude or feeling" [original emphasis] (MacIntyre, 2007, pp. 11–12) and so tend to be without criteria. One of the key characteristics of "the emotivist self" is, according to MacIntyre (2007, p. 33) that she lacks "any ultimate criteria" and so "the self is now thought of as criterionless" lacking even a sense of rational history. The public are managed and controlled through emotivism. This is evident, for example, in the manner that politicians and their agencies regularly exaggerate the perceived evils of those who oppose their policies. For example, protesters against government sanctioned vaccine mandates in Australia, New Zealand and Canada have been labelled as anti-vaxxers, anti-science, far-right extremists and fascists (Roose, 2021). Using such emotive language, along with a manufactured crisis and fear (Dodsworth, 2021), the public were encouraged to hate such protestors and what they stood for. It becomes easy to hate people once they have become labelled in this way and it is one reason why Antifa, who identify themselves as anti-fascist, has adopted the slogan to 'punch a Nazi' (Bray, 2017; Shaw, 2020) because this is so emotively charged and appeals to a 'hate' that has long been crafted against the Nazi's of the Second World War. Such 'hate' is believed to be easy to tap into through the simple use of the label 'Nazi' even although this label can be used quite arbitrarily. Therefore, there is no need to reason, deliberate or discuss out of any sense of respect for the other, but instead, Antifa encourage violence against who *they* identify as being a fascist or a Nazi.

The current 'cancel culture' of our time is dismissive of entering into civilized discussions and debates and instead aggressively demand the silencing of the other by labelling their views as phobic or demonstrating 'hate speech' and require that their own emotive views and preferences be the accepted norm. Of course 'hate speech' is not rational and would be classified by MacIntyre as being criterionless. Antifa represents one of the more extreme examples of cancel culture where, according to Bray (2017, p. xv) they shun the principle of the right to free speech because instead they have "committed themselves to fighting to the death the ability of organised Nazis to say anything." However, educators would rather have citizens become transformed through deliberations rather than having them silenced (Webster, 2011, 2021).

The point being made here is that the analyses being made by Chomsky and MacIntyre indicate that our current populations of the West are being manipulated and indoctrinated through emotivism, and is producing a great deal of doublethink which has been famously portrayed through Orwell's *Nineteen Eighty Four*. It is through doublethink that people can accept that war is peace, freedom is slavery and 2 + 2 = 5 *because* these are all matters of efficiently managed, obedient, emotive belief and *not* understandings which have been arrived at through critical, skeptical and careful thought. Such critical thinking is only possible through giving opportunity to doubt that the concepts being considered, such as 'peace' and 'war', are legitimately related or may alternatively not be so agreeable. The very first stage of critical thinking is to doubt and with this of course comes the fear of the crowd because one may not comply with *their* norms.

Undertaking thoughtful doubt about various concepts, ideas and suggestions which are presented through mass culture, requires criteria to enable one to evaluate and make judgements as to their validity and value. As such the educated person does not simply accept and uncritically believe because she was the recipient of some direct instruction. The unification of one's life as a whole, in terms of how the meaning and purpose of a *good*, ethical and fair life might be understood, thus provides the framework and criteria from which one can think and judge. MacIntyre, by referring to Kierkegaard, argues that this integrated and holistic unifying understanding of one's life as a whole, is an essential defense against manipulating forces. In summary MacIntyre (2007, p. 203) states:

> ...unless there is a *telos* which transcends the limited goods of practices by constituting the good of a whole human life, the good of a human life conceived as a unity, it will *both* be the case that a certain subversive arbitrariness will invade the moral life *and* that we shall be unable to specify the context of certain virtues adequately. These two considerations are reinforced by a third: ...the virtue of integrity or constancy. 'Purity of heart,' said Kierkegaard, 'is to will one thing.' This notion of singleness of purpose in a whole life can have no application unless that of a whole life does.

Here MacIntyre identifies that people can protect themselves from being manipulated by emotive appeals to various virtues by having a unity within themselves regarding ultimate meanings and purposes of life – or a *telos*. Interestingly he likens this unifying moral life to Kierkegaard's notion of purity of heart which shall now be considered in light of his existential dialectics in order to come to an understanding as to how a life of doubt, dancing with the thought of one's death, as characterized by Johannes, is so valuable for being educated.

EXISTENTIAL CHOOSING AND DIALECTICS

One of the key differences between the existential choice offered by both Sartre and Kierkegaard is that Sartre portrayed it as an event that one could participate in, while Kierkegaard argued that it is something that one *is*. For example, in his novel *Iron in the Soul* Sartre's (1949, p. 202) character Mathieu, who appears to be in a hopeless situation during the Second World War, considers that he is going to die and thinks to himself, "I have decided that death has all along been the secret of my life, that I have lived for the sole purpose of dying. I die in order to demonstrate the impossibility of living" (p. 203). These are the reflective thoughts on the event of dying which Mathieu has chosen or decided is to *happen* to him as if it were something external that is going to take something (i.e. life) away from him.

In contrast, Kierkegaard's presentation of existential choices and decisions are very much an aspect of one's life as a whole. He considered that existential choice, followed by conviction and commitment, was able to define who the individual actually *is*, what one values and what one aspires towards. MacIntyre (2001, pp. 340–1), with reference to Kierkegaard, concedes that his book *After Virtue* "ignored the complexity of the relationships... the self that makes that choice, and the self that is constituted by that choice" and now appreciates Kierkegaard's position where "the choice... constitutes me." Kierkegaard's own focus was upon Christianity and so he understood that Christians live their lives in total commitment and devotion to the way of life that they had chosen and decided upon, and that such a decision is not a one-off event but is something that continues to be chosen every moment in one's life. This led to his concept of purity of heart which he presented in his book *Upbuilding Discourses in Various Spirits*.

In this book Kierkegaard identifies himself as the author and offers various reflections for readers to consider while they strive to make their own lives more meaningful. One idea he presents is that of regret. Kierkegaard (1993, p. 13) writes, "So strange a power is regret, so sincere is its friendship, that there is in fact nothing more terrible than to have escaped it entirely" to indicate that in order for us to truly learn from our mistakes (or regrets) they must not be forgotten because they are our 'friends' who can help us grow and improve. This involves ongoing thoughtful reflection which engages with one's ultimate sense of value and one's current activity, and leads to a unity of value and purpose for oneself. Kierkegaard continues by arguing that "one cannot *confess* without this unity with oneself" (p. 20) to indicate that confession, perhaps either to a priest or counsellor, involves one responding to one's regrets with all of one's being. Interestingly he goes on to consider confession before God and claims that "the Omniscient One does not find out anything about the person confessing, but instead the person confessing finds out something about himself" (Kierkegaard, 1993, p. 22). Similarly with prayer which he suggests does nothing to change God but it does change the one who does the praying.

Through critical self-reflection perhaps involving regret, confession and prayer, Kierkegaard (1993, p. 24) then reaches his key point which is that "purity of heart is to will one thing." He supports his claim with the scripture in James chapter 4:8 which reads "Keep near to God, then he will keep near to you. Cleans your hands, you sinners, and purify your hearts, you double-minded" (cited by Kierkegaard, 1993, p. 24). He uses this sinful condition of being 'double-minded' as the problem that hinders us from personal growth. Such double-mindedness, which is different to Orwell's doublethink, can be understood as having ulterior motives and consequently not being genuine with others or even with ourselves. Kierkegaard concludes that "everyone who in truth is to will one thing must be led to will the good" because "the person who wills the good for the sake of reward does not will one thing but is double-minded" (pp. 35 & 37). Clearly he was against those who chose to become Christians for the purpose of being saved and going to heaven because what they ought to focus upon is being in a good relation with God and fellow humankind as a singular goal and purpose, without having the ulterior motive of receiving a reward of dwelling in heaven. The calling then, is to focus on who one is and the advice given is to live with a purity of heart by seeking and willing one thing – the good. By referencing both Augustine and Kierkegaard, Westphal (1996, pp. 40–1) suggests that because evil is "a perversity of the will" then a change of heart to one that is more pure must focus upon renewing "the direction of the will." This requires an ongoing dialectic with profound ideas that becomes a characteristic of educated individuals. So a purity of heart is characterized by willing one *good* thing which unifies oneself into a whole.

This notion of purity of heart from Kierkegaard is also found in the works of Dewey. While Dewey uses different terminologies he does offer some further details on what this might entail. With reference to the self which seeks the good he argues that "In truth, only that self is good which wants and strives energetically for good consequences; that is, those consequences which promote the well-being of those affected by the act" (Dewey, 2008, p. 288). This is quite different to passively complying with what others or authorities may demand. Both Dewey and Kierkegaard promoted the notion that one ought to choose *because* one has thought about, understands, is convicted of, and freely commits oneself out of a sense of who one is rather than what one must do to 'do the right thing' according to public opinion.

Considering life within Kierkegaard's highest stage of the religious can lead us to better appreciate how his existential dialectics is significantly different from the dialectics proposed through Hegel's system. The thinking which occurs via Hegel can be likened to a dialogue between a thesis and an antithesis, which, because it is engaging with an objective truth, is able to be resolved through a synthesis of these opposing views. Kierkegaard's approach to dialectics begins in a very similar manner with a subjectively experienced encounter, but because the possibilities which one must grapple have to do with one's very *being*, meanings and personal purposes for life, it is unable to lend itself to a resolution because it is fundamentally subjective in nature. Therefore, a key aspect of such an existential encounter is a deeply felt anxiety or angst because each individual is unable to place one's confidence upon a solid foundation, which many approaches to epistemology seek to attain. So unlike Hegel's dialectics which initially begins with subjective uncertainty and ends through establishing knowledge through resolutions, Kierkegaard's existential dialectics remains within this initial phase because, rather than seeking an impersonal and even 'objective' form of knowledge, it continues to grapple with who one really is and how one should conduct one's life each moment to reflect this identity. It is this thoughtful, reflecting grappling that is being likened to a dance.

Unlike many forms of dancing which have their characteristic steps, movements and styles, the sort of dancing which Kierkegaard uses to describe dialectics or thinking, seems to be far more free-flowing, uncertain, tentative and even playful. In the first section of this chapter it was noted how it was likened to Johannes stumbling as he attempted to walk through the streets while holding up a great and fragile stack of weights. Consequently it can be appreciated that this sort of dancing is more uncertain with each step rather than having the confidence of following a customary pattern of steps and movements or even imitating the movements of others. This is because the dancing represents existential thinking about one's very existence with its limits such as death, which is simultaneously a very weighty topic and without a sure procedure to follow.

THE TASK OF BEING A SELF DEPENDS UPON WILLING THE GOOD

The freedom involved in being able to choose who to be, how to relate and how to act in matters of ultimate importance and value, is understood to be an existential experience in the sense that the meaning of one's existence is being worked out in the absence of any absolute certainties. Kierkegaard identifies that this choosing takes place between one's actuality (who one is up to this moment), and one's possibilities (regarding who one might become). This experience between actuality and possibility, is described as being one of existential doubt due to the moment of decision – whichever way it is to go. It involves the exercising of one's freedom which, because of conviction and commitment, can be understood as employing more of one's *will* rather than only one's imagination. Existential decisions extend beyond mere wishes and instead involve convictions and commitments, hence why the notion of one's *will* is so important. With reference to this sort of freedom, Dewey (2008, p. 305) claims that it "is connected with possibility of growth, learning and modification of character" which aligns very well with Kierkegaard's view.

Appreciating this insight, Barnett (2007, p. 15), who promotes the value of ontology over epistemology, concludes that "'Will' is the most important concept in education." He appreciates the existential perspective and argues that "higher education calls upon students to come to their own interpretations, actions, judgements and arguments" (p. 32). He even goes so far as to state that in "… the language of existentialism… The idea of commitment is, I contend, central to the idea of higher education…" (p. 48). He explains that the role of higher education is to enable students to stand on their own feet, so to speak, in an individually responsible manner while he adds that higher education "requires the student to state her reasons for her point of view" (p. 54). Educators ought to see the relevance for this in contexts in addition to higher education. This is because critically thinking about and understanding one's reasons for one's point of view immediately differentiates the educative (and democratic) individual from the compliant masses as portrayed in Orwell's *Nineteen Eighty Four*.

Clearly one's will is entwined with one's initiative to step out and enact what one believes to be important as an individual rather than as a member of a crowd or a conforming and obedient servant. This is partly why doubt is experienced because there is always risk when committing oneself to live a particular way without being sure as to where this might lead. Conforming to group think is a very powerful force working against existential freedom and this has been famously demonstrated through psychological experiments such as those conducted by Milgrim (1974) and Ashe (1951). Even before these published experiments Bertrand Russell (2010) recognized back in the 1930s that early school culture has a very strong influence for causing young people to develop the habitual disposition to conform to what he described as 'the herd'. He too associates happiness with easy-going conformism, but invites his readers to fight some of the corruptions and evils in this world. He exhorts his readers to lift their sights higher rather than on simply seeking happiness and pleasure for themselves and to instead take on the troubles and burden of being involved in bigger projects which make the world a little bit better.

So dancing with the thought of death means giving serious thought to the weightier ideas as to what is ultimately important. Such thinking involves doubt that perhaps who we are currently and what we value and are choosing to do, ought to be re-evaluated. The weighty concerns which are to be 'danced with' include seeing our death as representing the sum of who we are and who we have become. We have no other possibilities for changing ourselves once our death occurs. The sort of thinking that the dancing represents pertains exclusively to our existential concerns. This is recognized by Dewey (2008, p. 275) who eloquently suggested that such thoughtful "Deliberation is dramatic and active, not mathematical and impersonal" and so depends upon individual initiative. Consequently such deliberation over existential concerns contribute to "making a difference in the *self*, as determining what one will *be*, instead of merely what one will *have*." (p. 274).

One of the most significant insights that this offers is that the participation in existential dialectics help form who one is by making coherent and unifying all that one chooses to believe and value. The thinking, choosing and exercising of the will all contribute to determining who we are. The alternative, as encouraged in authoritarian societies, is to simply be credulous and obey. As Winston, the main character in Orwell's (2016, p. 77) *Nineteen Eighty Four* stated, "In the end the Party would announce that two and two made five, and you would have to believe it."

Democracy, on the other hand, depends upon an educated population who think for themselves rather than simply follow what the government proclaims are the laws, rules and requirements. As Dewey (2008, p. 280) contends, "Rules are practical; they are habitual ways of doing things. But principles are intellectual; they are the final methods used in judging suggested courses of action." Here he indicates that grappling with principles is related to who one is. He offers the insight that "In committing oneself to a particular course, a person gives a lasting set to his own being. Consequently… one is in reality choosing what kind of person or self one is going to be" and "the self reveals its nature in what it chooses" (p. 287). This seems to be understood clearly by Orwell's (2016, p. 96) Winston who is struck with the thought "that in moments of crisis one is never fighting against an external enemy, but always against one's own body." So we are left to consider that when grappling, thinking and 'dancing' with thoughts of weighty ideas, ideals and principles upon which to base our lives, we are in fact engaging in an educative and moral process of becoming a particular person.

In addition to being important for the moral and educative growth of persons, engaging in existential dialectics is also essential for democracy. This is recognized by Alexander (2013, p. 202) who explains that,

> the core of the democratic virtues lies in the ability to learn the art of living meaningfully, cultivating experience so that society can intelligently act for those consummatory experiences which realize the deepest sense of embodied value and meaning in our existence.

He then encapsulates this in terms of our thinking, choices, will, commitment and passion in a united sense of identity by citing the existential theologian Tillich who declared that "No love is real without a unity of *eros* and *agape*" (cited by Alexander, 2013, p. 398). In short, we are what we love and are devoted towards. Alexander continues to argue that "When Eros engages culture as education (itself the dialogue of death and life…) it transforms into care, the selfless giving by the past in the present to the future, that is, Eros becomes *agapē*" (p. 394).

This led Alexander to suggest that the notion of 'conversational teleology' can be understood to represent this art of living meaningfully. It is contended that Climacus's notion of 'dancing with the thought of death' is this same sort of 'conversational teleology' which is characterized by doubt and leads to revealing who one is via a very openly thoughtful and considered set of values and principles which are united in such a way as to offer the criteria by which one can evaluate and make judgements in a responsible and accountable manner.

CONCLUSION

It would appear then, that dancing with death, as thinking about the weightier and ultimate existential concerns, is a big ask for educators and teachers. However, this is precisely the primary role of the educator, to assist and guide the moral and educative growth of all individuals, and that this is in fact an imperative for those of us who are pursuing a democratic way of life. This view is also shared by Alexander (2013, p. 418) who argues that the "function of culture… is ultimately a dialogue between death and life. … Education exists because of death. Teaching is not just one career option among many. *It goes to the root of what we are.*" Having the thought of our own death and other existential weighty matters as our dancing partner, helps us to craft a life worth living which is able to actively demonstrate its inherent goodness through the choice of commitments and activities we undertake in education as we pursue the public and ultimate good.

REFERENCES

Alexander, T. M. (2013). *The human eros.* Fordham University Press.
Asch, J. E. (1951). Effects of group pressure upon the modification and distortion of judgement. In H. Guetzkow (Ed.), *Groups, leadership, and men.* Carnegie Press.
Barnett, R. (2007). *A will to learn.* Open University Press.
Bray, M. (2017). Antifa: *The anti-fascist handbook.* Melbourne University Press.
Burnham, J. (1941). *The managerial revolution.* Lume Books.
Chomsky, N. (1989). *Necessary illusions: Thought control in democratic societies.* Anansi.
Chomsky, N. (2001). *Propaganda and the public mind.* Pluto Press.
Chomsky, N. (2016). *Who rules the world?* Hamish Hamilton.
Corske, M. (2011). *Engines of domination.* Mark Corske.
Dewey, J. (1985). Democracy and education. In J. A. Boydston (Ed.), *John Dewey the middle works, vol 9: 1916.* Southern Illinois University Press.
Dewey, J. (1988). James Marsh and American Philosophy. In J. A. Boydston (Ed.), *John Dewey the later works, vol 5: 1929–1930* (pp. 178–196). Southern Illinois University Press.
Dewey, J. (1989). How we think. In J. A. Boydston (Ed.), *John Dewey the later works, vol 8: 1933.* Southern Illinois University Press.
Dewey, J. (2008). Ethics. In J. A. Boydston (Ed.), *John Dewey the later works, vol 7: 1932.* Southern Illinois University Press.
Dodsworth, L. (2021). *A state of fear: How the UK government weaponised fear during the Covid-19 pandemic.* Pinter & Martin.
Freire, P. (2000). *Pedagogy of the oppressed* (M. B. Ramos, Trans.). Continuum.
Furlong, J. (2013). *Education – an anatomy of the discipline.* Routledge.
Gatto, J. T. (2010). *Weapons of mass instruction.* New Society Publishers.
Giroux, H. A. (2015). *Dangerous thinking: In the age of the new authoritarianism.* Routledge.
Herman, E. S., & Chomsky, N. (2002). *Manufacturing consent.* Pantheon Books.
Kierkegaard, S. (1983). *Fear and trembling* and *Repetition* (H. V. Hong & E. H. Hong, Trans). Princeton University Press.
Kierkegaard, S. (1985). *Philosophical fragments* (H. V. Hong & E. H. Hong, Trans). Princeton University Press.
Kierkegaard, S. (1993). *Upbuilding discourses in various spirits* (H. V. Hong & E. H. Hong, Trans). Princeton University Press.

Kierkegaard, S. (1998). *The point of view* (H. V. Hong & E. H. Hong, Trans). Princeton University Press.

Kierkegaard, S. (2001). *Johannes Climacus* (T. H. Croxhall, Trans). Serpent's Tail.

MacIntyre, A. (2001). Once more on Kierkegaard. In J. J. Davenport & A. Rudd (Eds.), *Kierkegaard after MacIntyre* (pp. 339–355). Open Court.

MacIntyre, A. (2007). *After virtue* (3rd ed.). University of Notre Dame Press.

Milgrim, S. (1974). *Obedience to authority*. HarperPerennial.

Mouffe, C. (2013). *Agonistics*. Verso.

Orwell, G. (2016). *Nineteen Eighty Four*. Text Publishing.

Peters, M. A., & Besley, T. (2021). Making democracy safe for the world? Philosophy of war, peace and democracy. *Educational Philosophy and Theory*. doi: 10.1080/00131857.2021.1960503

Pilger, J. (2016). *The new rulers of the world*. Verso.

Roose, J. (2021). 'It's almost like grooming': how anti-vaxxers, conspiracy theorists, and the far-right came together over COVID. *The Conversation*. https://theconversation.com/its-almost-like-grooming-how-anti-vaxxers-conspiracy-theorists-and-the-far-right-came-together-over-covid-168383.

Russell, B. (1922). *Free thought and official propaganda*. Watts & Co.

Russell, B. (2010). *Education and the social order*. Routledge.

Sartre, J-P. (1949). *Iron in the soul* (G. Hopkins Trans.). Penguin Books.

Schostak, J., & Goodson, I. (2020). *Democracy, education and research*. Routledge.

Shaw, D. Z. (2020). *Philosophy of anti-fascism: Punching Nazis and fighting white supremacy*. Rowman & Littlefield.

Webster, R. S. (2011). Must Dewey and Kierkegaard's inquiry for world peace be violent? *Educational Philosophy and Theory, 43*(5), 521–533.

Webster, R. S. (2021). *Caring confrontations for education and democracy*. Routledge.

Westphal, M. (1996). *Becoming a self*. Purdue University Press.

Windholz, E. (2020). Governing in a pandemic: From parliamentary sovereignty to autocratic technocracy. *The Theory and Practice of Legislation, 8*(1–2), 93–113.

CHAPTER THREE

Education, Attention and Transformation*

Death and Decreation in Tolstoy and Weil

PETER ROBERTS

Leo Tolstoy (1828–1910) is best known for his two great novels, *War and Peace* and *Anna Karenina*, but he also has much to offer educationists.[1] He addressed educational themes in his non-fictional work, linking these with his broader ethical, political and religious concerns. In his *Confession*, for example, written in his fifties, Tolstoy speaks about learning, literacy and knowledge, contrasting the agonies he experienced via a life of reason with the faith embraced by those who worked on the land. In his later years, he continued to question emerging educational and social trends. In an essay on the essence of religion, for instance, he argues against the "learned men" who "have decided that religion is not necessary and that it will be replaced by science"; "[a] rational being," he says, "cannot live without religion because it is only this that gives him the essential guidance as to what to do first and what follows" (Tolstoy, 1987, p. 86). Tolstoy did not merely write about education; he also had an intense practical commitment to it. He established a school on his estate, emphasizing progressive ideals such as freedom,

---

* Chapter 3 is reprinted by permission from Springer Nature: *Studies in Philosophy and Education*, 'Education, attention and transformation: Death and decreation in Tolstoy and Weil', *40*(6), 595–608, Peter Roberts, Copyright © 2021 Springer Nature.
1 *War and Peace* was first published, in Russian, between the years 1863 and 1869; *Anna Karenina* appeared between 1873 and 1878. The English translations referenced in this chapter are, for *War and Peace*, Tolstoy (1972), and for *Anna Karenina*, Tolstoy (2000).

creativity and child-centeredness.² Tolstoy stressed the significance of feelings and passion in education, and of attending to children's interests and experiences. He raised concerns about the excessive reliance on reason, particularly in the earlier stages of human development, and he resisted the notion that education could be turned into a science.³ Education for Tolstoy was closely linked with moral and spiritual development, and he felt that schools had an important role to play in building a better society. Beyond these direct connections to education, there is in Tolstoy's corpus an abiding concern with how we come to be formed as human beings, with what we come to value, and with what we should strive to achieve. Key characters in *War and Peace* and *Anna Karenina* – Pierre in the former and Levin in the latter – undergo a process that is clearly educational, reflecting on their lives and maturing in their thought as their narratives unfold. One of Tolstoy's most moving short stories, *The Death of Ivan Ilyich*, can be seen in a similar light: as a work of fiction focused on the educational growth of a character as he negotiates the challenges life brings.⁴ In Ivan Ilyich's case, it is the ultimate challenge he must face: his own death.

Among educational philosophers, there has been surprisingly little exploration of death and dying.⁵ The reasons for this relative neglect are not clear. Perhaps the question of death is seen as irrelevant to educational inquiry. It is possible also that the emotions often associated with death – sadness, helplessness, shock, and anger, for instance – make it too 'difficult', too sensitive, to take on as a subject for investigation. Or, it may be the case that death has been present as a theme all along, but often in a more subsidiary role. The notion of death, or related ideas such as mortality and immortality, may appear as part of a broader examination of a thinker's philosophy. Considerations of this kind could be evident in work by educationists on Plato, Kierkegaard, Nietzsche, Heidegger, or Arendt, to name but a few examples. Whatever the explanation, there is merit in contemplating what might be gained by allowing death to occupy a more prominent position in the field of philosophy of education. One way of approaching this task has its roots in ancient history. Socrates maintained that philosophy prepares us for death, and this, as noted elsewhere (Roberts, 2020), implies an educational process. We *learn*, through living philosophically, how to die. But we can also begin with a slightly different question: What does death – as a concept, as observed

---

2   The most comprehensive examination of Tolstoy's educational thought to date has been provided by Moulin (2014). See also, Cohen (1981) and Kazemek (1998).
3   For a detailed discussion of education and the limits of reason in Tolstoy's work, see Roberts and Saeverot (2018).
4   *The Death of Ivan Ilyich* was published in 1886. The edition cited throughout this chapter is the English translation by Richard Pevear and Larissa Volokhonsky (Tolstoy, 2009).
5   Exceptions include Blacker (1998), Dahlbeck (2015), Peters (2019), Puolimatka and Solasaari (2006), Roberts (2012, 2020), Shim (2020), and van Kessel and Burke (2018).

among others, as anticipated for ourselves – have to teach us? This is, however, not merely a conceptual exercise. We can, this chapter will suggest, learn something worthwhile *from dying* – i.e., from the experience of moving towards the moment of death. Tolstoy's *The Death of Ivan Ilyich* provides a vivid illustration of this point. Ivan Ilyich, in dying, undergoes a profound process of educational transformation.

At the heart of Ivan Ilyich's transformation, it will be argued here, is the idea of learning to pay attention. This thesis will be developed in the light of ideas from the French philosopher and pedagogue, Simone Weil (1909–1943). Tolstoy and Weil are united, among other ways, by the fact that they both adopted their own distinctive approaches to Christianity. Having been raised in the Russian Orthodox tradition, Tolstoy would later grow increasingly alienated from the Church. Weil was raised in an agnostic Jewish household, but in the last years of her short life made frequent reference to Christian ideas in her work. She formed a firm friendship with a Catholic priest, Father Perrin, but did not want to join any Church. Both Tolstoy and Weil were strongly committed to addressing what they saw as the key social injustices of their times. Both became highly critical of rigid class differences and endeavored, in their own idiosyncratic ways, to support those whom they saw as less fortunate than themselves. They were both widely read, and did not hesitate to offer their frank assessments of other thinkers, past and present. Tolstoy's interest in education was also shared by Weil, who was employed for some years as a teacher, and who addressed educational themes in her written work. She, like Tolstoy, was something of a rebel in her pedagogical ethos, caring little for grades and institutional formalities. Both were restless souls, who agonized over ethical, ontological and metaphysical questions. In both cases, the theme of death looms large over their lives. Weil addressed this directly in her aphorisms, essays and letters, and for Tolstoy, death is present throughout his corpus of published writings, both fictional and non-fictional. Tolstoy declared in his *Confession* that his existential and spiritual angst had taken him to the brink of suicide, and Weil's refusal to nourish herself sufficiently contributed to her own premature death.

Weil passed away at just 34 years of age, but she left behind an original and influential body of work, much of which has only appeared posthumously. The most substantial publication she prepared in her own lifetime, *The Need for Roots* (Weil, 2002), was a commissioned study of social renewal. But some of her most powerful and lasting ideas have only been put together in book form through the efforts of others. *Gravity and Grace* (Weil, 1997), with its carefully selected and organized collection of Weil's aphorisms, is perhaps the best illustration of this point. The letters and essays published in *Waiting for God* (Weil, 2001) likewise offer a perspective on religious, ethical and educational matters that is immediately identifiable with Simone Weil. There is striking economy to Weil's writing in places, with short, pithy statements lending themselves well to ongoing reflection by scholars across multiple disciplines. Her ideas have been engaged by philosophers, theologians, political scientists, classicists, and educationists, among others. Weil's work may have been incomplete, but that does not mean a coherent philosophy cannot be constructed from the writings she left behind. Tolstoy and Weil differed on some points of aesthetic and ethical detail, but in many respects, they were kindred spirits. Weil's concepts could be fruitfully applied in seeking to more deeply understand a number of different Tolstoyian works, but they offer a particularly helpful framework for analyzing *The Death of Ivan Ilyich*.

The first part of Tolstoy's story sets the scene for Ivan's death, and paints a vivid picture of disconnectedness: between the unreflective routine of everyday life and the sudden, shocking confrontation with the reality of death. It is Ivan's realization that this is *his* death, and not death in the abstract, that provides the substance for his traumatic experience. As his condition worsens, his suffering intensifies, and he is filled with anger, confusion, and despair. Gradually, through acts of attention (his own and others'), he moves toward a position of greater equanimity in facing the death that awaits him. Ivan's eventual acceptance of death is by no means a straightforward process. His experience is consistent with the passage from what Weil calls "gravity," through the void of intense suffering, toward a state of grace. Educational transformation, this story suggests, is often difficult, uneven and incomplete. From Tolstoy, and from Weil, we can learn that right up to the moment of our death, there is always more work to do.

A STRANGER COMES KNOCKING

Leo Tolstoy's *The Death of Ivan Ilyich* is widely regarded as one of the most important and insightful portraits of death and dying in world literature. When Tolstoy sat down to write this famous story, he had nothing left to prove in a literary sense, with *War and Peace* and *Anna Karenina* having already established his place in history as one of greatest writers of his age. The story was composed between 1884 and 1886 and had its origins in the sudden, real-life death in 1881 of a 45 year old man, Ivan Ilyich Mechnikov. Mechnikov had worked as a prosecuting attorney in Tula, a city about 12 kilometers from Tolstoy's estate (Pevear, 2009, p. xviii). The two men had, in fact, met with each other, Mechnikov visiting Tolstoy on one occasion, the latter finding the former a rather odd character. As Pevear points out, the Ivan Ilyich of the story is initially portrayed in quite a different way – as a "most ordinary" man – only to be utterly transformed as he undergoes the process of dying (p. xviii).

How, then, does Tolstoy tackle the question of death, this most difficult of subjects, a theme with which he was intimately familiar from both his earlier literary works and his own confessional musings (Tolstoy, 1972, 1987, 2000)? In *The Death of Ivan Ilyich* he begins with the death having already taken place: it is a subject that comes up for discussion among a group of Ivan Ilyich's former colleagues at the law courts one day. On hearing the news, the first thoughts of those present are about the promotions or transfers that might now open up for them following Ivan Ilyich's death. They also feel relieved that they have escaped the same fate that befell their colleague. One of these associates, Pyotr Ivanovich, prompted by a sense of obligation to a man he had known since boyhood, feels he must attend the funeral and go through the usual religious rituals and acts of condolence. He feels nothing when viewing Ivan Ilyich's dead body and is already thinking about the evening card game he has planned. Discussion also turns to plots of land that might be purchased. A sudden statement from Ivan Ilyich's widow, Proskovya Fyodorovna, about how terribly her husband had suffered during the last few days of his life, screaming incessantly, brings him to a temporary halt. Looking at his dead colleague's body again, he is terrified at the prospect that at any moment, he too could be confronted with similar pain. But he quickly removes such unpleasant thoughts from his mind, acting as if death was something relevant only to Ivan Ilyich and not to him (Tolstoy, 2009, p. 45). Both Pyotr Ivanovich and Proskovya Fyodorovna busy themselves with talk about the gruesome details of Ivan Ilyich's suffering – a matter of interest to the widow mainly for the affect it had on her nerves – and questions of money.

The scene of the present having been set, Tolstoy goes back to the recent past to tell us about Ivan Ilyich and how he came, at the age of 45, to die. We discover that as the middle son of three, he had enjoyed a relatively uneventful upbringing, and had negotiated the demands of law school and passions of youth relatively unscathed. With the help of his father, a government employee, he secures a post in the provinces and discharges his duties with appropriate restraint. His seriousness in his job is replaced by a joviality in social situations. He adopts a deferent posture with his superiors, but partakes of all the approved indulgences of men of his professional class. Consistent with the unbroken run of successes in his life to date, he is, within five years, appointed to a new post as an examining magistrate. This entails a move to another province but he is more than happy to make that sacrifice given the benefits associated with such a post. His position is held in high regard by others, and Ivan Ilyich is able to build connections with influential people and, in turn, play his part in influencing others.

He meets Praskovya Fyodorovna, who falls in love with him. He decides to marry her, both because her views of life accord with his own and because having a wife will be a fitting addition in his social circles. This pleasant little plan is disrupted somewhat by unexpected tendencies to jealousy and fault-finding from his new wife. At first he tries to ignore her outbursts but finds he cannot do so completely and is filled with terror: marriage, he comes to realize, is a disruptive force in his life. He takes a pragmatic approach, accepting the home comforts and social approval associated with marriage, and removing himself to his own private world whenever unpleasant incidents would arise. Children arrive, and Ivan is transferred to a post in another town. His salary has increased but the cost of living is higher, and his wife finds their new circumstances troubling. Apart from brief periods of amorous affection, Ivan and Praskovya exist in a state of estranged enmity. Ivan devotes himself to his work and tries to spend as little time as possible with his family. He finds himself intoxicated with the professional power that rests in his hands, and finds satisfaction in his superior ability to argue cases.

Having found a way to balance the mixed blessings of home life with the demands and rewards of his profession, Ivan continues to build his standing among his colleagues. His oldest child (a daughter) is by now 16, another has died, and his young son is, at the insistence of Praskovya, sent to preparatory school. But despite Ivan's success in his professional role, he is passed over, twice, for promotion. His bitterness over this snubbing is compounded by financial difficulties. He resolves, in avenging fashion, to secure an even better post for himself and is successful in doing so. This good news brings temporary cheer to Ivan and Praskovya's marriage, and as they immerse themselves in their new life in Petersburg, they acquire a taste for fine things, fashion their lodgings to their liking, and fall into a state of comparative contentment. They continue to argue from time to time but have fewer problems than had previously been the case.

This state of relative calm is punctured by the emergence of a new complication: Ivan has started to feel some physical discomfort in his stomach and has a strange taste in his mouth. He becomes more easily irritated, leading to further arguments with his wife, and eventually seeks medical advice on his condition. The doctor is inconclusive in his verdict, but Ivan has a feeling of dread and sadness. He finds the medicine prescribed for him does not help and grows increasingly desperate. Praskovya makes light of his experiences, jokingly blaming Ivan himself when speaking of his troubles to acquaintances. He senses that people are starting to make allowances for him, and he feels alone with his illness, others completely unable to understand the nature of his pain. Others who have not seen him for some time notice his changed appearance and when Ivan himself looks in the mirror, he too is shocked. He has been advised that his problems have to do with his appendix, but as he is lying in bed, trying to sleep, he comes to the startling realization that what he is really facing is a question of life and death. He can longer deceive himself: he is dying, and light will be replaced by darkness (p. 68).

ANGER, AGONY AND ACCEPTANCE

Ivan's sudden, stark realization that he will die – that death is coming, not just as an abstract idea, but in reality, *for him* – signals a decisive shift in the narrative. From this point onwards, it is not so much how Ivan has lived that will be the focus but how he will die. At first, when confronted with the stranger that is death, Ivan is perplexed and resistant. If death means nothingness, Ivan does not want it (p. 68). He is angry that others do not seem to comprehend what he is going through. But he too, in despair, cannot understand death. Death has always presented itself to him, where it had entered his consciousness at all, as merely something in the abstract; for death to now be something he, Ivan, a living, thinking, feeling human being, would have to face, was horrific. In all his previous dealings with the prospect of death, Ivan had managed to push such thoughts aside, but this was impossible now. No matter what else he was doing, death would make its presence felt. Unable to function properly at work or at home, he would retire to his study, and there he would experience the chill of finding himself alone with "*it*" (p. 72).

He comes to feel, more and more, as if others are simply waiting for him to die; waiting for him to relieve them of the need to deal with his presence. He sleeps less and less, and doses of morphine prove ineffective in ridding him of the torment that is worse than physical pain. He is no longer able to cope with normal bodily functions. Special food is prepared for him but eating becomes repugnant to him. In the middle of this rapidly declining state of affairs, a small ray of hope appears in the form of the butler's young helper, Gerasim. Gerasim has the unpleasant task of clearing up after Ivan. Embarrassed and weak, Ivan speaks to Gerasim, who undertakes his work quietly, willingly and attentively, with a lightness in his step. Where Ivan detects in others a falseness – a denial even that it is death he is facing – he sees in Gerasim sincerity and genuine empathy.

As Ivan's condition deteriorates, he finds that there is no escape from his torment. He has brief glimpses of hope, only to find that despair and pain once again intervene. In his anguish he wants to reach out to others, yet he knows that their company will only make it worse (p. 78). With the exception of Gerasim (and later his own young son), no one seems to understand him. When the doctor goes through the routine of examining him, Ivan sees nothing but deception and denial. Praskovya complains about Ivan not taking his medicine on time. Far from feeling love towards his wife, Ivan hates her. As he sees it, anything she does for him, she is really doing for herself. When people visit him, an uneasy silence hovers in the air, and he is disgusted by those who allow themselves to argue in front of him.

His anger and resentment grow, and the relentless pain and suffering persist, until finally the damn bursts and he cannot contain his tears. He weeps because he feels lonely and helpless, and he is angry at the cruelty of God – an absent God – and of other people (p. 83). He lashes out, without having a clear target, crying: "What have I done to You?" (p. 83). This moment of great distress is replaced by a new calmness. He listens attentively to a voice that seems to be his soul speaking, hearing the question "What do you want?," to which he replies: "Not to suffer. To live" (p. 84). His attention at this point is such that even his pain cannot distract him, and when he prompted further by his inner voice as to *how* he wants to live, he realizes that the best moments of his life had been in his childhood, a time he can no longer recover, a time that seemed to be experienced by a different person. As he reflects on his life, he comes to see that the more he had moved away from his childhood, the shallower his joys had become. The more he moved up in the world, the more he had in fact moved downwards. He wonders now what the point of it all had been, why life had been so odious and devoid of meaning. Why, he thinks, after such a life, should he then just suffer and die? (p. 84). His awareness that he has not lived as he should have lived becomes more acute, but he cannot find an answer to the question of how that should have been.

By now unable to move from the sofa, Ivan Ilyich lies, facing the wall, and continues his inner ordeal. He is alone, confronting an insoluble thought. Asking himself what it is that he is facing, he hears an inner voice confirming that it is death. As to why he is so tormented, he is told: "Just so, for no reason" (p. 85). He hears nothing further. Having previously swayed between hope and despair, now hope seems to have been destroyed. He is looking squarely at the face of death, and he is doing so in utter solitude. His mind returns repeatedly to the past, the most distant memories again proving the most pleasant. He remembers small details of how his senses were stimulated in childhood: the taste of French prunes, his toys.

The pain now so intense that he is wailing, Praskovya calls on him, and as she starts to talk about medicines, he stares at her spitefully and pleads to be allowed to die peacefully (p. 87). Their daughter, who arrives in the room at this time, feels sympathy for her father but is irritated that his pain is also tormenting her and her mother (p. 87). When a doctor tries to give Ivan something to ease the pain, the latter refuses his offer angrily. He reflects further on his life, coming to the conclusion that he has ruined all that has been given to him. He feels that everything about his life had been wrong. His wife pleads with him to take communion, and, despite his initial reluctance, he does so. It does little to dispel his feelings of hatred and disgust. Thereafter, his cries of pain are continuous. In his mind, he thrashes about violently, struggling against the black sack of death clutching for him. He keeps trying to tell himself that he had lived a good life, but this is what holds him back and torments him more than anything else.

Suddenly, he feels a powerful force against his chest and he is pushed into the black hole where death dwells. At that moment, his young son enters the room, sees his father suffering terribly, and as the sick man's hands thrash about, one lands on the boy's head. His son seizes the hand, holds it to his lips, and weeps. Falling inwardly, he sees a light and realizes that while he could have made more of his life, all is not lost. He feel sorry for his wife and son (p. 90). He wants to speak of forgiveness, utters the word "Forgo" instead, and does not have the strength to correct himself. But in that instant he obtains utter clarity: he now wants to act to deliver others in his family from their suffering, and in so doing, do the same for himself (p. 91). Now, finally, he finds himself able to attend to his pain and accept it. He no longer has any fear of death. He has no fear because there is "no more death"; instead there is light (p. 91). "So that's it!," he proclaims; "What joy!" (p. 91). For the dying man, this all occurs in an instant; for those standing near to him, the agony continues for a further two hours. Then, after a gurgling sound in his chest, and a few more moments of twitching, there is a gradual subsidence. Someone declares: "It's finished!" (p. 91). Ivan hears these words, repeats them inwardly, saying "[d]eath is finished … [i]t is no more," stops mid-breath, stretches out, and dies (p. 91).

DECREATION, ATTENTION AND TRANSFORMATION: THE EDUCATIVE STRUGGLE WITH DEATH

One of the striking features of *The Death of Ivan Ilyich* is its realism. Tolstoy does not 'airbrush' his characters, avoiding their most detestable features; nor does he romanticize the process of dying. While qualities such as kindness, thoughtfulness and compassion are evident in the thoughts, words and deeds of some who appear in the story, there are also plenty of examples of self-centeredness, selfishness and egoism. These characteristics are particularly prominent in the scene described at the beginning of the story, with Ivan's former colleagues and even his wife demonstrating a distinct lack of genuine care and concern over his passing. They seem to feel little sadness for Ivan and are more focused on themselves; on what the death means for them, on what they can gain from it, or on how it inconveniences them. They are more interested in the satisfaction of material wants and desires, through entertainment, money and property. They demonstrate an inability to place themselves in Ivan's position. They cannot imagine what it must it have been like to suffer as he did, even if they were present when he did so. They cannot truly *feel* his pain, cannot see it for what it was *for him*. Indeed, it is as if they cannot see Ivan at all. He is, in a sense, invisible to them as someone who existed as a complex thinking and feeling being. They are, in short, subject to the powerful force of what Weil (2001) refers to as *gravity*.

Gravity in the moral sphere operates in the same way as gravity in the physical sense: it drags us downwards. Gravity is at work when we take the easiest or most expedient path instead of the morally just, but more difficult, path. We feel the effects of gravity when we favor superficiality or sensationalism over depth and complexity. With gravity exerting its influence over us, we frequently fall prey to simplistic explanations and find ourselves readily swayed by the movements of the crowd. Gravity dulls our critical senses and lessens the significance of truth in our lives. We serve our own interests, and we pay little attention to the needs of others. Our focus is on satisfying our immediate wants, and we are unable to see how our preferences might be shaped by cultures of greed and consumption. Gravity is everywhere and always present. It is our 'normal' state of affairs, and something exceptional is required to reduce its effects. For Weil, the only deliverance from gravity is via *grace*. Grace is goodness; it is selflessness and love. Grace is mysterious; it can be felt but never fully defined. Grace is all-giving, all-encompassing, but if we try to 'pin it down', it eludes our grasp. Grace extends our perception of what is possible, without us ever quite knowing how it does so. Grace cannot be 'bought' or 'sold'. It cannot be destroyed, nor can it be acquired aggressively, through an act of conquest. Grace finds us, when we are ready.

Weil (1997, 2001) speaks of a tearing out that is often necessary if grace is to intervene. It is sometimes when we seem to be at our lowest ebb, suffering inconsolably, with no apparent relief in sight, that grace makes its presence felt. This is the case for Ivan, who cries out at the severe and unending physical pain he experiences and deep inner turmoil he feels. Ivan stares into what Weil calls the *void*, a point of no return, where all the usual rules about time and space seem to disappear. "To accept a void in ourselves," Weil says, "is supernatural" (Weil, 2001, p. 56). In facing the void there may be a sense of dread, perhaps of crippling fear, but there is also possibility. Everything that had gone before, shaping the ideas and patterns of behavior we take for granted, is called into question. Everything, in the midst of the void, is open for change. To enter the void is to prepare ourselves for the possibility of a profound transformation. Encountering the void is like staring into the abyss; it is, in Weil's words, "the dark night" (p. 56). Weil knew from first-hand experience how debilitating and painful, yet also potentially revealing and reinvigorating, a "dark night of the soul" could be (cf. Kovitz, 1992). Among other ailments and difficulties, she suffered from excruciating headaches, and sometimes found herself in a state of utter despair. Under such circumstances, in facing the void, we may feel as if we will fall forever. Yet, from this darkness, the ultimate unknowability of the void, light can emerge.

The journey Ivan undertakes from the moment death first comes knocking at his door resembles, in many respects, the process of *decreation* described by Weil. In Ivan's case, the process of decreation is particularly intense, all the more so as he feels death advancing ever closer. Decreation involves a movement from a state of self-centeredness toward a more selfless existence. It is by "decreating ourselves," Weil says, that "[w]e participate in the creation of the world" (Weil, 2001, p. 80). Decreation is not simply a whimsical choice, or an accidental occurrence; it is a prolonged, difficult, painful process. It can be conceived as a kind of death, or, more precisely, a form of *dying*. In explaining this, Weil uses the example of a seed that must die "in order to liberate the energy it bears within it, so that with this energy new forms may be developed" (p. 81). The same is true for human beings: "we have to die in order to liberate a *tied up* energy, in order to possess an energy which is free and capable of understanding the true relationship of things" (p. 81). Decreation requires both a harrowing confrontation with our own flaws and a readiness to change. If this path for transformation is to be cleared, humility, "the most beautiful of all the virtues" (Weil, 1997, p. 5), is necessary. Humility is not merely an indispensable starting point; it must be constantly reaffirmed as the forces of moral gravity – arrogance, excessive certainty, self-centeredness – threaten to intervene.

Cultivating our capacity for *attention* is the surest way of bringing about the kind of transformation Weil has in mind.[6] Attention cannot be forced; it is not a matter of, as it were, squeezing it out of ourselves. We must be patient, even in pain, and learn how to watch and wait. Equanimity and calmness are needed. Attention has both epistemological and ethical dimensions (Roberts, 2011). Through attention, we come to know in a new way. Attention is a matter of seeing ourselves and the world in a fresh light. It is also what is most needed when we face others who are afflicted. Our concern, Weil argues, should be with what the other is going through. We need to learn how to look at others, without prejudice or judgement, and to *see* them as if through innocent eyes. In an attentive gaze of this kind, "[t]he soul empties itself of all its own contents in order to receive into itself the being it is looking at, just as he is, in all his truth" (Weil, 1997, p. 65). Our focus, when attending to others in this way, should be on *them*, on *their* words, *their* gestures, *their* pain. This is not easy, for often, even as we listen to others, we are frequently preoccupied with other thoughts. We may be distracted with our own worries, or may, while someone is speaking to us, have already shifted our attention to what we will say in response to them. Weil counsels us to, as far as possible, suppress the insistent voice of the ego, and to immerse ourselves fully in the moment of the encounter with an other.

Ivan struggles violently with death, experiencing great pain, suffering within as well as without. The quiet acts of attention from others – the gestures of kindness shown by Gerasim, and the genuine concern demonstrated by his young son – are pivotal in helping him to gain a sense of perspective on his situation.

---

6 On the educational significance of attention in Weil's work, see Eppert (2004), Jesson (2014), Lewin (2014), Roberts (2011), Rytzler (2019), von der Ruhr (2006) and Yoda (2017).

With death approaching, Ivan is able to attend more closely to particulars, to the small details of his surroundings, his discourse with others, and his own inner conversation. At the same time, attention enables him to gain some necessary distance from the elements of his life that he comes to see as less important: ambition, advancement, wealth, and power. Ivan only begins to make a breakthrough in dealing with his situation when he realizes that he cannot win his desperate contest with death. Once he stops fighting, with himself more than anyone else, he can begin to see what had hitherto been obscured from him. His life before death's unwelcome visit has been characterized by a great deal of external 'noise': the demands of his career and family, the weight of social expectation, the hustle and bustle of career activities. The same constant 'chatter' continues during the initial stages of his illness, partly from without but also from within. Ivan is tormented not just by his physical pain but by the thoughts and emotions cascading through him. As he begins to apply his capacity for attention, he gradually learns how to slow down, to wait and to watch.

Even if we frequently fall short of the ideal, this does not mean progress cannot be made. Weil points out that though it may not be apparent at the time, no genuine effort of attention is ever wasted (Weil, 1997, p. 58). Our endeavors may not bear fruit immediately, and we may continue to struggle – sometimes for months or even years at a time. But the effects of sincere attentive effort will sooner or later be felt, sometimes in a domain seemingly disconnected from the one where they were initially applied. Weil maintains that "every time … a human being succeeds in making an effort of attention with the sole idea of increasing his grasp of truth, he acquires a greater aptitude for grasping it, even if his effort produces no visible fruit" (p. 59). Weil speaks of engaging "for ten years in an effort of concentrated attention that was practically unsupported by any hope of results" (p. 23). She describes the profound effect one form of attention – the regular repetition of a prayer – had upon her. She would recite the "Our Father," in Greek, over and over, both each morning and during the day while working in a vineyard. At times, she admits, her attention would wander or wane. But in such instances, she would begin again until she could repeat each word with absolute attention. "The effect of this practice," Weil observes, "is extraordinary and surprises me every time, for, although I experience it each day, it exceeds my expectation at each repetition" (p. 29). Weil continues:

> At times the very first words tear my thoughts from my body and transport it to a place outside space where there is neither perspective nor point of view. The infinity of the ordinary expanses of perception is replaced by an infinity to the second or sometimes the third degree. At the same time, filling every part of this infinity of infinity, there is silence, a silence which is not an absence of sound but which is the object of a positive sensation, more positive than that of sound. (p. 29)

What might attention to death yield for us, in an educational sense? In one his last diary entries, Tolstoy wrote: "I felt very vividly how beneficial for life is the thought that death may occur every instant" (Olney, 1972, p. 101). We retain this idea to the present day, usually stated in the form: "Live every moment as if it were your last." It is easy for such statements to become trite corporate catch-phrases, but for Tolstoy this notion had deep existential significance. As Olney observes, "In the midst of life, Tolstoy had the peculiar experience of feeling himself always in death, and that changed for him the very meaning of life itself" (p. 102). As Tolstoy saw it, we all exist under the shadow of death. The idea that one could be blasé about this, ignoring the "imminence and terrible reality of death" was, from his perspective, incomprehensible (p. 102). Some years later, Miguel de Unamuno (1972) would advance an even stronger view along similar lines, arguing that those who claimed not to care about death were monsters. For Unamuno, death was an obsession, and the prospect of nothingness was horrifying. In *The Death of Ivan Ilyich*, Tolstoy provides a vivid portrait of the terror that can be experienced in the final stages of life. For his protagonist, however, this only emerges when death comes knocking; for most of his existence, Ivan gives no thought to the question of his own demise. His lack of attention to death wraps him in a sort of protective shell. Tolstoy's 'awakening' to the reality of death came much earlier in his adult life. Death is everywhere in his work, as it is in the work of his fellow Russian novelist Dostoevsky. In Tolstoy's fiction, characters die through war and suicide, they consider questions of mortality and immortality in relation to the meaning of life, and they experience slow symbolic deaths through the tedium and routine of their everyday lives. Death provides the flame around which myriad Tolstoyian narratives and characters circle.

What bearing did Tolstoy's perception of the ever-present prospect of death have on the way he lived his life? In his case, and for Unamuno too, an awareness of existing always under the shadow of death was in some senses a source of great discomfort and anxiety (cf. Pachmuss, 1961). Thinking about death did not make Tolstoy's life any easier or happier or more straightforward; to the contrary, it made his existence more complicated, difficult and distressing than it might otherwise have been. On the face of it, this seems to provide a powerful argument for avoiding thoughts of death, or at least for avoiding the kind of thinking undertaken by Tolstoy. In his *Confession*, Tolstoy (1987) finds something of an antidote to his angst in the approach taken by the peasants with whom he associated: death did not seem to concern them, for they had faith. Unlike Tolstoy, they did not question the beliefs at the heart of their faith; they simply accepted them and got on with their lives. And yet, as has been noted elsewhere (Roberts & Saeverot, 2018), Tolstoy is less than convincing in his advocacy of this type of faith. He romanticizes the lives of those to whom he is referring and fails to adequately account for the irreversibility of a reflective mode of existence. Tolstoy could never adopt a 'simple' faith or comfortably dismiss his nagging doubts about what might happen to him after his death. He juxtaposed faith to reason, questioning the latter, but in doing so, logically, carefully and systematically, he simultaneously affirmed his commitment to rational thought. Tolstoy, like Unamuno, provides a sobering reminder that the voice of critical reason, once activated, can never be switched off. This point has broader pedagogical significance: with critical education, it can be argued, there is *no going back*.[7] A critical awareness of death, once activated, cannot be dismissed; rather, one must learn to live with, and *work* with, what this awareness has to offer. From Weil, we can learn that if that work is to be productive for us in educational and moral terms, it must be attentive.

Death is sometimes seen as a form of darkness, but, like the void in Weil's philosophy, it can also be seen as a source of light. The theme of light is significant for Weil, as it is for Tolstoy in *The Death of Ivan Ilyich*. Weil argues:

> If there is real desire, if the thing desired is really light, the desire for light produces it. There is real desire when there is an effort of attention. It is really light that is desired if all other incentives are absent. Even if our efforts of attention seem for years to be producing no result, one day a light that is in exact proportion to them will flood the soul. Every effort adds a little gold to a treasure no power on earth can take away. (Weil, 1997, p. 59)

In Tolstoy's story, the revelatory effects of attention, as light, are experienced in dramatic fashion. As the story concludes, truth, light and death converge. "To love truth," Weil suggests, "means to endure the void and, as a result, to accept death. Truth is on the side of death" (p. 56). For Weil, light – in the form of grace – enters where there is a space to be filled. Ivan creates that space, that void, having undergone a painful process of decreation. Having done so, he discovers new truths about himself and others.

Tolstoy, like Weil, held himself to a very high standard of truth, and there is also a link in his work between truth and death. For Tolstoy, as for Weil, there was little room for compromise. Truth, for both thinkers, was not merely a matter of convention or convenience but of 'life and death'. Both Tolstoy and Weil were dismissive of what they regarded as trivial pursuits in the name of entertainment. Tolstoy was adamant, for example, that art should not just be about beauty but should fulfil a spiritual purpose.[8] While their personalities differed in some respects, both approached life – and death – with a strident seriousness that did not always endear them to others. Tolstoy's "unflinching search for absolute truth" led him into conflict with the Church, and he was formally excommunicated in 1901 (Edmonds, 1966, p. 15). This followed the publication of his novel

---

7 See further, Roberts (2013).
8 This view is conveyed in *What is Art?* (Tolstoy, 1995).

Resurrection, a tale of a man, like Tolstoy, on a desperate search for redemption, but also a damning critique of social injustice and the institution of the Church.[9] As Edmonds observes, "[t]o the end of his life ... [Tolstoy] persisted in confining his quest to the ethical plane, until even his intrepid 'purgings of the soul' could advance him no farther and he found himself at a full stop – confronted by the cataclysmic choice between resurrection and – death" (p. 14).

The clarity Ivan attains in his last moments aligns with Weil's conjecture that "the instant of death is the center and object of life" (Weil, 2001, p. 22). "For those who live as they should," Weil says, the moment of death "is the instant when, for an infinitesimal fraction of time, pure truth, naked, certain, and eternal, enters the soul" (p. 22). In the course of a human life, birth and death are the "only two instants of perfect nudity and purity" (Weil, 1997, p. 84). Human life, Weil maintains, is "impossibility, absurdity," but impossibility can provide a door to the supernatural (p. 148). In undertaking the difficult work of decreation, we "make something created pass into the uncreated" (p. 78). Decreation is a kind of preparation for the moment of death. In living, we bear the weight of time, but in death we encounter "an instantaneous state, without past or future" (p. 84). To live in a world structured by the logic of time is to suffer, but this need not be pointless pain. Weil claims that "the transforming power of suffering and of joy are equally indispensable"; "[w]hen either of them comes to us we have to open the very center of our soul to it" (p. 79). This too mirrors Ivan's experience, but only at the very last. It is only as death is about to take him that Ivan is finally able to be at peace with his pain. In his last moments, he is, the story implies, calmer, clearer and more honest than at any other time in his life. He is able to forgive himself and others, face death with detached curiosity, and accept its embrace.

What is at stake here in educational terms? In the introduction to this chapter, the potential significance of death for educationists was signaled. From Tolstoy and Weil, it was suggested, we can learn that "right up to the moment of our death, there is always more work to do." In examining *The Death of Ivan Ilyich* closely, it is perhaps now clearer that 'dying' through decreation *is* the work that needs to be done, and that this is a profoundly educational process. Weil argues that the suffering we experience when others die is due to the "pain of a void," a sense of "lost equilibrium" (Weil, 1997, p. 66). But our own death, she adds, is the same. "The object and the reward are in the future," and deprivation of the future creates a void, a loss of equilibrium. "That is why," she says, "to philosophize is to learn how to die"; this is also why "[t]o pray is like a death" (p. 66). Prayer, as invoked in this context, is a form of *attention*. But the point Weil is making

---

9   *Resurrection* (Tolstoy, 1966) was first published in 1899, just one year after *What is Art* appeared.

does not apply to prayer alone; all attention, of the educative kind conceived by Weil, contributes to the process of learning how to die. This amounts, then, to a reconceptualization of the purpose of education. Weil (2001) makes it plain that all studies, whatever the subject area, are ultimately concerned with the development of our human capacity for attention. But if this possibility is to be realized, we must, as it were, clear the ground for grace to intervene, and this involves engaging in acts of decreation. 'Dying' in this way means learning to let go of that which drags us downwards in the moral sphere; of gradually overcoming the force of 'gravity' as Weil understands that term. We need the humility, the patience, the equanimity that Ivan Ilyich finally attains in his last moments. We need to learn how to step back from our usual self-interested inclinations, to watch, and to wait. Death, the deepest, darkest mystery in many lives, is not the cancellation of this process but its culmination; death is the moment where, in a single instant, the meaning of all the work we have undertaken is revealed.

CONCLUSION

In Tolstoy's beautiful, harrowing story, we witness an educative struggle with death. Ivan Ilyich, when faced with the sudden realization that he will die, is at first in a state of shock and disbelief. He goes on to experience anger, hatred, horror, and disgust, among other emotions. Over time he reaches a state of greater acceptance in the face of his own death, but this is not a simple, linear movement from one well-defined, clearly ordered stage to the next. Ivan's educational metamorphosis is complicated, messy and difficult. He finds himself on the edge of an existential abyss, struggles desperately with himself and others, and undergoes a painful process of decreation. For much of his life, he has never given the question of his death a moment's thought. He is swept up in the process of 'getting on' in the world; of attaining success in the eyes of others, and of advantaging himself relative to them. He is in the company of colleagues who seek similar goals. His marriage too seems, at least in part, to be one of convenience. Ivan's goals are, as it were, all external to him. Until the stranger that is death comes knocking, he has found no need to turn inwards, to examine himself. Death forces him to refocus his priorities, to *attend*, for the first time, closely to himself, to his relations with others, and to the deeper meaning of his life. Attention enables him, within the limited time he has left to live, to learn and to grow in ways he previously could not have imagined. The clarity that emerges for Ivan just before his death, at the moment when, in Weil's terms, he is in closest company with truth, is the culmination of a multifaceted process of transformation: from the gravity of unreflective superficiality and selfishness to the unbounded love and light granted by grace.

REFERENCES

Blacker, D. (1998). Education as immortality: Toward the rehabilitation of an ideal. *Religious Education*, *93*, 8–28.

Cohen, A. (1981). The educational philosophy of Tolstoy. *Oxford Review of Education*, *7*(3), 241–251.

Dahlbeck, J. (2015). Educating for immortality: Spinoza and the pedagogy of gradual existence. *Journal of Philosophy of Education*, *49*(3), 347–365.

Edmonds, R. (1966). Introduction. In L. Tolstoy, *Resurrection* (R. Edmonds, Trans.) (pp. 5–16). Penguin.

Eppert, C. (2004). Altering habits of attention in education: Simone Weil and Emmanuel Levinas. In H. A. Alexander (Ed.), *Spirituality and ethics in education: Philosophical, theological and radical perspectives* (pp. 42–53). Sussex Academic Press.

Jesson, S. (2014). Simone Weil: Suffering, attention and compassionate thought. *Studies in Christian Ethics*, *27*(2), 185–201.

Kazemek, F. E. (1998). Classics reconsidered: Tolstoy in the middle school classroom. *Voices From the Middle*, *5*(2), 34–39.

Kovitz, S. (1992). Simone Weil's dark night of the soul. *The Midwest Quarterly*, *33*(3), 261–275.

Lewin, D. (2014). Behold: Silence and attention in education. *Journal of Philosophy of Education*, *48*(3), 355–369.

Moulin, D. (2014). *Leo Tolstoy*. Bloomsbury.

Olney, J. (1972). Experience, metaphor, and meaning: 'The Death of Ivan Ilyich'. *The Journal of Aesthetics and Art Criticism*, *31*(1), 101–114.

Pachmuss, T. (1961). The theme of love and death in Tolstoy's *The Death of Ivan Ilyich*. *American Slavic and East European Review*, *20*(1), 72–83.

Peters, M. A. (2019). Against death. Longevity forever! *Educational Philosophy and Theory*, *51*, 1–4.

Pevear, R. (2009). Introduction. In L. Tolstoy, *The death of Ivan Ilyich and other stories* (R. Pevear & L. Volokhonsky, Trans.) (pp. ix–xxiii). Vintage.

Puolimatka, T., & Solasaari, U. (2006). Education for death. *Educational Philosophy and Theory*, *38*, 201–214.

Roberts, P. (2011). Attention, asceticism and grace: Simone Weil and higher education. *Arts and Humanities in Higher Education*, *10*(3), 315–328.

Roberts, P. (2012). *From West to East and back again: An educational reading of Hermann Hesse's later work*. Sense Publishers.

Roberts, P. (2013). Happiness, despair and education. *Studies in Philosophy and Education*, *32*(5), 463–475.

Roberts, P. (2020). Philosophy, death, and education. In G. W. Noblit (Ed.), *Oxford research encyclopedia of education* (pp. 1–21). Oxford University Press.

Roberts, P., & Saeverot, H. (2018). *Education and the limits of reason: Reading Dostoevsky, Tolstoy and Nabokov*. Routledge.

Rytzler, J. (2019). Turning the gaze to the self and away from the self – Foucault and Weil on the matter of education as attention formation. *Ethics and Education*, *14*(3), 285–297.

Shim, S. (2020). The existential meaning of death and reconsidering death education through the perspectives of Kierkegaard and Heidegger. *Educational Philosophy and Theory*, *52*(9), 973–985.

Tolstoy, L. (1966). *Resurrection* (R. Edmonds, Trans.). Penguin.

Tolstoy, L. (1972). *War and peace* (C. Garnett, Trans.). Pan Books.

Tolstoy, L. (1987). *A confession and other religious writings* (J. Kentish, Trans.). Penguin.
Tolstoy, L. (1995). *What is art?* (R. Pevear & L. Volokhonsky, Trans.). Penguin.
Tolstoy, L. (2000). *Anna Karenina* (R. Pevear & L. Volokhonsky, Trans.). Penguin.
Tolstoy, L. (2009). *The death of Ivan Ilyich and other stories* (R. Pevear & L. Volokhonsky, Trans.). Vintage.
Unamuno, M. de (1972). *The tragic sense of life in men and nations* (A. Kerrigan, Trans.). Princeton University Press.
van Kessel, C., & Burke, K. (2018). Teaching as an immortality project: Positing weakness in response to terror. *Journal of Philosophy of Education, 52*(2), 216–229.
von der Ruhr, M. (2006). *Simone Weil: An apprenticeship in attention.* Continuum.
Weil, S. (1997). *Gravity and grace* (A. Wills, Trans.). Bison Books.
Weil, S. (2001). *Waiting for God* (E. Craufurd, Trans.). Perennial Classics.
Weil, S. (2002). *The need for roots* (A. Wills, Trans.). Routledge.
Yoda, K. (2017). An approach to Simone Weil's philosophy of education through the notion of reading. *Studies in Philosophy of Education, 36*, 663–682.

CHAPTER FOUR

Immortality, Uncertainty and Education

Unamuno Revisited

PETER ROBERTS

Few thinkers have demonstrated a more passionate and sustained concern with the question of death than Miguel de Unamuno. The problems posed by death loom large over Unamuno's work, reflecting the prominent role they played in structuring his thought, his personality and his professional priorities. Death was a source of both anguish and hope for Unamuno. He had a desperate longing for immortality but was also well aware that from a rational perspective, this idea was an absurdity. This tension, between the prompting of our wants and feelings on the one hand and the voice of critical reason on the other, was, as Unamuno saw it, at the heart of the tragic nature of human existence. A towering figure in the history of Spanish letters, Unamuno served for many years at the University of Salamanca, as a Professor of Greek and as Rector. He is best known in the English speaking world for his philosophical treatise, *The Tragic Sense of Life* (Unamuno, 1972), but he also wrote novels and short stories (e.g., Unamuno, 1996, 2000) and newspaper articles (see Earle, 2019). He was fluent in multiple languages and was an active commentator on social and political affairs. He was never afraid to speak his mind, and his views did not always endear him to others in positions of authority. Unamuno had a commanding presence, both in person and in his writing. He asserted himself very much as an individual, and it was the distinctive 'I' that only he could be that he wanted to hold on to for all eternity. The possibility of individual immortality was, for Unamuno, essential in giving life meaning. He felt that if we could be certain that after we die there is complete nothingness, our lives would be pointless. Retaining some uncertainty – not being able to entirely rule out the prospect of immortality – is what gives us hope. It allows us to act as if life matters (Bubens, 2021).

As a thinker, Unamuno defies easy categorization but his work shares much in common with other philosophers and novelists in the existentialist tradition (Barrett, 1990; Cooper, 1999; Flynn, 2009; Kaufmann, 1975; Marino, 2004; Saeverot, 2013; Webster, 2009). His religious views have generated considerable discussion (Baker, 1990; Evans, 2013; Longhurst, 2015; Oya, 2020a; Rodgers, 2015; Summerhill, 1978). Unamuno was neither a straightforward man of faith nor an avowed atheist; he *wanted* to believe in God, but could not dispense with his doubts. His own struggles are reflected in the agonies experienced by his literary creations, most notably the priest depicted in his novella *San Manuel Beuno, Mártir* (in Unamuno, 1996; see also, Hollingsworth, 2013; Larubia-Prado, 2014). As a Spaniard, he was deeply affected by his countryman Cervantes' classic novel, *Don Quixote* (Cervantes, 2005), and his own stance on religious matters has been seen by some as Quixotic (Alessandri, 2018). Unamuno's thought has also been considered in relation to questions of gender (Barnes, 2013), art (Gómez, 2007), and politics (Shanley, 1977). His ideas have been compared with those of Kierkegaard (Evans, 2013), Dostoevsky (Mermall, 1978), Tolstoy (Roberts & Saeverot, 2018), Nietzsche (Oya, 2020b), Schopenhauer (Gómez, 2007), Bergson (Fraser, 2007), Marcel (Longhurst, 2015), and Camus (Dienstag, 2006), among others.

Unamuno's work has attracted some attention from scholars with an interest in educational questions, but there is plenty of scope for further inquiry (Boyles, 2016; Hughes, 1978; Luarsabishvili, 2019; Roberts, 2016; Roberts & Saeverot, 2018). His memorable description of consciousness as a "disease" (Unamuno, 1972) has important ontological implications, and his complex position on the nature and significance of knowledge poses ongoing questions for those with an interest in epistemological matters. Unamuno also has something significant to offer current debates over the question of identity and its connections with memory (cf. Longhurst, 2011). Most of all, Unamuno demonstrates how a central concern with the question of death can provide the animating force for a meaningful life. Unamuno's writings can prompt us to reconsider how we understand the nature and purpose of education, what we should expect of teachers, and how we see ourselves as learners. Unamuno helps to see that education extends well beyond the classroom; it is, his work suggests, very much a lifelong process, to which we become committed through grappling with the problems posed by the question of death. Death may not be in the forefront of our minds as we undergo the process of education, but it is, from Unamuno's point of view, always there in the background. All of our activities, he believes, are driven by an underlying quest for immortality, whatever form that may take. This chapter begins with a brief overview of Unamuno's stance on immortality, situating this in the context of his broader ontological and epistemological position, before turning to a more detailed exploration of some of the ethical and educational implications of his ideas.

CONSCIOUSNESS, CONTINUITY AND THE TRAGIC SENSE OF LIFE

Unamuno's ontological starting point is not an abstract concept of being human, or the idea of a collective, shared 'humanity'; his focus is on the concrete, specific individual – the living, conscious person "of flesh and blood" (Unamuno, 1972, p. 3). (Unamuno uses the term "man" in place of "person".) The specific person, Unamuno maintains, is both the subject and the object of all philosophy, whether this is acknowledged or not. What makes someone a certain person – distinctively that person and not someone else – is the combination of two principles: unity and continuity. Unity is the sense of purpose that guides our lives, even if this may change from one moment to the next. Continuity, for the individual, can be explained by reference to memory. Memory forms the basis of an individual's personality, "just as tradition is the basis of the collective personality of a people." "We live in memory and by memory," Unamuno says, "and our spiritual life is simply the effort of our memory to persist, to transform itself into hope, the effort of our past to transform itself into our future" (pp. 11–12).

For Unamuno, the notion of wanting to be someone other than the person one is does not make sense. We might wish to have something another possesses – e.g., knowledge or wealth – but the being that is ourselves is something to which we cling, even in the face of adversity. Unamuno elaborates: "It has often been said that every man who has suffered still prefers to be himself, with all his misfortunes, than someone else, even without those misfortunes" (p. 12). Misfortune is preferable to non-being, to nothingness. We strive to persist, to be, no matter what life throws at us. Unamuno wants to remain the flawed, suffering, longing, joyous, idiosyncratic individual being that he is. Becoming part of a larger whole, at one with everything else, is not enough for him. He wants to hold on to particulars that make him, his life and his memories, distinctive. A person might change significantly, Unamuno adds, but "only within the stream of his continuity" (p. 13). Unamuno acknowledges that people can undergo personality changes but argues that such cases are pathologies, demanding specialized treatment. Where changes of this kind occur, individual continuity has a physical basis only and the function of memory in shaping personality and consciousness disappears. For the victim, an illness of this kind is the equivalent of death.

If it is the instinct for self-preservation – hunger – that is fundamental to the individual human being, it is the instinct for perpetuation – love – that is fundamental to human society. From this proposition, Unamuno goes on to suggest that just as individual human beings grasp what is necessary to continue living, so too is there a sense within social groups of what is needed to keep a society going (p. 30). The perceptible world – the world the individual comes to know, driven by hunger – is complemented by an ideal world, an invisible and intangible reality, perceptible only by inner senses that exist in the service of perpetuation. These senses are often dormant, but they are there nonetheless, and "social consciousness" can be stirred. For Unamuno, the ideal world that can be known via our existence as social beings is as real and important as the physical world we perceive with our senses. It is from this world, a world of imagination and fantasy, that reason is born. As the world changes, we change too and our ability to think, to reason and reflect, continues to adapt and develop. We cannot know exactly what we will need to know 1000 years hence, but from what we understand of human history we might predict that something new will be revealed. We can reasonably foresee that we will come to know more of reality as this becomes necessary in maintaining our existence.

Knowledge, for Unamuno, is both a dead weight we must carry with us – the whole history of human thought dragging behind us – and also the source of our redemption. Our capacity for reflective knowing is a burden but one from which we cannot escape. To rebel against this simply digs us further into a pit of despair. As reflective, conscious beings, we suffer, and we must, according to Unamuno, live with the perpetual tension between, on the one hand, what we want and feel and, on the other, what reason tells us is true. The despair borne out of reflective consciousness, while individually structured and experienced, is nevertheless shaped by our relations with others. In considering questions of existence and non-existence, reason and reflection can only take us so far. Unamuno argues that we cannot "conceive of ourselves as non-existent"; consciousness cannot make sense of its own destruction, cannot comprehend the idea of "absolute unconsciousness" (p. 43). For Unamuno, the universe we perceive with our senses is too restrictive; his wish is to gain much more space to move, much more air to breathe: "I want to be myself and, without ceasing to be myself, to be others as well, to encompass the totality of all things visible and invisible, to extend myself to the limitless in space and prolong myself to the endless in time" (pp. 43–44). An expression of this longing for eternity in our everyday relations with others is *love*, for "whoever loves another desires to become eternal in this other" (p. 44). Love allows us to see the vanity of the present world, the world of appearances that will pass; it permits us a glimpse of something more, something beyond the limits imposed by fate and circumstances.

As individual men and women, the most important problem we face, each in our own way, is our own mortality: What will become of us when we die? Deep within us all, Unamuno suggests, is a longing for immortality. Unamuno has no patience for those who claim otherwise; he shares Pascal's view that anyone who adopts a posture of indifference toward the question of death is a "monster" (p. 46). For Unamuno, the certainty of physical death and the uncertainty of what, if anything, remains of our consciousness after this shapes everything else. As he sees it, this question haunts all efforts at constructing elaborate philosophical systems, even those seemingly far removed from notions of mortality and immortality. Unamuno detects in the work of Spinoza and Nietzsche, for example, distinctive forms of rationalism but also a richness of feeling, a fullness of life and an underlying desire for eternity. Referring to Spinoza's claim that the free person thinks of everything but death, Unamuno sees an act of denial that is characteristic of all philosophical work. Spinoza was thinking precisely of death; his philosophizing was an attempt to free himself of this thought, but in this he failed. To be free in the sense proposed by Spinoza is in fact to be dead, a slave to freedom (p. 45). Spinoza's work, far from being a serene meditation on life (the hallmark of wisdom as Spinoza sees it), is in fact a philosophy of despair – and this is a fate that awaits any deeply reflective human being.

Unamuno suggests that to resign oneself to the inevitability of final death – that is, annihilation of the self we become – is a sign not of strength but of weakness. Among those who are strong, he claims, "the urge toward self-perpetuation overrides the doubtfulness of achieving it, and their over-abundance of life overflows the boundaries of death" (p. 57). If we deny the possibility of life after death, or if we are overwhelmed by doubt, we tend to seek other ways of preserving ourselves for posterity. We want our names to be known, our memories to remain. This can be witnessed in the push among so many to distinguish themselves, a struggle that from Unamuno's perspective is "terrifying" (p. 59). This is evident among intellectuals in their obsession with originality, a tendency that involves an attempt to establish one's superiority over not just one's contemporaries but also those who are dead (pp. 59–60). The desire for this form of immortality thus extends not just into the future but back to the past. Driven in this way, we often fall prey to envy in the face of those who have already achieved intellectual immortality. We demonstrate our own insecurity as we seek to establish our own place among such immortals, and become bitter when we think we will fail to do so. For the sake of preserving our name, we will sacrifice not only happiness but our lives. We want to prolong ourselves more in time than in space. If we could choose between shining for an instant throughout the whole Universe and lasting forever in our own little corner, we would choose the latter. And we would do so for the same fundamental reason that drives those who seek life after death in the Christian sense: we are terrified of extinction. "We aim at being everything," Unamuno says, "because we feel it is the only way to escape being nothing" (pp. 63–64).

WAKE UP! UNAMUNO AND THE PURPOSE OF EDUCATION

The dominating presence of death as a key theme in Unamuno's work is difficult to deny. Death hovers over almost everything he wrote, fictional and non-fictional. But death for Unamuno does not mean *dying*; to the contrary, it is, or can be, a life-giving force. The thought of death drove Unamuno to think, to feel, to act; it provided the key to finding meaning in life. Not knowing what will happen to us when we die was a source of great agony for Unamuno, but the idea of not *caring* about this was intolerable. This is where a clue to discovering the educational significance of Unamuno's work lies. From Unamuno, we can gain a clearer sense of why death ought to matter to us all. Unamuno teaches us, but we must brace ourselves if we are to learn from him. Unamuno was, as William Barrett (1972) puts it in his Afterword to *The Tragic Sense of Life*, engaged in a *contest* with death (p. 361). Death was a combatant; an opponent in a titanic struggle. In reading Unamuno, we also enter into the fray with a formidable opponent. An encounter with Unamuno's work leaves us "shaken and winded" (p. 361). Unamuno comes at us "head on," and yet, "the man himself is so simple, direct, beguiling – a true friend, but a troubling friend" (p. 361). Being troubled in this way is at the heart of Unamuno's implied theory of education.

Unamuno's educative purpose was to *wake us up*. "My aim," Unamuno says in *The Tragic Sense of Life*, "is to make all men live a life of restless longing" (Unamuno, 1972, p. 349). Unamuno refers to an "invasive, overmastering, aggressive, inquisitorial ethic," where the spirit of one person is imposed on others (p. 306). We should, he argues, do everything we can to avoid lulling our fellow human beings to sleep; rather, we should seek to "arouse them to the anguish and torment of spirit" (p. 306). Our role is to offer our own suffering as "nutriment and consolation" for the suffering experienced by others (p. 306). The best way to address suffering, Unamuno believes, is through more suffering. We should not be turning to drugs to reduce or eliminate our pain; instead, we should be placing "salt and vinegar in the soul's wound" (p. 307). Unamuno is not suggesting that we should be inflicting physical pain; rather, his focus is on the inner turmoil we experience. His point is that we must avoid falling asleep; we need to keep feeling the pain that burns inside us, for in feeling, we exist – and continuing to exist is what matters most. This is, it must be noted, an ethic of *mutual* imposition: "All men should strive to impose themselves upon one another, to give their spirits up to one another, to leave their seals on one another's souls" (p. 307). Unamuno stresses that there is no one way of living in this ethic, and observes that in the animal kingdom, mastery can take many different forms, from the fierceness of the tiger to the cunning of the fox and the speed of the hare. For we humans, patience and resignation can also be "weapons of conquest," provided they are "informed by inner action and longing" (p. 308).

While Unamuno generally refrained from providing systematic ethical principles, there are some exceptions to this rule. If we accept, as Unamuno did, that the deepest longing we have is for our consciousness to persist, beyond death and forever, we can formulate a moral imperative of this kind: "Act so that in your own judgement and in the judgement of others you may deserve eternity" (p. 285). We should, Unamuno argues, make ourselves irreplaceable. We should act as if we were about to die but would then survive and live forever. These are, however, not abstract notions or ideas that exist simply in the service of a theory. We live the desire for immortality not just in our minds but through our conduct. Virtue does not arise from dogma; rather, it emerges in our actions. Similarly, faith does not create martyrs but is, rather, created by them. And 'conduct' for Unamuno is not just conduct of any kind; it is "passionately good conduct" (p. 285). Unamuno argues that if anything is good, it is good *for something* – that is, conducive to a particular end – and that end, as he sees it, is the desire for immortality. 'Good' conduct, then, is conduct that leads to, or is consistent with, this end. Beyond this, Unamuno remains rather vague. This too, however, is in keeping with his underlying ethic. Unamuno does not want to supply others with ready answers, for that would defeat his educational purpose. He *wants* others to struggle, in an inner sense, seeking answers to the most searching questions, for themselves. The point is not to resolve doubt but to cultivate it and to allow it to be maintained. Uncertainty is, from Unamuno's point of view, not merely permissible but highly desirable: "uncertainty, doubt, the perpetual wrestling with the mystery of our final destiny, the consequent mental despair, and the lack of any solid or stable dogmatic foundation, may all serve as basis for an ethic" (pp. 283–284).

It is the longing itself that provides the starting point for an educational journey, but as beings endowed with the capacity for critical reason, we cannot settle into a comfortable relationship with our desires. We must learn to live with the uncertainty thrown up by the conflict between reason and passion; this tragic tension is what defines us as human beings. Unamuno is clear that he does not wish, at the moment of his death, to see his consciousness annihilated or absorbed into some greater whole. He wants his longing – his hope – to last forever; to neither be fulfilled, nor obliterated (p. 278). In longing, there is life; there is striving, and suffering, and joy. In a life of longing, there is always a sense of something being missing, and with this, a deep, ever-lasting sorrow. "Our life," Unamuno observes, "is hope continually changing into memory which in turn again engenders hope"; "[a]n eternity which would be like an eternal present without memory or hope, would be death" (p. 278). Unamuno seeks not an eternal Paradise, with an end to all our suffering, but more a permanent Purgatory (p. 279). This is not to suggest that suffering of all kinds is desirable, or justifiable. Unamuno's concern, as noted above, is with the particular kind of suffering that emerges from the conflicting impulses within us. There is, he believes, no final or adequate 'solution' to these difficulties. Our condition is tragic, but it is this tragedy that gives meaning, substance and purpose to human life.

Unamuno felt a special kinship with Kierkegaard. He regarded the great Danish thinker as a 'brother' and drew inspiration not only from his writings but the way he lived his life. He learned Danish specifically with the goal of reading Kierkegaard in his original language. Unamuno saw Kierkegaard as a man of great integrity who committed himself wholeheartedly to the problem of existence. Their respective 'answers' to the problem of existence differed somewhat, but they were united in the view that our formation as unique individuals is a key task. "I came into the world to create myself," Unamuno says (1972, p. 52). This idea is important when pondering the link between immortality and education. If we are to uphold Unamuno's ethical imperative of making ourselves worthy of immortality, we must continually work on ourselves. This is a lifelong process; indeed, it is, from Unamuno's perspective, a life-sustaining process. We are, as individual human beings, necessarily incomplete; there is always more work to do. As circumstances change, new demands are placed on us. We change too, but something of us continues, connecting us with our past as we respond to the challenges of the present. Education occupies the space between past and future. It does not allow us to forget, continually reviving and refreshing our memories, and in doing so, exposes us to the possibility of despair as well as joy. But education also prompts us to anticipate what could happen, to explore alternatives, to imagine better worlds (Roberts & Freeman-Moir, 2013). In this sense, it offers hope. For Unamuno, the uncertainty that arises from our existence as conscious, reasoning, questioning beings is precisely where this hope resides. If we have, or feel we have, complete certainty, there is no need to learn, no need to inquire and investigate. The existence of doubt keeps us alive, open, ready to explore.

Unamuno wants to sustain life – existing conscious life, with all of its frailties and difficulties – and this implies *movement*. We can, if we take Unamuno seriously, never sit still, never fully relax; we will *always* be restless, always be a little 'on edge'. We can never know in any final or absolute sense, but must keep searching and struggling. Indeed, there is merit in shifting our focus from knowing to *learning*. If we know something, or think we know it, we tend not to reflect and probe and inquire further. Knowing means, in a way, that we can 'forget' things; we can park what we know to one side, making it unconscious. Unamuno wants to perpetually wake up the conscious self; he wants us to be forever reminding ourselves that we exist, and that we are beings endowed with the capacity to think, to feel, to want, and to act. Learning, as a process of remembering, but also of exploring unfamiliar terrain, can be our "highest pleasure" (p. 249). The joy, we can say, lies in the process of discovery, but this is only possible with some sense of our own identity as discovers – as searchers, engaged in "ceaseless learning" (p. 250). We can acknowledge that we change over time while also recognizing a connecting thread between what we are now and what we were 10, 20 or 50 years ago. Extending Unamuno's point, we might say that just as we may wake in the morning from the unconsciousness of sleep, "ceaseless learning" persistently rouses us from the tendency to forget. All learning becomes a matter of *re*learning our past, in the light of the problems posed by the present. Through learning we constantly remind ourselves to remember who we are and why we are here. The appropriate stance for someone committed to learning, then, is one of humility and openness. A learner is always willing to keep asking questions. Knowledge can be stored away in archives, but learning is always ongoing.

ASKING CRITICAL QUESTIONS OF UNAMUNO

On the face of it, Unamuno's educational prescription – offered as a means to cope with the "disease" that is consciousness – is startlingly strong medicine. Here is a writer who not only admits to his own inner torment but appears to want to make others suffer too. It is not that Unamuno is trying to be cruel or sadistic, as if he enjoys seeing others in pain. He is simply trying to describe what it means to exist as a human being. For Unamuno, the tragic tension he identifies between our desire for immortality and the voice of critical reason is not merely an expression of individual anguish; it is, he believes, something shared by us all (even if we cannot always see this clearly). This is not a form of suffering that any other creature endures; it is distinctive to human beings. In experiencing suffering of this kind, then, we live as we should: we fulfil our human destiny. We might accept this for ourselves, but Unamuno's position raises ethical questions when we consider the role we might play – as teachers, for example – in shaping other lives. How far should we go in prompting others to 'wake up', knowing this will make them suffer? There is no straightforward answer to this question. Every educational situation is unique. Teachers need to consider the age of the students with whom they are working. They need to think about the students' prior experiences and learning, the type of course or program they are completing, and the other relationships they have in their lives. What is possible and appropriate in a university will be very different from what we might reasonably expect to do in a primary school or early childhood center. There is sometimes a fine line between stimulating critical thought and bullying, and this may vary not just from one educational level to the next, but from one student to the next. It can be said, nonetheless, that teaching and learning are *always* risky processes. Teachers can never know exactly how their actions will affect others, and if we are committed to a process of learning that is more than mere drill or memorization, we open ourselves up to the possibility of being unsettled, disturbed, troubled. Even if the goal is rote learning, that too carries risks, for there are often negative consequences, both for individual learners and for wider society, of not being encouraged to pose problems or ask difficult questions.

Unamuno's work was sustained by the principle of struggle. The idea of death as the end, as nothingness, was so horrific to him that he fought with every fiber of his being against this. Unamuno could never go gently toward some eternal darkness. His struggle was not merely with death but also with himself. He responded with anger, frustration and despair to his own reasoning consciousness. For Unamuno, reason was, at times, an enemy, with whom he was engaged in mortal combat. The idea of struggle can be seen as fundamental to education (Kuhlman, 1994), but is it possible to sustain the same impulse for activity, the same tension between reason and longing, without the contestation and resistance that characterized Unamuno's life and work? Perhaps this need not be an 'either/or' question; we can be both resistant and accepting. Unamuno argued that we must learn to accommodate the disease that is consciousness, but there may be more than one way of doing this. We share certain features in common as human beings, but we are, Unamuno would be the first to admit, also distinctive individuals. Each of us must find our own way of learning to live with uncertainty and struggle, with death, and with ourselves. There is a sense in which we can accept that we may, at times, be resistant, restless, despairing. 'Accepting' in this context does not imply a stance of passivity; what is at stake here is a kind of 'active' acceptance. Nothing about Unamuno seemed to be calm, at least not in an inner sense; as a man, and as a writer, he was often not merely restless but openly agitated. But where for Unamuno facing up to the question of death, and the anguish that went with this, was a confrontation, for others it can be a calming process. We can learn to pay quiet, patient, deliberate attention to death, as an object for study or contemplation. Death can then, in turn, teach us – if we are ready to hear what she has to say. The tensions that structure our lives can be treated in the same way. We can attend with full self-awareness, as active participants in the process, while attempting to gently reduce the intrusion of the ego into our contemplative activity (cf. Murdoch, 2001; Weil, 1997, 2001). Attentive, educative inner activity of this kind may not eliminate the tension – indeed, Unamuno would say, we should not want to do this – but it can change our relationship to it. We can, in other words, perhaps live on better terms with ourselves, and with the tragic nature of our existence, than Unamuno's work suggests we might.

We can also question the extremes to which Unamuno is willing to go in articulating his wish to live on. Unamuno claims that "it is better to live in pain than peacefully cease to be at all" (1972, p. 49). But just how much pain would he be prepared to endure, and for how long, before he would rather disappear into nothingness? Those who live with severe chronic pain sometimes not only accept the possibility of death but positively look forward to it for the relief that it will bring. We might agree with Unamuno that to live is to suffer in certain respects, and we might see some educative value in suffering. But there are different forms of suffering and Unamuno provides relatively little guidance in distinguishing between these variations. His main focus is on the one form of suffering that matters most *to him*: the tragic tension we experience between our longing for immortality and the doubting voice of critical reason that says this is an impossibility. He suggests that he was "never made to tremble by descriptions of hellfire, no matter how terrible," and that he could not imagine "a more authentic Hell than that of nothingness and the prospect of it" (p. 49). But his preference for Hell over nothingness is perhaps partly explained by his confession that he "could not believe in this atrocious Hell, an eternity of punishment" (p. 49). Unamuno is, as it were, let off the hook by his own lack of belief in the dire warnings of eternal damnation. This is, for him, just a fanciful idea that need not be tested against his expressed preference to live on. He knows he wants to live on, and wants to keep wanting to do so, not in the abstract but as the particular individual that he is, with all of his troubles and idiosyncrasies. But what if his difficulties were far greater than those with which he was familiar – where would his limits lie? His answer appears to be that there are no limits; that no matter how much we suffer, and in what ways, and for how long, provided we continue to live on, this is preferable to nothingness. What he does not do is consider whether he might still want to make this claim if an "eternity of punishment" – either in "Hell" or in incessant severe pain here on Earth – *really did await him*. He fails to adequately acknowledge the extent to which his view of the world is shaped – and limited – by his own experiences and circumstances.

There is perhaps an element of bravado in Unamuno's claims, underpinned by a tendency to construe human problems as a clash of opposing positions. Reason and faith cannot, in Unamuno's mind, happily co-exist. Attempts to prove the existence of God or the afterlife on the basis of rational argument are, in his view, fruitless. They simply provide consolation when faced with the tragic nature of the human condition. For Unamuno, reason and science stand opposed not just to faith but to everything that is active and vital in us: our deepest, most important feelings and desires. Unamuno's combative nature comes through in some of the contrasts he draws between himself and other thinkers. He has little patience for Nietzsche, who was himself not known for his moderation when dealing with intellectual opponents. Nietzsche's vision of a kind of superman who would overcome the weakness of Christian morality, living fully in this world without illusions of another better world to come, was, as Unamuno saw it, anything but a manifestation of strength. To the contrary, he argued: it was a pathetic cry from a weak human being who could not face up resolutely to the tragic nature of the human condition. Being willing to live with the doubt created by the tension between our longing for immortality and the voice of critical reason was, in Unamuno's terms, a real show of strength. But framing the problem in this way – as a kind of contest to show who is stronger – is not the only approach open to us. We can *value* 'weakness', if this is conceived as a kind of gentle acknowledgement of our shared fragilities as human beings. A calmer, gentler path starts not with a contest of wills, but with an expression of openness, humility and a willingness to learn from others.

The propensity to view all of life as a battle also emerges in Unamuno's ethical position, and this has important pedagogical implications. Unamuno, it will be recalled, speaks of imposing one's spirit on others by being "invasive, overmastering, aggressive, [and] inquisitorial" (1972, p. 306). It must be acknowledged that Unamuno's focus, at least in *The Tragic Sense of Life*, is not directly on pedagogical matters. We can infer a pedagogical theory from what he has to say, and we can see Unamuno himself as a teacher, shaking us up as readers, playing his part in creating the life of restless longing that he regards as desirable. But he is not writing about schools or universities, or about the students who inhabit those institutional spaces, or even about teaching *per se*. Nonetheless, if we imagine what an application of Unamuno's ideas might look like in contemporary classrooms, we come up against some immediate ethical and practical problems. Teachers should, if we take Unamuno's words to heart, not only be prepared to challenge the students with whom they work; they should see this as their central task, and they should uphold this responsibility in an invasive, inquisitorial, aggressive manner. As noted in earlier discussion, critical thought can be encouraged, but sensitivity to the particulars of the context in which one is working is essential. Just as there is more than one way to wake up from our sleep at night (for example, with the singing of the birds, the change in light, a gentle nudge from a bed partner, or a loud alarm), so too might we say that there is no one best way to 'wake up' students. An ethic of aggression, applied in a classroom context, would be likely in our current age to bring formal warnings and probable dismissal. But even if we worked in professional environments where strategies of this kind were permitted, something important could be lost in pedagogical terms. Imposing ourselves as overbearing inquisitors could, for some students, be counterproductive, deterring them from embracing the restless life of searching and longing so valued by Unamuno. For those who are especially sensitive, the experience of being publicly and persistently challenged by a teacher could be traumatic, shutting down any tendency they might have had to probe and explore their ideas further. We can accept that all teaching in educational institutions such as schools and universities involves intervention, but intervening is not the same as imposing. If we are to gain something valuable from Unamuno in our work as teachers in contemporary classrooms, acknowledging the roles we play in influencing the lives of young people, we need to pay appropriate attention to the subtleties of human relationships in pedagogical situations. Questions of consent and understanding are important. Opportunities for discussion and debate need to be in place and the power dynamics at work in such interactions need to be examined. Prior knowledge and experience need to be considered. Teachers need to not only teach, but also listen and learn from the students with whom they work. For Unamuno, it is 'all or nothing', and this will often be inadequate when dealing with the complexities of educational life.

CONCLUSION

The combative tendencies in Unamuno's thought and character played themselves out not just in his writing but also in the war he had with himself. Unamuno was hard on himself, realizing that he sometimes fell short of his own ideals, but he did attempt to learn from his failings. He recognized the dangers of excessive certainty and argued against dogmatism. He wanted no part in movements that denied the right to question, and he was suspicious of anyone who claimed to possess absolute truth. Emphatic dismissal of the possibility of the existence of God, or of eternal life, was as distasteful to him as blind unreflective faith. When Unamuno declares that he wants to create lives of restless longing, his mission is not, as Evans (2013) points out, to destroy but to *disturb*: "Unamuno does not want anyone to be resigned to a particular dogma because, for him, all of life is a longing that should never be assuaged" (p. 33). Sustaining a life of longing, it has been argued in this chapter, is also a pedagogical commitment. While pedagogical questions were not Unamuno's primary focus in his magnum opus, *The Tragic Sense of Life*, there is in that important philosophical work a kind of teaching going on. Unamuno, in keeping with his ideals, wakes us up. He teaches by disquieting his readers. We may disagree with him at times but he speaks to us with such conviction that it is difficult to ignore what he has to say. We cannot remain indifferent with Unamuno. If we meditate on his words, reading him slowly and carefully, he leaves a permanent mark on us: we can never be the same again, having encountered Unamuno. That is surely a worthy goal for any teacher, and in this sense, but perhaps in other ways as well, Unamuno continues to live on.

REFERENCES

Alessandri, M. (2018). Interpreting Unamuno's Quixotism as a religion. *Philosophy Today, 62*(3), 899–919.

Baker, A. F. (1990). Unamuno and the religion of uncertainty. *Hispanic Review, 58*(1), 37–56.
Barnes, J. C. (2013). Spiritual mother or complete human? Gender and existence in Miguel de Unamuno's *San Manuel Bueno. Mártir. Hispanófila, 169,* 19–34.
Barrett, W. (1972). Afterword. In M. de Unamuno, *The tragic sense of life in men and nations.* (A. Kerrigan, Trans.) (pp. 361–374). Princeton University Press.
Barrett, W. (1990). *Irrational man: A study in existential philosophy.* Anchor Books.
Boyles, D. (2016). Absurdities, contradictions, and paradoxes in Miguel de Unamuno's *Amor y pedagogía. Educational Theory, 66*(5), 619–639.
Buben, A. (2021). Unamuno on making oneself indispensable and having the strength to long for immortality. *International Journal for Philosophy of Religion.* Early online version: https://doi.org/10.1007/s11153-021-09794-y
Cervantes, M. de (2005). *Don Quixote* (E. Grossman, Trans.). Vintage.
Cooper, D. E. (1999). *Existentialism: A reconstruction* (2nd ed.). Blackwell.
Dienstag, J. F. (2006). *Pessimism: Philosophy, ethic, spirit.* Princeton University Press.
Earle, E. R. (2019). *"With weapons of burning words": The rhetoric of Miguel de Unamuno's newspaper writings.* Doctor of Philosophy Dissertation, Texas A&M University.
Evans, J. E. (2013). *Miguel de Unamuno's quest for faith: A Kierkegaardian understanding of Unamuno's struggle to believe.* Pickwick Publications.
Flynn, T. (2009). *Existentialism: A brief insight.* Sterling.
Fraser, B. (2007). Unamuno and Bergson: Notes on a shared methodology. *The Modern Language Review, 102*(3), 753–767.
Gómez, M. A. (2007). Unamuno and Schopenhauer: Art, artistic imagination and the relation to modernism. *Confluencia, 23*(1), 43–61.
Hollingsworth, C. A. (2013). *Theological existentialism in* San Manuel Beuno, Mártir. Doctor of Philosophy Dissertation, Wayne State University.
Hughes, R. (1978). Education and the tragic sense of life: The thought of Miguel de Unamuno. *Educational Theory, 28*(2), 131–138.
Kaufmann, W. (Ed.). (1975). *Existentialism from Dostoevsky to Sartre.* Plume.
Kuhlman, E. L. (1994). *Agony in education: The importance of struggle in the process of learning.* Bergin & Garvey.
Larubia-Prado, F. (2014). Sanctity, heroism, and performance in Miguel De Unamuno's *San Manuel Bueno, Mártir. Hispanófila, 171,* 217–236.
Longhurst, C. A. (2011). Unamuno on identity: Personal and national. *Hispanic Research Journal, 12*(1), 48–62.
Longhurst, C. A. (2015). '¿Qué es eso de creer?' Religious belief in Miguel de Unamuno and Gabriel Marcel. *Bulletin of Spanish Studies, 92*(4), 527–548.
Luarsabishvili, V. (2019). Miguel de Unamuno and John Dewey: The system of education and personal liberty. *Kultura i Wartości, 28,* 277–291.
Marino, G. (Ed.). (2004). *Basic writings of existentialism.* The Modern Library.
Mermall, T. (1978). Unamuno and Dostoevsky's Grand Inquisitor. *Hispania, 61*(4), 851–858.
Murdoch, I. (2001). *The sovereignty of good.* Routledge.
Oya, A. (2020a). Unamuno and James on religious faith. *Teorema, 39*(1), 85–104.
Oya, A. (2020b). Nietzsche and Unamuno on *Conatus* and the Agapeic way of life. *Metaphilosophy, 51*(2–3), 303–317.
Roberts, P. (2016). *Happiness, hope, and despair: Rethinking the role of education.* Peter Lang.
Roberts, P., & Freeman-Moir, J. (2013). *Better worlds: Education, art, and utopia.* Lexington Books.

Roberts, P., & Saeverot, H. (2018). *Education and the limits of reason: Reading Dostoevsky, Tolstoy and Nabokov*. Routledge.

Rodgers, E. (2015). The Christ of Velázquez and the Christ of Unamuno. *Bulletin of Spanish Studies*, *92*(1), 51–63.

Saeverot, H. (2013). *Indirect pedagogy. Some lessons in existential education*. Sense Publishers.

Shanley, M. L. (1977). Death and politics in the work of a twentieth-century philosopher. *Polity*, *9*(3), 257–278.

Summerhill, S. J. (1978). Death and God in Unamuno: Towards a theory of creative symbolic imagination. *Revista Canadiense de Estudios Hispanicos*, *3*(1), 47–74.

Unamuno, M. de (1972). *The tragic sense of life in men and nations* (A. Kerrigan, Trans.). Princeton University Press.

Unamuno, M. de (1996). *Abel Sanchez and other stories* (A. Kerrigan, Trans.). Regnery Publishing.

Unamuno, M. de (2000). *Mist: A tragicomic novel* (W. Fite, Trans.). University of Illinois Press.

Webster, S. (2009). *Educating for meaningful lives through existential spirituality*. Sense Publishers.

Weil, S. (1997). *Gravity and grace* (A. Wills, Trans.). Bison Books.

Weil, S. (2001). *Waiting for God* (E. Craufurd, Trans.). Perennial Classics.

CHAPTER FIVE

Educating the Horizon of Understanding

Through Death Anxiety

R. SCOTT WEBSTER

The subject of death tends to be avoided in education as well as in everyday discussions. Hence, it is the likes of Pascal and his philosophy that can interrupt and even disrupt this tendency by presenting us with his wager[1] as to whether there may indeed be life after death. As such, death may be worth investing some of our attention especially for what it can offer education. For educators, the primary challenge is *not* to offer an answer, content or argument upon which such a wager might rest, but rather it is to give consideration as to why taking notice of, and engaging with, the various possibilities related to death is valuable for our state of becoming educated, particularly through the anxiety that is often associated with this activity. This is recognized by Bauman (2008, p. 37) who lamented that it is everyone's tendency to "avoid looking inwards and keep running in the vain hope of escaping face-to-face encounter with [our] predicament… philosophers insist that it takes exclusive, sparsely awarded qualities like a 'noble mind', solid knowledge and strong character (sometimes also nerves of steel) to resist that temptation" to avoid this. From this it can be recognized that becoming educated perhaps requires a great deal of effort and even strength of character.

As educators perhaps our central concern ought to be upon who we are becoming rather than what we simply might know or can do. Consequently this

---

1   Blaise Pascal (1623–1662) proposed a wager to argue that believing in the existence of God was more beneficial compared with not believing in his existence.

involves a serious engagement with what it might mean to be a human person and in particular what it might mean to be an educated person. Referring to tertiary education Barnett (2007, p. 26) claims that "both our practices and our thinking about higher education are in urgent need of an ontological turn. To put it more straightforwardly, we are in desperate need of thinking and practices that take the student as a human being seriously." In his own examination as to what this involves, Barnett (2007, p. 32) draws upon existential philosophy to argue that "[b]eing a student is to be in a state of anxiety." Hence he sees great value for anxiety in the pursuit of becoming educated. It has similar relevance for education more generally, and in this chapter this insight is extended through engaging with death anxiety because it is considered to have significantly valuable potential for becoming educated. What makes death anxiety unique amongst the various forms of anxiety, is that it is closely related to how one understands the meaning and purpose for one's own life and indeed for life overall.

EDUCATION FOR AUTHENTICITY

In this first section the existential notion of authenticity as it relates to education is explored. Then consideration shall be given to death anxiety before investigating how this can enhance existential authenticity and therefore education. Education is valuable for both individuals and for society, and so individuals ought to be understood as social beings rather than as hyper-individualistic beings. This important point needs to be clarified at the outset because existentialists accentuate the importance of the individual, especially in terms of freedom and choice, but it ought to be appreciated that this is always within a social context. To undertake this exploration insights shall be made by drawing primarily on the existentialism of Kierkegaard, Heidegger, Sartre and Nietzsche, along with the pragmatism of James and Dewey.

Every theory of education draws upon an understanding of human nature. This is because at its core 'education' is the pursuit of an improved or even a *good* life. It aspires to a state of being which is regarded to be more worthwhile than an uneducated or uncultivated state. Educational ideals are therefore articulations of what is thought best for being human and typically consist of characteristics such as an appreciation for the pursuit of truth, being critically thoughtful, careful, considerate, and the like. Such characteristics depend upon understandings as to what it means to be human and what it might mean to be a good person and a good society.

For existentialists, our ontology – or being – is considered to be primarily hermeneutical. That is, people are viewed as meaning-making creatures who are able to exercise freedom to *choose* how to make sense of their experiences and of their existence. Consequently, from an existential perspective, to be educated involves the capability for being able to make and choose well-crafted and wise meanings. It is important that the emphasis is upon the *capability* for *making* good meanings rather than acquiring or possessing universally good meanings, because the existentialists understand the importance of the context for each person. As Heidegger (1999, p. 17) explains, the actual conditions of our existence in which we find ourselves, which he describes as our 'facticity', works against trying to universalize and so he claims that "we avoided on principle the expression 'human' Dasein or the 'being of man'." Therefore, hermeneutics becomes central for engaging with one's particular context and to do so requires what Heidegger describes as a 'wakefulness'. In contrast to a disposition for simply going along with the 'crowd' (usually in the form of mainstream media, politicians and those who form popular culture) and complying to what they expect for oneself, a wakeful disposition is one which takes seriously the task of giving meaning and choosing what one ought to do and therefore who one ought to become.

It is important to recognize that while existential philosophy champions the importance of individual freedom it does not promote the sort of freedom which attempts to transcend one's reality. This limitation is stressed by Sartre (1958, p. 520) who stated that the authentically free individual "must choose itself by taking into account these circumstances [of one's world]." One's situational context is accepted as a given and is described as one's facticity in which one is 'thrown' into in the sense that we are not free to pretend that we do not already have bodies, parents, ethnicity and various other relations with entities in our environment. We are inescapably embedded into some aspects of reality including our own past. As Sartre (1958, p. 29) states, "[i]n freedom the human being is his own past..." indicating that we cannot transcend beyond our current context including how we arrived at this. However, even although we cannot change our existence, what we are free to do is to give various meanings to our relations and experiences. This is what existential freedom is all about – choosing what we ought to value and be committed to, and what sense and meaning to give to all of our experiences, including the meaning and purpose of our lives.

This insight of existential freedom has also been developed by Frankl in a more extreme manner. As a prisoner in German concentration camps during the Second World War, Frankl accepted that he could not, as a prisoner, change anything about his physical circumstance. However, the freedom he could exercise was how he related to his situation and he discovered that despite the physical restrictions he was still able to choose what meanings to craft in order to make his life meaningful and bearable. He summarized his situation with the following insight, "There is nothing in the world, I venture to say, that would so effectively help one to survive even the worst conditions as the knowledge that there is meaning in one's life" (Frankl, 1984, p. 126). Throughout the terrible context in which he found himself 'thrown' and for which an unbearable situation might be made bearable (Webster, 2017a), he was nevertheless able to exercise some freedom to give his life a greater sense of meaningfulness through such mental and attitudinal activities such as reciting poetry and reflecting upon the love he had for his wife.

Embarking on a life of authenticity, that is, of choosing oneself rather than accepting from others who one ought to be and how one ought to live, must be accompanied by a recognition that with such existential freedom comes a certain level of anxiety or anguish. This is a major theme as identified by Sartre (1958, p. 29) who explains;

> Kierkegaard describing anguish in the face of what one lacks characterizes it as anguish in the face of freedom. But Heidegger, whom we know to have been greatly influenced by Kierkegaard, considers anguish instead as the apprehension of nothingness.

Sartre clarifies that the positions of both Kierkegaard and Heidegger are complementary and are not contradictory. This notion of nothingness from Heidegger, is identified by Sartre as originating from Hegel who referred to it as being an empty abstract and therefore able to be nullified. However, Sartre (1958, p. 15) developed this concept further arguing that such nothingness needed to be "emptiness of something" and from this linked this notion of nothingness to one's future possibilities which remain 'nothing' until chosen. Hence his existential relation between our being and our nothingness or future possibilities which lie ahead of us as we live our lives forwards.

> Anguish in fact is the recognition of a possibility as *my* possibility; that is, it is constituted when consciousness sees itself cut from its essence by nothingness or separated from the future by its very freedom (Sartre 1958, p. 35).

Nevertheless, we are free to choose the meaning we assign to our relations with various entities within our environment.

Kierkegaard's own philosophical position is one which recognizes that it is relatively easy to give meaning and sense to our lives when we look *back* through our history and are able, through hindsight, to give a narrative which gives a sense of unity. However, he understood that the challenge for everyone is to live life *forwards*. For each moment we step into the future there is no 'looking back' to a past narrative or set of meanings which can provide any sense of certainty as we move into the future, unless of course we are perhaps tranquilized rather than being wakeful. Heidegger elucidates on this moving *forwards* in wakefulness when considering Aristotle's claim that humans are rational as is especially recognized through the use of the term *logos*, which Heidegger (1999, p. 17) points out "never means 'reason,' but rather discourse, conversation". Here he promotes the idea of an ongoing conversation in one's context, indicating a never-ending process of meaning-making and meaning-revision, which reflects this characteristic of living life *forwards* as Kierkegaard has pointed out.

This insight of the existentialists regarding living life forwards in a mode of uncertainty and in perpetual 'conversation' with one's environment, makes significant links with the philosophies of pragmatism. Gadamer (1989, p. 122) notes that the Greek term *pragma* is "entangled in the praxis of living" and is more focused on the individual using her own initiative rather than the more universalizing concept of praxis. So this etymological root of pragmatism allows us to see that it has much in common with existentialism as both focus on individual freedom and 'practical lived philosophy'. Indeed in his book titled *Pragmatism* James recognized some of the similarities between these two philosophies and this recognition was then taken up by Dewey. Reflecting on this, Alexander (2013, p. 40) argues that Dewey took up this challenging way of living as described by Kierkegaard, and "was trying to show how we could also understand in the forward direction, that is, that knowledge is inherently temporal." Consequently Alexander (2013, p. 41) concludes that for humans who are able to live well, "learning is more significant than knowing." This is echoed by Koerrenz (2017, p. 1) who, by drawing upon the existentialism of Bollnow, explains "[h]umans are… primarily determined by their openness to what is new and challenging – in other words, by the fact that they can (and do) *learn*" [original emphasis]. However, this cannot pertain to just any sort of learning – because after all animals can be observed to be 'learning' – and so clarification is required regarding existential learning or rather 'growth'. This existential growth involves the exercising of one's initiative in order to make meanings which are essentially important, and this requires genuine interest. Sartre (1958, p. 477) too accentuates the importance of "intention, which is fundamental structure of human-reality" which is only possible by being fully present in experiences. From this it can be concluded that, from an existential point of view the educated (i.e. improving) person is one who remains open in such as way so as to be continually learning from one's journeying step by step, and is not one who simply knows or understands. That is, one is able to be in a conversation with one's self and environment in a way that one is able to make well-crafted and wise meanings. Hence, the process of 'education' is to include improving one's ability to remain 'open' to conversation and give meaning to our lives as we continue to encounter new experiences.

A key concept of existential philosophy is 'authenticity' which pertains to living a life in a worthwhile manner. Authenticity involves the willingness and courage to actively and freely choose, and in particular, to *choose* to be oneself. For Heidegger (1996, p. 265) his "Da-sein… has chosen itself" which is reflective of Kierkegaard's argument that it is not enough to simply know oneself as per the ancient Greeks, but one has to actively *choose* oneself. Included with this is the choice of what one will value. Nietzsche went to great length in his book *Beyond*

Good and Evil to discuss this very point of exercising one's will to power or free will, to choose and even create one's own values. But the exercising of one's will to determine one's own values can be a very anxious affair and is even described by Nietzsche as a 'dangerous formula' which can only be undertaken by strong characters or by 'nerves of steel' as suggested by Bauman in the introduction.

Authentic choice is not limited to actual events of choosing. Rather, it is evident as a disposition, a way-of-living or way-of-*being* which is an aspect of one's very identity or character. Hence why educators and philosophers place an emphasis on authenticity rather than on authentic choices. According to Barnett (2007, p. 18) the state of a person's authentic *being* involves her will, commitment and energy which he even suggests could be understood as our 'spirit'. Such spirituality, characterized by a commitment, will and energy which moves one to participate in life in a wakeful manner offers the strength for authenticity. This is the sort of 'free spirit' that Nietzsche (1966) encourages in his aspirational ideal for the educated, in order that they resist becoming slaves to the status quo of compliance.

This existential view of authentic freedom and choice is held in contrast to submitting inauthentically to the expectations of others. These others are often referred to as the 'crowd' or 'herd' to differentiate between society's mass who simply accept the norms, expectations and roles which are placed upon them by various authorities, rather than actively choosing for oneself how one ought to live. Such inauthenticity is likened to being 'spiritless' by Kierkegaard (1980, p. 95) who claims that " [i]n spiritlessness there is no anxiety, because it is too happy, too content." Heidegger suggests that for the majority of our lives we are not authentic but we simply conform to the 'they-self' because it is easier and without anxiety. He even argues that he himself was not usually "the who of Da-sein" but instead he was for the most part in everydayness "the they-self" (Heidegger, 1996, p. 247). Sartre represented this through his famous statement that 'existence precedes essence', meaning that one's essence, identity and values are unable to be determined until one freely *chooses* them. Hence his emphasis upon being free as an individual to perpetually choose one's own identity and the meanings that one should live one's life with in each micro-moment of life, rather than have these imposed by various authorities including 'everyday' cultural norms.

This notion of authenticity is also closely aligned to the importance of living life *forwards*. When one is part of the crowd or mass living inauthentically, one gives meaning to oneself at the present moment by reaching *backwards* to the traditions and norms which are to be accepted, inherited or obeyed from various 'authorities'. In contrast, both existentialists and pragmatists seek to give sense and meaning as they venture forwards, which may involve giving consideration to traditional customs, values and practices, but rather than simply accepting these as givens, they instead 'test' the value that these may have for the present context.

This can be presented through Nietzsche's description of taking a hammer to past idols to sound them out. This doesn't mean that the existentialists and pragmatists are violent towards cultural and traditional norms but rather they 'test' their relevance and usefulness for the present situation. After such evaluation the educated person, living in authenticity, judges and freely chooses how to relate to them and remains personally responsible for this choice. Rather than passively conform to what society expects of us, educated authentic individuals exercise a strength of character to work through the *fear* and anxiety of their own freedom, as Fromm (1942) has described, freely choosing what to value and who to be. This however, involves a great deal of anxiety due to the lack of authorities and certainties involved.

DEATH ANXIETY

This section will address the concept of death anxiety before providing the argument why it has importance for becoming educated in the sense of authenticity. Firstly, there is a need to explain that existential anxiety and experiencing angst towards one's own death, are not the same as a fear of dying, nor do they involve dwelling in morbid despair over death. Death anxiety is simply an accepted clarity that one will inevitably die. As such, psychologist and professor, Shapiro (2016, p. 56) explains, it is "a normal, healthy component of life related to awareness of life's true limits." Dying one day, is a given and the better we are orientated to this fact then the more likely it is that we can be psychologically healthy. As Van Ranst and Marcoen (2000, p. 68) in their studies on well-being, report that the "[e]lderly who enjoyed high levels of Psychological Well-Being were more likely to accept death as an inevitable reality of life." Therefore the sort of anxiety that is being referred to in the expression 'death anxiety', represents one's relationship to this limiting fact about one's future.

To explain the potential positive nature that such anxiety might have for education in addition to psychological well-being, it is important to reflect on the value of a certain amount of anxiety in general. Shapiro reports that in experimental psychology the two terms 'anxiety' and 'arousal' are almost synonymous with each other. He identifies that in psychology it is understood that if anxiety, or arousal, is either too low or too high, then one's ability to perform at one's optimal level is hampered. The extremes which lie on this spectrum are ennui at one end and neuroticism at the other, and both are regarded to be unhealthy as well as unhelpful. In sport and the performing arts for example, it is recognized that a certain level of nervous tension – or anxiety and arousal – enables participants to perform at their best. Being overly anxious can lead to a loss of perspective and nervous tension while not being anxious enough can lead to overconfidence and carelessness. However, if one's anxiety/arousal is about midway between these extremes then one is more likely to be able to perform at one's optimal potential.

With regards to one's own death, an excess of anxiety can lead to neurosis, inhibiting one's ability to think and act well primarily due to a burden of fear. Similarly if one lacks sufficient anxiety towards one's death then one can lose a seriousness of attitude for one's limited time of being alive and instead be distracted by superficiality and/or a purely materialistic outlook. Both extremes are unhelpful for living an examined life and one that is meaningful. Death anxiety is an existential experience involving inner reflection and contemplation. However, this existential dimension can be overlooked when the thought of death is universalized, such as through the "nationalizing of death" as observed by Bauman (2006, p. 36–7) who adds that national patriotism, which is important for "mass conscript armies and universal military duty" can reduce the significance that death might have for each individual because they are 'lost' in the crowd of the nation. Hence some contemplative seriousness towards one's own personal death, assisted by an appropriate level of anxiety, holds an important key for living an authentic and therefore educated life. This has been recognized by Heidegger who encapsulated this disposition through what he referred to as our being-towards-death.

One of the key features that Heidegger offers through this concept of our being-towards-death or our death anxiety, is that through it we are better able to grasp our life as a totality including being limited by having an end, and that this grasping is with our whole being. It involves accepting that our existence has limits within which we have responsibility. This is considered to be a valuable way-of-being because it adds a realistic dimension of limitations for living an authentic life. The alternative to this, which is to live inauthentically in a more superficial mode of everydayness, is described by Heidegger as being similar to being in a 'tranquilized state', lacking the sharp awareness that comes with clear thinking. Nevertheless, he does acknowledge that we tend to adopt this state of being tranquilized by the norms of society through our everyday life in our casual relations with those around us. He explains that society tends to encourage strategies and attitudes to be used for evading any serious contemplation about our death. This occurs to such a degree that the avoidance "dominates everydayness" and is discouraged by others living inauthentically, because society does not support "the courage to have Angst about death" (Heidegger, 1996, pp. 234, 235). This is so generally accepted that even when a person is clearly dying Heidegger contends that those around him or her tend to speak as if the person can still escape death by returning again to life, usually in another dimension, in an effort to offer some comfort. While Heidegger's own understanding of a potential existence beyond death is quite different to other existential philosophers such as Kierkegaard, he nevertheless identifies this disposition in people for avoiding serious contemplation of death, even in the face of one currently dying.

A key point for understanding the educational significance of death anxiety is that this is not limited to moments of quiet reflection, but rather it is an integral aspect of living each moment of our lives being lived forwardly. In a concise manner Heidegger (1996, p. 245) states that "Being-towards-death is essentially *Angst*" [original emphasis] which is not limited to a mere emotion but is embodied in one's very being. He explores how our conscience receives a call to reflect on our death in such a way that the call is 'attuned' by this angst. Importantly he explains that this 'call' is actually a discourse, it is a hermeneutical back-and-forth contemplation within experience which embraces that our very existence is limited by a temporality which may at any moment, include our death. This is partly captured by Mulhall (1996, p. 117) who clarifies that:

> From the outset, Dasein is thrown into the possibility that each present moment will be its last. It projects itself into every future moment in the face of the possibility that it may not be actualized… Death is Dasein's ownmost possibility in that it most intensifies the mineness of existence.

Here is a reminder of the earlier discussion on the importance of living life *forwards* which necessarily requires grappling with uncertainties. One of the most important of which is the possibility of our own dying at any moment. Therefore, there is the possibility that this current experience or the very next one we are about to embark upon could be our very last before our existence is ended.

Referring to 'the call' made possible by the opening made through courageously contemplating one's own death, Heidegger (1996) argues that one positive and important aspect that might emerge is the opportunity to grow in greater authenticity. For Heidegger an important aspect of authenticity is that it is an orientation which incorporates 'totality'. That is, while we might focus upon particular relations which have various purposes or relevance (e.g. a hammer has the purpose of hammering a nail, and a timber frame has the relevance of attaching a roof to a building), totality refers to the big picture perspective of all the 'relevances' being accumulated together, of how everything hangs together so to speak. That is, it pertains to the overall relevance and purpose that our entire life might have, knowing that our current existence is temporal.

In order to offer the opportunity for authenticity, death anxiety has significant value. This is because only the individual can die her own death. As recognized by Sartre (1958, p. 532) "death… does not remain simply human; it becomes *mine*. By being interiorized it is individualized." While death itself is universal the actual experiences of dying and contemplating one's own death, are uniquely personal and therefore they help accentuate our individuality. Dying is a unique experience for each individual and so it is often considered as an individuating event which separates us from the universal. This is summarized by Derrida (2008, p. 42) as follows:

> Death is very much that which nobody else can undergo or confront in my place. My irreplaceability is therefore conferred, delivered, 'given', one can say, by death. It is the same gift, the same source, one could say the same goodness and the same law. It is from the site of death as the place of my irreplaceability, that is, of my singularity, that I feel called to responsibility.

More insightfully perhaps than Derrida here, Sartre (1958, p. 534) extends this notion of irreplaceability by claiming that "love is, like death, irreplaceable and unique; nobody can love for me" just as nobody can die for me. Nevertheless, it would appear that Derrida too recognizes the significance that death has for the existential perspective – of singularity and individual uniqueness, and also for responding to the call of responsibility and therefore authenticity. It could also be argued that it is important to note that he regards death as a gift, as something of great value which is being pursued here especially in relation to education.

This gifting of death and the anxiety of our death invoke a response from within ourselves. Our innermost being where we hold our most precious values and principles closest to us and is the source of our authenticity, has opportunity to respond to this call of death. As recognized by Anz (1998, p. 47)

> If we allow ourselves to be educated by anxiety, then we will come to understand that dying is not a process that happens to us from outside; rather it is our own ownmost being, which as a not-yet-grasped possibility 'concerns' us in anxiety.

This helps identify that we are not focusing only upon the reality of our physical body ceasing to live, but instead our focus is upon our anxiety towards this event, how we actively relate to this. It is the actual first-hand experience of death anxiety that opens us up to becoming further educated.

Perhaps the most significant insight that death anxiety offers is a reminder that our very next moment may be our final one. This insight should not be dismissed as either trivial or unnecessarily morbid but instead be seen as potentially very valuable for two main reasons. Firstly it encourages a disposition of wakefulness in the sense that we need to invest some serious thought and responsibility for participating in the current experience in the way that we are, and secondly, it invites us to think how our various current activities are to be evaluated in terms of what we consider is of most value to us personally. That is, are we investing our time and energy into activities which we have already carefully concluded are some of the most worthwhile things that we could spend our life doing, including potentially, our final moments alive? It ought to be appreciated as providing the opportunity to help live life to the fullest, with our full devotion to what is of most value – because it may be our last. This is essentially the 'good news' aspect that the existentialists offer through the metaphor of looking down into the abyss of meaninglessness. The important point is not to dwell on the abyss or to become mesmerized by life's apparent nihilism, but instead we can turn and walk away from the edge and forge our own authentic path in life in a way that we actively choose how to make it significantly meaningful. What death anxiety adds is some assistance for being wakeful to appreciate the importance of living as fully, creatively and as responsibly as possible in the present moment.

HORIZON OF UNDERSTANDING

As will be recognized, the educative growth of authenticity requires wisdom and not just an accumulation of *any* information, attitudes or choices due to the inherent anxiety that comes with existential freedom. Therefore, in this section the basis of our meaning-making capacity shall be explored before further examining the educative role that death anxiety might have for the educative growth of this capacity. Specifically a focus on Gadamer's concept of a horizon of understanding will be addressed, which is considered similar to the concepts of James's 'sameness' and Dewey's 'attitude of anticipation'.

In his *Principles of Psychology*, James (1890, p. 488) tried to describe what it must be like for a baby who is 'thrown' into the world full of sensations and stimuli, and argued that the world must appear like "one great blooming, buzzing confusion" until the baby infant is able to fuse separate impressions together through a meaning-making process he described as 'sameness'. Perhaps the metaphor of a jigsaw puzzle is useful here where the noticing of potential fitting together of separate pieces becomes an essential skill to gives sense to and construct the collection of pieces into a complete and whole picture. According to James (1890, pp. 272 & 459) this sameness involves connecting "a multiplicity of objective appearances" into a singular 'reality' that combines both thought and practical reality, and thus he concluded that it is "the very keel and backbone of our thinking."

Following on from James, Dewey (1991, p. 128) described this same tendency for fusing separate impressions together as involving "an attitude of anticipation" where in our everydayness we anticipate what to expect in our routine activities based upon the meanings we have already made from previous experiences. This is very much related to his concept of a continuum of experience where the meanings of past experiences can be used to guide and give sense to the meanings of subsequent experiences (Dewey, 2008a). This activity of interpreting observed 'facts' or data is not a purely cognitive affair because as Dewey (1989) explained they make judgements, and as such they include valuing. So with reference to a jigsaw puzzle, the observer is understood to value some pieces over others, typically those with corners, edges or with images that can be used for anchoring parts of the picture. Therefore, his continuum of experience can be likened to a looking backwards for meanings that have been made in the past, to see if they are appropriate for the present task at hand.

Our horizon of understanding is the base or framework from which we are able to perceive and give meanings. Gadamer refers to this framework as a horizon because it represents the limits to what we can 'see'. This connection between 'seeing' and 'understanding' has been made by several philosophers who refer to the expression 'now I see' which is another way of saying 'now I understand'. So we are limited to what we can 'see' and understand using the horizon as a metaphor. Gadamer (1989, p. 302) warns of the uneducated state where "a person who has no horizon does not see far enough and hence over-values what is nearest to him." He holds this in contrast to one who is becoming educated and who has a horizon. He states,

> On the other hand, 'to have a horizon' means not being limited to what is nearby but being able to see beyond it... The concept of 'horizon' suggests itself because it expresses the superior breadth of vision that the person who is trying to understand must have. To acquire a horizon means that one learns to look beyond what is close at hand – not in order to look away from it but to see it better... (Gadamer, 1989, pp. 302 & 305).

Therefore, having a horizon, and to have one's horizon expanding and fusing with others, are key characteristics for becoming educated.

We can improve our horizon by climbing a tower or a hill, enabling us to see much further. An immediate implication of this is that we can expand our horizon of understanding when we are able to relate to others and seriously consider their own perspectives. Seeing things from the point of view of others is an educative experience in itself because we are introduced to different understandings which expand our existing horizon.

In addition to the simple extension or addition to our view Gadamer (1989, p. 374) refers to the "fusion of horizons" which is experienced when we are able to engage with the questions and concerns of others in order to 'see' better from their perspective. Gadamer put a great deal of emphasis in his understanding of hermeneutics in the direction of the past. Hence he encouraged studying the writings of those from the past who have gone before us. This was in contrast to Kierkegaard and Heidegger who focused more on moving forwards into the future. In addition, by referring back to the ancient Greeks, Gadamer argued that all aspects of one's horizon of understanding ought to be interrelated and unified through a religious perspective. He notes this unification includes all of one's views on politics and ethics as well as knowledge in general. Gadamer (1999, p. 39) clarifies that for the ancient Greeks "[t]he religious vocabulary... is not intended to make a statement about god or the gods, but rather to designate the order of being about which they are inquiring; the whole, the all, being."

A significant problem for those living inauthentically is that even although they may be happy and content on a superficial level, they can develop a fragmented identity. This is because they are in the habit of passively and uncritically complying with what society expects of them as moral or upright members of society who are disposed to doing 'the right thing' – which inevitably means being compliant. When passively and uncritically conforming to the various demands expected by society, one can emerge as a patchwork or collage of contradictory views. In contrast, because the authentic person seriously and critically questions how she ought to conduct herself, freely deciding the criteria to employ for 'doing the right thing', she develops a more unified horizon of understanding and sense of herself. This can be identified to a degree in Kierkegaard's (1987, p. 361) journal where he discussed authenticity and declares "What matters is to find my purpose… the crucial thing is to find a truth that is true *for me*, to find *the idea for which I am willing to live and die*" [original emphasis] indicating that one's whole self, including ones values, ought to be united in an overall purpose and *raison d'être*.

Interestingly this understanding of the religious as a unifying perspective for one's horizon of understanding, is also reflected in Dewey's own discussion of a religious attitude. Dewey went to length to indicate that the adjective 'religious' is significantly different to the noun 'religion' thereby aligning his own view to being similar to how the ancient Greeks understood the religious as described above by Gadamer. He states that the "fundamental question, I repeat, is not of this and that article of intellectual belief but of intellectual habit, method and criterion" (Dewey, 2008b, p. 24). So for Dewey both the religious attitude and a scientific way of testing ideas ought to exist together as they certainly do not exclude each other. The experimental disposition to be scientific, tests the validity of various ideas while the religious attitude seeks to maintain an overall coherence or unity to all of one's beliefs. This latter aspect becomes all the more challenging as particular beliefs are changed and reformulated. Therefore, from this we can appreciate the potential value that can be added to an educational curriculum by including such a religious dimension (Webster, 2010, 2013).

This unifying religious attitude was seen by Dewey to be important for what he refers to as an integrated character. Like the existentialists Dewey (1988, pp. 120 & 121) argued that growth can only be achieved "with the individual himself" and that "it is impossible to develop integrated individuality by any all-embracing system or program" such as is identified with religions and worldviews. He was concerned with the predominance of conformity throughout the society of his day because he recognized it to be an "artificial substitute used to hold men together," and added that it is an "artificially induced uniformity of thought and sentiment [which] is a symptom of an inner void" (Dewey, 1988, pp. 82 & 83). Hence the filling of the inner core of oneself is understood to fill the void and be a defense against being manipulated by others to conform to their expectations. It is this inner core of one's *being* where authenticity is to be forged and which therefore has great importance for education.

With his emphasis upon looking backwards, perhaps Gadamer is placing too much emphasis upon simply fusing one's horizon with others because in doing so one might lose one's sense of authenticity. Gadamer (1989, p. 305) acknowledges that "it requires a special effort to acquire a historical horizon" which we can attest to when studying and learning. But Dewey adds a significantly important dimension to this. Typically formal education primarily involves the study of subjects or disciplines so that one gains knowledge and understandings from them. This is sometimes referred to as being disciplined by the disciplines because one learns to think and act according to what one has learned directly from these subjects. Dewey (1989, p. 179) identifies that this can be understood as 'conformity' which he explains occurs when;

> The mind becomes logical only by learning to conform to an external subject matter… the pupil learns the definitions one by one and, progressively adding one to another, builds up the logical system, and thereby is himself gradually imbued, from without, with logical quality.

Consequently Dewey (1989, p. 179) warns educators to be wary of placing too much emphasis "upon studies rather than attitudes and habits" because this can inadvertently lead to lives which are essentially *conformist* in nature. Instead educators ought to place more focus upon the attitudes and habits of students because, as we understand existentially, the exercising of these attributes in making critical judgements and choices is essential for authenticity.

REFORMULATING THE HORIZON OF UNDERSTANDING

In this chapter the case is being made that death anxiety can be valuable for authenticity and the educative growth of our horizon of understanding. To appreciate the particular impact that this anxiety can have, a review of how our conceptual understandings might transform and grow is considered helpful. This is because this approach is at odds with many predominant approaches to learning theory. It can be appreciated that the 'fusion' of horizons to which Gadamer refers, might represent the mere extension of an existing horizon with the addition of another. However, it is the *re*formation of our horizons that is of importance when it comes to the potential value of death anxiety.

Learning theories are replete with ideas regarding how learners are understood to progress their learning from simple and superficial beliefs to more complex understandings. The majority of these theories assume an implicit linear system of inputs and outputs, where the inputs are often reduced to various forms of teaching, while learning is considered as the main output (Biesta, 2006, 2017), often literally stated as outcomes. Consequently the work of Piaget has remained very influential within learning theory in general as is evident in the varieties of constructivism in contemporary theories as well as in slightly older models such as Biggs and Collis's (1982) SOLO (Structure of the Observed Learning Outcome) model which in turn, has been adopted more recently by the likes of John Hattie (2009) who is popular with government agencies. These approaches tend to reflect the belief that learning is cumulative. That is, learning involves the acquisition of information which is relatively simple at first, but becomes more complex or deeper through the accumulation of these simple 'blocks' being built upon one another.

The vast majority of learning theories currently dominating approaches to curriculum work in schools and even universities, rely upon this approach of building ideas and information from the simple (and sometimes 'concrete') to the more complex (and often abstract). Not only has this approach dominated learning theory but it has marginalized understandings of 'education' as depicted in Biesta's (2006) concept 'learnification'. This predominant linear process of accumulation initially requires an empty vessel where a collection of knowledge provides the foundation for further knowledge building or construction. Importantly, it also represents thinking as being primarily inductive, in which general principles, patterns and insights, are constructed *after* making several 'neutral' observations. This is encouraged by Hattie (2009, p. 208) who relates approaches of inductive teaching to the inductive reasoning of students, claiming that a meta-analysis shows 'positive effects' between these two phenomena. This has led to Hattie and Yates (2014) making the case that memory is more important than thinking, and consequently teachers ought to be focused on bolstering the memorizing capability of students. This is because what is most important for Hattie (2009, p. 249) is making learning 'visible', which means superficial, and hence he acknowledges that his own work is "particularly effective at measuring surface features… but rarely effective at measuring the construct representations" or conceptual understandings.

Vygotsky (1986, p. 100) also recognized the problems associated with such linear approaches and reports that "[m]emorizing words and connecting them with objects does not in itself lead to concept formation; for the process to begin, a problem must arise that cannot be solved otherwise than through the formation of new concepts." So Vygotsky here is making the case that a concept is not formed spontaneously when facts and information are accumulated. New concepts emerge when an individual's current conceptual understandings or horizon proves to be inadequate for giving sense and meaning to an encounter. As this problematic situation is experienced the individual realizes that her current conceptual understandings need to be adjusted, reformed or replaced altogether. Vygotsky (1986, p. 109) clarifies this further by stating;

> [t]he process of concept formation, like any other higher form of intellectual activity, is not a quantitative overgrowth of the lower associative activity, but a qualitatively new type... The quantitative growth of the associative connections would never lead to higher intellectual activity.

Vygotsky was well aware that concept formation involves the process of *re*formation of understandings. When problems and puzzlements are experienced due to one's current concepts proving to be inadequate to offer explanations or resolutions, then one's actual understandings need to undergo change and not merely be simply added to with more information. While Dewey (1989, p. 227; 1991, p. 119) explains that on occasion we participate in thinking to specifically grapple and "grasp meaning" he importantly identifies that with "every extension of knowledge makes us aware of blind and opaque spots, where with less knowledge all had seemed obvious and natural." Here Dewey warns us that when we have confidence in our understanding of things and feel well able to interpret, understand and explain various events we encounter, we nevertheless may have some blind spots. Consequently, it is not just observations, data and events that need to be grappled with in order for us to give sense and meaning to them, but the very horizon from which we are able to make meanings. Consequently, for education, the metaphor of the horizon indicates that we don't simply learn in a linear fashion but also we *re*shape and *re*formulate some of our fundamental conceptual understandings. Our beliefs, ideals and values therefore ought to be reflected upon from time to time, in order to uncover blind spots that are always part of our horizon of understanding and to provide opportunity to understand differently.

Such *re*formation of important understandings within a discipline, has been described by Kuhn (1970) as a revolution of paradigms. In his own historical research he focused specifically upon scientists and their discipline-specific understandings. He referred to the paradigm as being an encompassing horizon of understanding providing an over-arching umbrella to all of one's perceptions as well as one's conceptual understandings. He claims that "something like a paradigm is prerequisite to perception itself" and also to conceptual understandings (Kuhn, 1970, p. 113). He concludes that,

> Scientists, it should already be clear, never learn concepts, laws, and theories in the abstract and by themselves. Instead, these intellectual tools are from the start encountered in a historically and pedagogically prior unit that displays them with and through their applications. (Kuhn, 1970, p. 46)

Here Kuhn is identifying that for science, as with all disciplines, the perception of phenomena and conceptual understandings all emanate from a prior 'unit', paradigm or horizon. Hence there is not support here for inductive thinking where 'neutral' observations are made and *then* a conceptual understanding emerges – as is assumed by Hattie. This has also been explored by another philosopher of science – Karl Popper who went so far as to claim that "there is no inductive thinking" and therefore there can be no "un-interpreted raw facts." This is extremely important for how we might live *forwards* in an authentic manner. We are dependent upon our existing conceptual understandings to give meanings and sense to current and perhaps novel experiences and so we require a habitual disposition which allows us to re-evaluate our own horizon of understanding as well as evaluate the meanings of our current experiences.

When a discipline, such as science, makes perceived progress, Kuhn argues that what takes place is not mere shifts but are much more profound changes which he describes as revolutions because of the substantive changes that take place in order to conceptualize and understand various phenomena holistically. Through this it can be appreciated that these scientists don't contribute to the growth of the discipline simply through the collection and accumulation of data and information, but they are also involved in concept *re*formation and more profoundly in a revolution of paradigms because they all need to be adjusted to some degree in order to remain compatible and unified with each other.

Individuals are also able to undergo a 'revolution' to their thinking and understanding. This is made possible via the religious attitude to which Dewey and Gadamer refer, which is the individual wakefulness to investigate how *all* of one's beliefs and knowledge are to be unified into a 'total' picture of the world and one's place in it. This unified view rests upon what one considers is of ultimate value and can be recognized through the meaning and purpose that one has for life in general and for their own life in particular. Consequently a revolutionary change to one's horizon tends to have significant input upon their meaning and purpose of life.

Educative growth in contrast to the indoctrinated state, which tends to be static and impervious to evidence and argument, involves some *re*formation of conceptual understandings, such as explained by Vygotsky (1986) where individuals undergo *un*learning and *re*learning as concepts are reformulated. This non-linear approach represents thinking as deductive, in which there is already an existing underlying but dynamic set of beliefs which are drawn upon to give sense and meaning to various experiences which are encountered. This non-linear approach seems to be the preferred way for understanding how thinking and educative growth occurs. Indeed Popper (1992) has suggested that thinking is *only* deductive and goes so far to state that inductive thinking is a fallacy. Whilst an engagement with this claim is not being continued here, it is agreed that thinking is primarily deductive and consequently has huge implications for how we might understand learning.

EDUCATING OUR HORIZON OF UNDERSTANDING THROUGH DEATH ANXIETY

From an existential perspective one of the important characteristics of human persons understood is that we have the capacity to be open to continually learn at the conceptual level as well as learn perceptually. Therefore, becoming educated must involve enhancing this capacity so that we can make wise meanings. As has been discussed, all learning and meaning-making are framed by our horizon of understanding from which we deductively give sense and meaning to subsequent experiences. Importantly for educated people, the ability to re-evaluate our horizon of understanding and undertake conceptual *re*formation is crucially important. Indeed the survival of our species and the planet as a whole may well be dependent upon this enablement. Therefore, it is fundamentally necessary for people to change the way we act in this world because our current desires, appetites and activities are unsustainable. The ways in which we fundamentally view the world and our place in it perhaps needs a revolutionary re-evaluation and reformation.

The current dominant approach to formal education, to which government policies and literature are dedicated, is founded upon an assumption that the disciplines of knowledge have a degree of certainty to offer and which allow 'learning' to be easily 'measured'. The approach being adopted here is significantly different because of the acknowledgement that existence is unpredictable and uncertain and therefore any program worthy of the name of 'education' ought to enable societies to live well in such an ever-changing environment. This was the position of Dewey (1958, p. 41) who described that "Man finds himself living in an aleatory world; his existence involves, to put it baldly, a gamble. The world is a scene of risk; it is uncertain, unstable, uncannily unstable. Its dangers are irregular, inconstant, not to be counted upon as to their times and seasons." This acknowledgement of the nature of reality makes Dewey's views consistent with much of the work of the existentialists. For example, Kierkegaard (1992, p. 86) has argued that "one who is existing is continually in the process of becoming ... the perpetual process of becoming is the uncertainty of earthly life, in which everything is uncertain." The task of education then, is to enable us to live authentically, which involves being in a perpetual state of becoming further educated made possible through freedom and choice.

In one of his final works Kierkegaard (1998) explained directly rather than using one of his pseudonyms, that he wanted to compel his readers to notice and give serious attention to being able to live a meaningful life. Anz (1998, p. 39) picks up this point and suggests that to "compel someone to take notice, however, is not the same as giving advice" because the experience of "taking notice" directly implicates one's authenticity, while simply "giving advice" on the other hand, doesn't actually require much response – if any – from the one being addressed. This appeal to one's authenticity to take notice is recognized by Garrison (2010, p. 142) who states that "[m]otivation is never a problem. The problem is how to educate the human erōs to take an interest in truly valuable things." This education of our eros, interest and even will, is where death anxiety has great potential for helping individuals to 'take notice' and give serious attention to how they are living. It accentuates the importance of one's life because one accepts that one's existence is temporary and may, at any moment, come to an end.

Encouraging students to take notice and to invite their authentic responses requires an approach to education that is quite uncommon today. Frankl (1988, p. 28–9) has observed this too when he states that "education avoids confronting young people with ideals and values" and through this absence of confrontations the everyday experiences of education tends to "reinforce the existential vacuum" in their lives. This existential vacuum which is identical to the 'inner void' which Dewey referred to as discussed earlier, makes people vulnerable to being manipulated by authorities, media and peer pressure. Therefore, authenticity which requires an integrated character of unified ideals and aspirations is benefited by confrontations. Death anxiety is able to confront us with an acceptance that our life is finite and indeed potentially could end at very short notice. This anxiety can compel us to be fully present in the moment and to reflect and re-evaluate how we are making sense of and participating in life at this very moment. As Frankl (1984, pp. 131–2) sums up, "Live as if you were living already for the second time and as if you had acted the first time as wrongly as you are about to act now!"

It is through death anxiety that individuals can be more wakeful to give serious thought to the present moment and consider whether their current activity is worthwhile, especially with the anxiety that their life is potentially about to terminate. This reflection through death anxiety importantly provides opportunity to re-evaluate our fundamental meaning and purpose for how we conduct ourselves. For example, if our current moment is being spent in self-indulgent debauchery, death anxiety could offer itself as the stimulus to consider whether participating in this current activity is how we would like to be remembered doing as our last act? As another example, death anxiety allows us to be open to be confronted by the eyes of our young child who is seeking our attention which is at odds with our traditional 'busyness' in everyday life. Death anxiety confronts us at such times to ask if our priorities are what they ought to be. From these encounters with the limits of life, some recalibration can occur regarding what is valued and cherished. This is considered most pertinent for educators at a time when mere measurements are coming to dominate the work that we do (Webster, 2017b). This can lead to revolutionary growth in how we see life and its most important values, knowing that what is precious is also fragile.

If we have little concern for what lies beyond our death then perhaps self-indulgent debauchery may seem to have a place. However, it is through engaging with death anxiety that our horizon of understanding may have opportunity to reconceptualize our beliefs of what happens beyond death. Perhaps there is some form of life after death, as Pascal's wager challenges us. For Kierkegaard, his own horizon of understanding led him to view death as only an episode. In which case we might ask that if our horizons were to be fused with his, might we give some thought as to how are we are preparing for the possibility of life beyond the episode of death? One doesn't need to be convinced of such a possibility but one could remain open to it and this is where it is valuable in terms of *being* educated. This is the sort of openness that is encouraged by James (1982, p. 423) who argues that an openness to apparent mystery can "break down the authority of the non-mystical or rationalistic consciousness… open[s] out the possibility of other orders of truth…" This has since been picked by others (e.g. Fenwick, 2019) who continue to research into the function of unconsciousness after the physical brain ceases to function.

Heidegger argued that death is eternity and Dasein is temporal and united through death in the sense that Dasein as a project is 'completed'. In contrast, Kierkegaard did not consider death as eternal but saw death as being a moment towards coming before the face of God who is the eternal and omnipotent 'other'. Unlike Heidegger, Kierkegaard understood eternity as being an attribute of God and as a potential for *all* people and not just Christians. It opens up opportunity to continually dialogue with and re-evaluate our own horizon of understanding. This is important for what it might mean to *be* educated, as Anz (1998, p. 46) explains, "The 'eternal' is the basic relationship through which 'knowing' is converted into Socratic ignorance, in an experience of fear and trembling." So through death anxiety, rather than perhaps an extreme form of fear or dread, both our knowing and our capacity to grow in knowing, are opened up for examination of potential blind spots allowing for the readiness to open our horizon of understanding even further.

In addition to this sense of the eternal there is also the presence of the omnipotent other. Derrida (2008, p. 5) reflects upon Kierkegaard's position, describing it as "the relation of self as being before the other [where] the other is its infinite alterity…" He goes on to explore the impact that this openness might have on our *being* by arguing that,

> the Christian *mysterium tremendum* …[is a] more radical form of responsibility that exposes me dissymmetrically to the gaze of the other; where my gaze, precisely as regards me (*ce qui me regarde*), is no longer the measure of all things. (Derrida, 2008, pp. 28–29)

Here Derrida challenges us with the possibility that our own horizon of understanding will never be sufficient for providing sense and meaning, even of ourselves, if we are to come face-to-face with God. However, even outside of its given Christian context, there is the call to nevertheless be responsible for such a possibility which is something that Derrida considers is worthwhile. From this perspective of our own limits he concludes that "one is never responsible enough because one is finite" and yet death anxiety through a Christian perspective offers a "most powerful momentum for plumbing the depths of this abyss of responsibility" (Derrida, 2008, pp. 29 & 52). He therefore challenges us as to how we are responding to this responsibility that we have for potentially coming before God on the other side of our death.

The educative value for engaging with the eternal through death anxiety, is considered by Kierkegaard as being not just a useful and interesting activity but is essential if one is to live authentically. He claims that "Therefore he sins who lives only in the moment as abstracted from the eternal" (Kierkegaard, 1980, p. 93) indicating that we are a lesser being as a consequence of avoiding engaging with the possibility of the eternal. This is because such avoidance lessens our anxiety, and as identified throughout this chapter, a certain level of anxiety is necessary for being wakeful and able to live life forwards with responsible criticality. When death anxiety includes reflecting upon the eternal, a valuable type of anxiousness is embodied which enables us to achieve another degree of openness towards having our horizon of understanding re-evaluated and further educated.

Engaging with death anxiety enables the re-evaluation of some of the assumptions upon which our horizon of understanding is founded, and possibly is able to identify some prejudices or blind spots we may have, especially regarding our beliefs as to whether there is life beyond death and whether we may ever have to come face-to-face with an omnipotent God. Examples of blind spots might include a rejection of the possibility of the existence of God because perhaps we have had negative experiences with religious people who we assume represent the possibility of his existence. But perhaps the potential existence of God should not be judged through experiences with religious people or even with formal religion. Perhaps, being omnipotent and eternal by definition, God extends far beyond any religious horizon of understanding because, as Derrida has identified, he is the 'infinite alterity' and therefore by definition, is unknowable. How then might one prepare now in this lifetime for such a possible encounter, especially considering that our next moment may be our last one before this episode occurs?

CONCLUSION

Although it is generally avoided, death anxiety ought to be considered as a normal dimension of living which not only helps promote psychological well-being but it can also encourage educative growth. Being educated is understood from an existential perspective as authenticity, characterized by the free and responsible choice of valuing. The capacity for choosing and making meanings are dependent upon our horizon of understanding from which we view the world and our place in it. In addition to having the horizon grow by fusing it with other horizons, educative growth is also more profoundly possible by *re*-evaluating and *re*formulating the actual horizon itself, and that this is most likely to occur through the anxiety associated with our death. Educating our existential relation with our horizon of understanding through such death anxiety is recognized by Anz (1998, p. 47) who explains that "[i]f we allow ourselves to be educated by anxiety, then we will come to understand that dying is not a process that happens to us from outside; rather it is our own ownmost being, which as a not-yet-grasped possibility 'concerns' us in anxiety." Through this perspective of Anz, it can be appreciated that such anxiety can be our teacher for greater authenticity.

Death anxiety allows opportunity to pause, reflect and be wakeful in the current moment, considering whether it could be our final one and whether we are participating in life in the best way we can. Consequently, death anxiety provides opportunity to re-evaluate the values that we have chosen to base our understanding of ourselves and the world upon. Such a re-evaluation allows us to evaluate how we are investing ourselves according to our current commitments, and whether these commitments are the ones we ought to have. This can require a great deal of courage or 'nerves of steel' to contemplate our identity, values and commitments freely and beyond the compulsion to comply with society's norms, and also to accept our inevitable death and consider a possible encounter with the eternal. Facing such anxiety is able to enhance our authenticity and what it means to be educated.

REFERENCES

Alexander, T. M. (2013). *The human eros*. Fordham University Press.
Anz, W. (1998). Kierkegaard on death and dying. In J. Rée & J. Chamberlain (Eds.), *Kierkegaard: A critical reader* (pp. 39–52). Blackwell.
Barnett, R. (2007). *A will to learn*. Open University Press.
Bauman, Z. (2006). *Liquid fear*. Polity.
Bauman, Z. (2008). *The art of life*. Polity.
Biesta, G. J. J. (2006). *Beyond learning*. Paradigm Publishers.
Biesta, G. J. J. (2017). *The rediscovery of teaching*. Routledge.
Biggs, J. B., & Collis, K. F. (1982). *Evaluating the quality of learning: The SOLO Taxonomy*. Academic Press.
Derrida, J. (2008). *The gift of death* (2nd ed.) (D. Wills, Trans.). The University of Chicago Press.
Dewey, J. (1958). *Experience and nature*. Dover Publications.

Dewey, J. (1988). Individualism, old and new. In J. A. Boydston (Ed.), *John Dewey the later works vol. 5: 1929–1930* (pp. 41–123). Southern Illinois University Press.
Dewey, J. (1989). How we think (2nd ed.). In J. A. Boydston (Ed.). *John Dewey the later works vol. 8: 1933* (pp. 105–352). Southern Illinois University Press.
Dewey, J. (1991). *How we think* (1st ed.). Prometheus Books.
Dewey, J. (2008a). Experience and education. In J. A. Boydston (Ed.), *John Dewey the later works vol. 13: 1938–1939* (pp. 105–352). Southern Illinois University Press.
Dewey, J. (2008b). A common faith. In J. A. Boydston (Ed.), *John Dewey the later works vol. 9: 1933–1934* (pp. 1–58). Southern Illinois University Press.
Fenwick, P. (2019). *Shining light on transcendence*. White Crow Books.
Frankl, V. E. (1984). *Man's search for meaning*. Washington Square Press.
Frankl, V. E. (1988). *The will to meaning*. Plume.
Gadamer, H-G. (1989). *Truth and method* (2nd ed.) (J. Weinsheimer & D. G. Marshall, Trans.). Continuum.
Gadamer, H-G. (1999). *Hermeneutics, religion, and ethics*. (J. Weinsheimer, Trans.). Yale University Press.
Garrison, J. (2010). *Dewey and eros*. Information Age Publishing Inc.
Hattie, J. (2009). *Visible learning*. Routledge.
Hattie, J., & Yates, G. (2014). *Visible learning and the science of how we learn*. Routledge.
Heidegger, M. (1996). *Being and time* (J. Stambaugh, Trans.). State University of New York Press.
Heidegger, M. (1999). *Ontology – the hermeneutics of facticity* (J. V. Buren, Trans). Indiana University Press.
James, W. (1890). *The principles of psychology* (Vol. 1). Dover Publications.
James, W. (1982). *The varieties of religious experience*. Penguin Books.
Kierkegaard, S. (1980). *The concept of anxiety* (H. V. Hong & E. H. Hong, Trans.). Princeton University Press.
Kierkegaard, S. (1987). *Either/or, vol.2* (H. V. Hong & E. H. Hong, Trans.). Princeton University Press.
Kierkegaard, S. (1998). *The point of view* (H. V. Hong & E. H. Hong, Trans.). Princeton University Press.
Koerrenz, R. (2017). *Existentialism and education*. Rotterdam: Palgrave Macmillan.
Kuhn, T. S. (1970). *The Structure of Scientific Revolutions* (2nd ed.). The University of Chicago Press.
Mulhall, S. (1996). *Heidegger and being and time*. Routledge.
Nietzsche, F. (1966). *Beyond good and evil* (W. Kaufmann, Trans.). Vintage Books.
Sartre, J-P. (1958). *Being and nothingness* (H. E. Barnes, Trans.). Routledge.
Shapiro, J. L. (2016). *Pragmatic existential counseling and psychotherapy*. Santa Clara University.
Van Ranst, N., & Marcoen, A. (2000). Structural components of personal meaning in life and their relationship with death attitudes and coping mechanisms in late adulthood. In G. T. Reker & K. Chamberlain (Eds.), *Exploring existential meaning* (pp. 59–74). Sage.
Vygotsky, L. (1986). *Thought and language* (A. Kozulin, Trans.). MIT Press.
Webster, R. S. (2010). The right to inquire into the religious. In K. Engebretson, M. de Souza, G. Durka & L. Gearon (Eds.), *International handbook of inter-religious education* (pp. 1105–1120). Springer.
Webster, R. S. (2013). Improving the value of the national curriculum through ethics and the religious. *Journal of Australian Curriculum Studies, 33*(1), 31–41.

Webster, R. S. (2017a). Making the unbearable, bearable, through existential spirituality. In A-M. Pascal (Ed.), *Multiculturalism and the convergence of faith and practical wisdom in modern society* (pp. 81–98). IGI Global.

Webster, R. S. (2017b). Valuing and desiring purposes of education to transcend miseducative measurement practices. *Educational Philosophy and Theory, 49*(4), 331–346.

CHAPTER SIX

Learning From the Death of Others

Levinas and Heidegger on Educating for the Good Beyond Being

JOHN QUAY

THE EDUCATIONAL CHALLENGE PRESENTED BY CATEGORIAL MURDER

Categorial Murder and Ontological Categorization

This chapter is concerned with murder – the unlawful and premeditated killing of a person or persons – and how education may be theorized and practiced in order to work against such killing. While murder happens in educational institutions, notably in the very public and tragic circumstances surrounding school killings (Katsiyannis et al., 2018), it is not murder in schools that is the primary focus. Instead, it is important to learn from situations exemplary of what Bauman (2004) refers to as "categorial murder," wherein "men, women and children were exterminated for having been *assigned to a category of beings* [emphasis added] that was meant to be eliminated" (p. 26). This is murder justified on the basis of ontological categorization.

Prominent amongst such extermination events is the Holocaust or Shoah, when "approximately six million Jews and by some accounts close to a million Gypsies, accompanied by many thousands [of] homosexuals and mentally retarded," were "shot, poisoned and burnt by the builders of the Nazi-designed New World Order" (Bauman, 2004, p. 25). Bauman, born into Jewish ancestry but not raised a Jew (Bielefeld, 2002), had personal experience of the Second World War as a soldier in the Polish Army. Beyond his own experiences, Bauman points to numerous other extermination events evident through relatively recent human history – including Rwanda, where "Hutus massacred their Tutsi neighbours," the Khmer Rouge killing fields in Cambodia, and the partitioning of India and Pakistan – all focused on removing an ontologically categorized group of people "because they did not fit the order about to be built" (2004, p. 25).

Bauman describes categorial murder as *"creative* destruction," because it is aimed at "eliminating everything out of place and unfitting," such that "order is created or reproduced" (2004, p. 37). He designates the places where extermination events occurred as "construction sites" (p. 25), to distinguish them from situations of combat involving confrontation between two forces. This distinction highlights how categorial murder is not only meant to deprive the appointed human targets of their lives, "but also, and a priori, to expropriate them from their humanity" (p. 26). This means that nothing the victims might do or not do could help them, "nothing could bring exemption from the fate common to the category to which they belonged" (p. 26). The killing of the victims is established in advance by the ontological categorization undertaken by the murderers.

Categorial Murder in the Experience of Levinas

Levinas had intimate experience of two catastrophic extermination events involving ontological categorization and categorial murder: the Russian Revolution and the Second World War. Levinas was a Jew born in Lithuania in 1906; his religion was an important category. He grew up in Ukraine during the Russian Revolution, studied in France and Germany, and lived as a French citizen, and a French soldier (and a prisoner of war) during the Second World War (Cohen, 1994, pp. 115–121). As described by Bauman, the Russian Revolution saw "ten million genuine or alleged 'kulaks' of Ukraine … starved to death for being a wrong sort of people with no room at all in the brave new world of classless conformity" (2004, p. 25). Levinas's family survived these occurrences by leaving Ukraine. And Levinas escaped the murder of the Holocaust because he was, as a prisoner of war, categorized as a French soldier, rather than a Jew. "I was directly restrained to a special status," Levinas (2001b, p. 40) recalled, "registered as a Jew but spared by my uniform the destiny of those who were deported." However, such an escape from death did not limit the impact the Holocaust had on Levinas's life, which, he reflected, was biographically "dominated by the presentiment and the memory of the Nazi horror" (Levinas, 1990, p. 291).

Levinas became aware that these two extermination events were the setting for the book *Life and Fate* by Grossman (1985), a Soviet writer and journalist. This was a novel which (according to an interlocutor) "overwhelmed" Levinas

(1999, p. 106), and he mentioned it in at least eight published interviews he participated in during the 1980s (Robbins, 2001). Levinas précised Grossman's book as a description of "the situation in Europe during the time of Stalin and Hitler" (Levinas, 1999, p. 106) in "800 pages offer[ing] a complete spectacle of desolation and dehumanization" (p. 107). Confounding for Levinas was how Marxism had "turned into Stalinism" (p. 107) such that the situation in Russia was in fact the consequence of a quest for human freedom. As with other extermination events, the categorial murder occurring under Stalin's influence and rule emerged from an intention to construct a new and better society; pursuing a goal that seemed good, via means which were evil. Levinas regarded Stalinism as "the greatest offence to the cause of the human, because Marxism bore the hopes of humanity" (p. 107).

Can Education Work against Categorial Murder?

Can education work against such creative destruction justified ontologically? Investigating this question requires engagement with ontology, in order to comprehend ontological categorization. For this, Heidegger's phenomenological ontology is central. Also implicated in such an investigation is ethics, and here Levinas's philosophy is key, because in formulating his position on ethics, Levinas engages closely with Heidegger's phenomenological ontology, especially as Heidegger expresses it in *Sein und Zeit*, or *Being and Time* (2010). But Levinas does not accept all of Heidegger's thinking, and he offers a critique of Heidegger's ontological position, an ethical critique informed by differing phenomenological interpretations of experiencing death. Levinas's central insight regarding Heidegger's phenomenology is his challenge to Heidegger's interpretation of experiencing death.

The key movements in the argument expressed in this chapter involve, firstly, explication of Levinas's critique of Heidegger, to highlight their different positions on ethics and ontology, via their differing phenomenological analyses of death. Then, secondly, to draw their work together – ontology and ethics – to identify the ethical and other ramifications of these differences, with an especial focus on the face to face relation. Thirdly, the philosophical positions of Levinas and Heidegger are applied to education, to suggest how they may work together to inform teaching and learning. The remainder of this introductory section provides a summary of these movements to forecast the broader philosophical argument to be detailed in the rest of the chapter.

Education through Ontology to Ethics

Energized by his experiences of extermination events, Levinas is chiefly concerned with issues of ethics, which underpin his critique of Heidegger's ontology.

Via this critique Levinas identifies and emphasizes "the face to face" as the basis for ethical relation (1969, p. 202), in contrast to the side-by-side ethical positioning of Heidegger's "being-with" (2010, p. 111) in a totality. These two ways of relating offer concrete exemplars of the two different ethical positions emphasized in the philosophies of Levinas and Heidegger.

Heidegger's ethical position is achieved chiefly through his interpreting of Aristotelian philosophy, conducted during the years leading up to and including the writing of *Sein und Zeit* and informed by his continuing and developing phenomenological analysis of Da-sein. Through this interpretation, Heidegger (2009a) merges politics with ethics, leading to his position that ethics is "determined as being-with-one-another" (p. 48). Heidegger argues that, in comprehending the Aristotelian position, "we must leave aside other modern concepts of ethics and politics, and understand the investigation as one that is primarily oriented toward being-along-with-others" (p. 87).

In contrast, the face to face is a central feature of Levinas's philosophy. From an educational perspective, it is significant that the face to face relation can breach or "rupture," as Levinas (1969, p. 226) describes it, the ontological totality that circumscribes the "along side" (p. 80) of being-with. This face to face rupturing reveals that there is more than just totality, even though the idea of totality suggests that it embraces all. Beyond totality, which is ontological, lies infinity, "*a surplus always exterior to the totality*" (p. 22). Hence the other person is more than can be ascertained by reference to the totality that ostensibly circumscribes the face to face relation and is, in fact, "infinite" (p. 230) in their possibility, an infinity made accessible by the face to face rupturing of the totality.

Concomitant with this rupturing of totality achieved face to face, revealing infinity, Levinas argues for the possibility of escape from being (2003); escape that ventures beyond the possibility of ontological categorization by acknowledging infinity outside totality. Philosophically, what lies outside totality is described in "the Platonic idea of the Good beyond Being" (1969, p. 293). Hence, for Levinas, the good beyond being is the infinity beyond totality. Here Levinas is careful to explain that "the Good as the infinite has no other, not because it would be the whole, but because it is Good and nothing escapes its goodness" (1978, p. 187fn). The good, for Levinas, is not another version of ontological totality but somehow beyond this, not as whole but as idea.

Levinas recognized that the idea of the good, exemplified in particular acts of goodness, plays a significant role in Grossman's narrative. A major theme he identifies in the book is that of "the impossibility of goodness as a government, as a social institution" (1999, p. 107). From experience, Levinas contends that every attempt to organize the human fails, making it vainglorious to believe that social proclamations involving ideology and plans could attain some ultimate goodness.

And he declares himself "very cautious about ideological socialism" (Levinas, 2001c, p. 136). Fallacious attempts to achieve such social organization contributed to the creative destruction underpinning ontological categorization and the extinction events Levinas experienced.

Yet Levinas also sees in Grossman's book that goodness is never completely lost, as it "holds on" (1999, p. 109) in instances of, not large but "little goodness" (p. 107) or "kindness" (p. 108). Amidst the decay of human relations characteristic of war, Levinas observes that "goodness persists" (p. 107); so "in the relation of one person to another person [face to face], goodness is possible" (p. 107). To highlight one example of such a little goodness or kindness, Levinas recounts an episode toward the book's end.

> When Stalingrad has already been rescued, the German prisoners, including an officer, are clearing out a basement and removing the decomposing bodies. The officer suffers particularly from this misery. In the crowd, a woman who hates Germans is delighted to see this man more miserable than the others. Then she gives him the last piece of bread she has. This is extraordinary. Even in hatred there exists a mercy stronger than hatred. (Levinas, 2001a, p. 89)

The essential thing in Grossman's book for Levinas, is voiced by the character Ikonnikov, who says, "'there is neither God nor the Good, but there is goodness'" which Levinas (2001a, p. 89) acknowledges, "is also my thesis." This persistence of goodness in the relation of one person to another is, for Levinas, the goodness of everyday life: "the only thing that remains vigorous" (1999, p. 107). And he is clear that "this saintliness of the human cannot be expressed on the basis of any [ontological] category" (p. 109). This is because little goodness, in contrast to goodness as government or social institution, is enabled by the face to face relation, where the face, rupturing being and revealing infinity, is the ethical "authority that commands me, 'Thou shalt not kill'" (p. 104). Displacing the truth supporting ontological categorization in a totality removes the justification for categorial murder.

Important to educators in this regard is the attention Levinas focuses on Heidegger's phenomenological interest in the truth of being, a notion of truth as disclosedness characterized via intelligibility, comprehension, understanding, knowing. Moving beyond being therefore means that the good, infinity, must go beyond the truth disclosed in a totality. "What more there can be than the question of being is not some truth," Levinas declares, "but the good" (1978, p. 9). This contrast between truth and the good is a version of the contrast between the idea of totality and the idea of infinity, and these "differ precisely in that the first is purely theoretical, while the second is moral" (1969, p. 83). For Levinas, theoretical references theory, intelligibility, comprehension, truth; while morality is enabled via infinity, the good.

Levinas's positioning of morality as beyond truth, and in this sense as "first philosophy" (1969, p. 304), is a pivotal contribution. The good sits "above every essence" of being, as "the most profound teaching, the definitive teaching, not of theology, but of philosophy" (p. 103). The good is "before being" (1978, p. 122) and is right at the center of the philosophical problematic (2001b, p. 54). For education, Levinas's philosophy positions moral questioning as more foundational than questioning truth within a specific totality. To decide between totalities involves moral questioning, going beyond being to the idea of the good. It requires the face to face as a rupturing of totality to reveal infinity.

This most profound teaching from Levinas has significant implications for teaching as a practice. Teaching, Levinas argues, is methodologically the production of infinity. "Teaching signifies the whole infinity of exteriority. And the whole infinity of exteriority is not first produced, to then teach: teaching is its very production" (1969, p. 171). Therefore, "teaching is not a ... hegemony at work within a totality," Levinas declares, "but is the presence of infinity breaking the closed circle of totality" (p. 171). Importantly, this means that the other is "the first rational teaching, the condition for all teaching" (p. 203), because the other, face to face, enables the rupturing of being, revealing infinity.

Can education work against categorial murder? Yes, but it requires teaching and learning to go beyond a focus on truth as intelligibility, comprehension, understanding, within a totality. Teaching and learning must engage with truths but must also hold these truths up to broader questioning concerned with morality, with goodness beyond the totality that is the specific learning situation – such as a subject in school. This means bringing education into conversation with infinity. And it requires educators to follow Levinas in, first of all, developing awareness of the various ontological features of education by way of Heidegger's philosophy, in order to, second, perceive the ethical lessons that Levinas provides.

LEARNING FROM DEATH

Learning from the Holocaust

Bauman and Levinas, informed by their life experiences, are aligned in their disdain for the ontological categorization of people which, according to Levinas, arises from the ontological "ground of totality" as "system" (1969, p. 80). Levinas understands such ontological categorization to be founded within an ontological philosophical position, as developed by Heidegger. To overcome ontological categorization, especially where this can lead to the extreme of categorial murder, the totality must be breached or ruptured, such that the other person "*is not under a category*" (1969, p. 69). This rupturing is an event of learning and of teaching, where "teaching," for Levinas, involves "breaking the closed circle of totality" (p. 171).

Levinas's insight in this regard is informed by his experience of the Holocaust, which he regards as "an event of still inexhaustible meaning" (1999, p. 161). Likewise, Bauman considers the Holocaust "an event of tremendous importance for the future shape of the world" (2004, p. 35), because it offers "a laboratory in which certain, otherwise diluted and scattered potentials of modern, widely shared forms of human cohabitation were condensed, brought to the surface and in view" (p. 35). And, Bauman warns, "if that significance is not acknowledged, the most important lessons of the Holocaust ... are bound to remain, to everyone's peril, unread"; lessons pertaining to "the genocidal potential endemic to our forms of life" along with "the conditions under which that potential may bring its lethal fruits" (p. 35).

Levinas attributes the inexhaustible meaning of the Holocaust to "thinking of the death of the other man" (1999, p. 162), via which he reflects on his engagement with Heidegger's phenomenological ontology. Levinas believes Heidegger to be "the one who pursued philosophical thought's reference to death the farthest" (p. 155). But in so doing, he regards Heidegger as problematically deducing "all conceivable meaning from the attitude of man *toward his own death* [emphasis added]" (p. 161), rather than the death of the other.

Levinas proclaims his admiration for Heidegger to be "above all an admiration for *Sein und Zeit*" (1985, p. 38). "In *Sein und Zeit*'s analyses of anxiety, care and being-toward-death, we witness a sovereign exercise of phenomenology," Levinas believes; an exercise that "is extremely brilliant and convincing" (pp. 39–40). "*Sein und Zeit* has remained the very model of ontology," he argues; "the Heideggerian notions of finitude, being-there, being-toward-death, etc., remain fundamental" (p. 41). And at the basis of Heidegger's ontology is, for Levinas, the "return to Being as a verb," achieved via "the ontico-ontological difference" (2001c, p. 131). Levinas recognizes that Heidegger's phenomenology emphasizes comprehension of being as verb, whereas before Heidegger the word being was habitually spoken of as a noun or "substantive, even though it is a verb par excellence." (p. 38). Hence, "with Heidegger, 'verbality' was awakened in the word being, what is event in it, the 'happening' of being" (p. 38).

Levinas sees nothing in Heidegger's new phenomenology, especially as "elaborated and developed in the magnificent opening pages of *Sein und Zeit*," that highlights "any political or violent ulterior motive" (1989, p. 486). However, he does raise concerns with the way in which Heidegger develops his analysis beyond these early sections. In this regard Levinas points out that being is positioned in Heidegger's phenomenology as "a reflexive verb: it is not just that one is, one is oneself" (1978, p. 16). And he therefore notes, with some disquiet, a "tensing of being back onto itself, a plot in which the reflexive pronoun, -self, is bound up"

(2000, p. xii). This reflexivity means that "what is at stake in the 'event' of being is that being itself," expressed as "persisting-in-being or the concern for being" (p. 209). Levinas (1999) interprets this persisting or concern as "the effort to exist, the aspiration to persevere in being," which he knew Spinoza had referred to as "the *conatus essendi*" (p. 166).

This problematic reflexivity in being as a verb is, for Levinas, further evidenced ontologically via Heidegger's notion of mineness, wherein "primordial importance is attached to *one's own being*" (Levinas, 2000, p. 211). Levinas recognizes Heidegger's "event or adventure or advent of *being that is concerned with being*" to be "a kind of fullness of the mine – a 'mineness' or *Jemeinigkeit*, in Heideggerian terms" (p. 212), where, as Heidegger (2010, p. 41) puts it, "the being [verb] of this being [Da-sein; see below] is always *mine*." Awareness of this reflexivity awoke in Levinas a philosophical urge to escape what he perceived to be ontological confinement, defining escape as "the need to get out of oneself, that is, *to break that most radical and unalterably binding of chains, the fact that the I is oneself*" (2003, p. 55).

Levinas's Concern with Heidegger's Analysis of Death

Da-sein as Inauthentic (Division 1) and Authentic (Division 2)

Heidegger refers to this being which we ourselves in each case are as Da-sein, or literally there-being; being is there-being. There-being, Da-sein, is mine. Mineness is important methodologically for Heidegger because, he argues, "the phenomenological interpretation must give to Da-sein itself the possibility of primordial disclosure and let it, so to speak, interpret itself" (p. 131). Heidegger's position as "the questioner" (p. 39) in this phenomenological investigation means that his analysis is focused on a particular there-being, a particular Da-sein: for Heidegger, Da-sein is concretely mine. Heidegger is interrogating his Da-sein, as an "individualization" (p. 35) of being. By analyzing his own Da-sein, Heidegger aims to uncover "the being of beings" (p. 33) via two analytical phases unfolding in the two divisions of *Sein und Zeit*: (1) the preparatory fundamental analysis of Da-sein, and (2) Da-sein and temporality.

The basic delineation between these two divisions can be seen in the distinction Heidegger draws within mineness, between "authenticity and inauthenticity" (2010, p. 53). Authenticity (the focus of division two) describes Da-sein being aware of itself as Da-sein: an important methodological achievement in a phenomenological sense because, for Heidegger, this gives Da-sein access to Da-sein as whole, in the reflexive way that Levinas problematizes. Inauthenticity (the focus of division one), while still mine, describes the publicness of Da-sein in its everydayness, which Heidegger attributes to an ontological sense he calls "the they" (p. 119), because "we enjoy ourselves and have fun the way *they* enjoy themselves," and "we read, see, and judge literature and art the way *they* see and judge" (p. 123). All that we do is done in the way of the they.

For Heidegger, "the self of *everyday* [emphasis added] Da-sein is the *they-self* which we distinguish from the *authentic self*, that is, the self which has explicitly grasped itself" (2010, p. 125). Division one is focused on this everydayness which emphasizes the inauthentic being of Da-sein, prescribed in various ways by the publicness of the they, although still mine. The move to the authentic self is a further methodological step.

Da-sein as Unwhole (Division 1) and Whole (Division 2)

Heidegger pursues his phenomenological analysis beyond the inauthentic self of division one, to the authentic self of division two, where Da-sein explicitly grasps itself as Da-sein. This is methodologically required, Heidegger believes, to further the analysis of Da-sein beyond the inauthenticity that characterizes division one of *Sein und Zeit*. The existential analytic of division one "*cannot lay claim to primordiality*" because it "never included more than the *inauthentic* being of Da-sein, of Da-sein as *fragmentary*" (Heidegger, 1996, p. 215). In order for the analysis to progress, "it will have to bring the being of Da-sein in its possible *authenticity* and *totality* existentially to light beforehand" (p. 215). This means that division two must first grapple with and build on a phenomenological view of "*all of* Da-sein" or "Da-sein as a whole" (p. 215), rather than Da-sein as fragmentary, as was the case in the analysis of Da-sein's inauthentic everydayness in division one.

It is worth noting that Heidegger describes his division one analysis of Da-sein as fragmentary because in division one he worked chiefly with care as a structural factor, arriving at the position that "care is the totality of the structural whole of the constitution of being of Da-sein" (2010, p. 223). But for Heidegger the analysis of division one is always only preparatory: "The analytic of Dasein which penetrates to the phenomenon of care is to prepare the way for the fundamental, ontological problematic, *the question of the meaning of being in general*" (p. 171). This is because care – especially the future orientation of care that Heidegger calls "*project*" (p. 140) – "tells us unambiguously that something is always *outstanding* in Dasein which has not yet become 'real' as a potentiality-of-its-being" (p. 227). Hence there is "a *constant unfinished quality*" in the basic constitution of Da-sein, and "this lack of wholeness means that there is still something outstanding in one's potentiality-for-being" (p. 227). It is in this sense that Heidegger speaks of "the 'unwholeness' in Dasein" (p. 235) and the need for further analysis in division two.

Resolving the methodological problem of the "possible being whole" of the there-being "which we ourselves in each instance are" (2010, p. 248) is what Heidegger aims to achieve in the early sections of division two via authenticity and totality, and this is where Levinas's concern with Heidegger's reflexivity is particularly focused. While, again, Levinas acknowledges "no formulation specifically traceable to the theses of National Socialism" in the pages of *Sein und Zeit*, he does note how "the construction includes passages in which they might find accommodation" (2000, p. 225). "I would mention, for my part," Levinas continues, "the notion ... of authenticity, of *Eigentlichkeit* – conceived in terms of the 'mine' ..., in terms of *Jemeinigkeit* ..., of the me in mineness ..., in terms of a *belonging to self* and *for self* in their inalienable self-belonging" (pp. 225–226). As a consequence of this reflexivity, Levinas registers "a profound need to leave the climate" of Heidegger's philosophy, whilst acknowledging the impossibility of leaving it "for a philosophy that would be pre-Heideggerian" (1978, p. 4).

Da-sein's Authentic Being-Toward-Death: Death as Mine

Levinas interprets Heidegger's phenomenological analysis to be saying that "the social is beyond ontology" (1985, p. 58). "Sociality in Heidegger is found in the subject alone," he (1987, p. 93) argues, "and it is in terms of solitude that the analysis of Dasein in its authentic form is pursued." This is because, in the Heideggerian sense of authenticity, "all 'relations with others' are dissolved or 'cancelled'" (2000, p. 226). Levinas's interpretation is, in this regard, chiefly informed by his reading of Heidegger's phenomenological analysis of dying and death in division two of *Sein und Zeit*. Here Heidegger analyses death in order to comprehend the wholeness of Da-sein, and in doing so he aligns death with mineness: "Insofar as it 'is,' death is always essentially my own," Heidegger (2010, p. 231) proclaims; because "in dying, it becomes evident that death is ontologically constituted by mineness and existence," not relation.

This was Da-sein's "*authentic* being-toward-death" (2010, p. 249), enabling achievement of wholeness, in contrast to inauthentic everyday understandings of death promulgated by "the they, which never dies" (p. 404). Being-toward-death as a project left nothing outstanding, a project Heidegger characterizes as driven by comprehension of one's death as the possibility of the absolute impossibility of being, which he believes can only be comprehended as my own, because one cannot directly experience the being-toward-death of someone else. "Death is a possibility of being that Dasein always has to take upon itself," Heidegger claims, because "with death, Dasein stands before itself in its *ownmost* potentiality-of-being," and "all relations to other Dasein are dissolved in it" (p. 241).

He summarizes his interpretation by stating that "death is the possibility of the absolute impossibility of Dasein," meaning that "*death* reveals itself as the *ownmost, nonrelational, and inseparable possibility*" (p. 241).

Levinas directly criticizes this passage in order to highlight the problem he sees with Heidegger's methodological attempt to gain the wholeness of Da-sein, where Heidegger aligns death, according to Levinas, with "an authenticity of the most proper being-able-to-be and a dissolution of all relations with the other" (2000, p. 214). Therefore, "Heidegger deduces all conceivable meaning from the attitude of man towards his own death," Levinas (1999, p. 161) argues; "and he thinks that my death for me can be nothing but the ultimate self," the authentic self. As a consequence, "the fundamental relation with being, in Heidegger, is not the relationship with the Other, but with death," Levinas (1985, p. 58) proclaims, a circumstance resulting from Heidegger's phenomenological attempt to attain Da-sein as whole.

Levinas's Challenge to Heidegger's Analysis of Death

Levinas sees a significant problem with Heidegger's phenomenological analysis of death. Where "Heidegger calls the extreme possibility of death possibility of impossibility," Levinas calls death "an impossibility of possibility" (1999, p. 155), neatly reversing Heidegger's positioning of possibility and impossibility. For Levinas, death is not a possibility like other possibilities, because death, he argues, "is an event without project. The 'project' one may have of death is undone at the last moment. It is death alone that goes the last leg. Not us. We do not, strictly speaking, meet it" (p. 155).

This statement highlights the profound difference between Levinas and Heidegger in their phenomenological interpretation and positioning of death. In contrast to Levinas, Heidegger believes that death can be included as a moment in there-being, the moment "when Da-sein reaches its wholeness in death" (2010, p. 229), enabling methodological access to the whole of Da-sein. Reaching wholeness in death thus means engaging with the moment of one's own death as a possibility, a moment that can't be shared. For Heidegger, then, death is the most individualized, nonrelational possibility. This prompts Levinas to again remark on the reflexive nature of Heidegger's being-toward-death, describing it as "the finite being ... moved *by* its finitude *for* that finitude itself" (2000, p. 131).

Levinas regards this Heideggerian interpretation of death as impossible. In contrast, Levinas believes that one's own death can never be known, as "it is resistant to knowledge, in an exceptional way," meaning that it remains a "mystery" (1999, p. 156) because one never actually meets death. As such, for Levinas, there-being can never be whole in the way Heidegger desires. This was, for

Levinas, a methodological bridge too far. For Levinas, there-being cannot be anything but fragmentary in everydayness.

In displacing Heidegger's division two analysis of death, Levinas contends that one can only experience death via the death of the other person. "The death of the other can constitute a central experience for me," Levinas argues, "whatever the resources of our perseverance in our own being may be" (1999, p. 161). Levinas considers the significance of the moment of death of the other to be "infinite, its emotion ethical through and through" (p. 162). It is in this regard that Levinas sees inexhaustible meaning in the Holocaust; for in speaking of the Holocaust, he was "thinking of the death of the other man" (p. 162). The death of the other is an expression of the face to face relation, rupturing being and revealing infinity.

When Heidegger does acknowledge experience of the death of the other through aspects of his analysis, his ethical commitments remain methodologically tied to ontology, to being-in-the-world, via the sense of being-with others in that world, a position Levinas disagrees with. Heidegger describes how, "in mourning and commemorating" someone's death, "those remaining behind *are with* him [the deceased person], in a mode of concern which honors him" (2010, p. 230) And while, "in such being-with the dead, the deceased *himself* is no longer factically 'there' … being-with always means being-with-one-another in the same world"; thus "it is *in terms of this world* that those remaining can still *be with him*" (p. 230). For Levinas, this signals how Heidegger positions the ethical relationship with the other as "conditioned by *being-in-the-world*, and thus by ontology" (2000, p. 213).

It is important to stress again that while Heidegger does acknowledge experience of the death of the other, he puts aside his analysis of the dying of others as it does not achieve his methodological requirement for the wholeness of Da-sein. Indeed, he believes that, by focusing on analysis of the dying of others, "the attempt to make the being a whole of Dasein phenomenally accessible in an appropriate way gets stranded again" (2010, p. 231).

In significant contrast, Levinas's analysis elucidates a different way forward, drawing on his position that one's own death remains a mystery, and that it is the death of the other which is philosophically important, opening to a very different version of ethics. "Fear for the [death of the] other person does not come back to anguish over *my* death," he argues; instead, it "transcends the ontology of Heidegger's *Dasein*" through "an ethical disturbance of being" (2000, p. 131). Levinas sees in eschatology a way to, and the need to, "breach … the totality" (1969, p. 23) created by the reflexivity in Heidegger's ontology, via an ethical disturbance of being. Levinas's ethical approach is the focus for the next section of this chapter, with the aim to elucidate its potential for mitigating ontological categorization and categorial murder.

ONTOLOGY AND ETHICS

Levinas's Ethical Concern with Heidegger's Ontology: From the Truth of Being to the Good Beyond Being

Imbued with experience of the Holocaust, and informed by the ethical deficiency he discerns in Heidegger's phenomenological ontology, Levinas expresses his philosophical disquietude in an important pair of juxtaposed questions: "Is the adventure of being, as being-there, as Da-sein, an inalienable belonging to self, a being *proper* – *Eigentlichkeit*, an authenticity altered by nothing …?"; "or, on the contrary, would not *to be*, that verb, signify – in *being-there* – non-indifference, obsession by the *other*, a search and a vow for peace …?" (2000, p. 207) – "a peace in which the eyes of the other are sought, in which his look awakens responsibility?" (pp. 207–208).

Levinas's thesis is inspired by this juxtaposition, which highlights the need to elevate the little goodness that persists in the relation of one person to another, in the goodness of everyday life about which Grossman had written; a persistence that can break through the horrors of extermination events. To find this goodness philosophically is a primary aim of Levinas's, and he believes that it lies beyond being. For "if philosophy is the questioning of Being" – which is Heidegger's question – "it is already a taking on of Being," Levinas (1978, p. 9) argues. And if philosophy is already a taking on of being, then it is obstructed by being. Hence, if philosophy "is more than this question, this is because it permits going beyond the question [of being], and not because it answers it" (p. 9). This beyond being lies philosophically, for Levinas, in the Platonic idea of the good beyond being. "What more there can be than the question of being is not some truth," he declares, "but the good" (p. 9). Therefore, Levinas positions the good above every essence, where the word essence derives from *esse*: be. The good beyond being is, for Levinas, the most profound philosophical teaching.

Levinas's critical juxtaposition of truth and the good is another expression of the juxtaposition addressed in his two questions above. Levinas knows that Heidegger has advanced his phenomenological analysis since *Sein und Zeit* with a progression in his questioning of being. The shift is from a focus on the meaning of being, where meaning signals being as intelligibility in a totality of relevance, to a focus on the truth of being, where truth conveys being as openness or disclosedness, disclosing this intelligible totality of relevance. As Heidegger himself states: "The thinking that proceeds from *Being and Time*, in that it gives up the word 'meaning of being' in favor of 'truth of being,' henceforth emphasizes the openness of being itself" (Heidegger, 2003, p. 47). Yet, for Levinas, both of Heidegger's questions, and thus Heidegger's entire philosophical project, align being with understanding or intelligibility, and thus with truth. "Being … is the light in which existents become intelligible," Levinas (1969, p. 42) interprets, meaning that "truth is in effect not separable from intelligibility" (p. 82). Heidegger expresses it similarly: "It is understanding that first of all opens up or, as we say, discloses or reveals something like being," and "we call the disclosedness of something truth" (Heidegger, 1982, p. 18).

In Levinas's interpretation, being, as truth, is intelligibility, meaning that being is always the way a being is understood or known. However, Levinas expresses this point more polemically, arguing that, therefore, "ontology consists in neutralizing the existent in order to *comprehend or grasp it* [emphasis added]" (1969, pp. 45–46). As a consequence of this comprehending or grasping – this neutralizing – other people are understood or known in being-with, and therefore in "an association of side by side, around something, around a common term and, more precisely, for Heidegger, around the truth" (1987, p. 41). For Levinas, this is "not a relation with the other as such but the reduction of the other to *the same* [emphasis added]" (p. 47). The same is an important concept for Levinas, which he draws from Heidegger's analysis of world as totality of relevance or referential totality (Levinas, 1996). The same is forged from the concrete relationship between an I and a world, which Levinas describes as "identification" (1969, p. 37), because the I "finds in the world a site and a home." He therefore refers to the same as a site, a medium, "a milieu of understanding" (2000, p. 5).

Neutralizing the other by reducing the other to the same is ontology's function, achieved via "totalization … in which nothing remains other for reason" (Levinas, 1999, p. 48). "Everything is here, everything belongs to me," in this milieu of understanding, this world of mine, this totality of relevance; "everything is caught up in advance with the primordial occupying of a site, everything is com-prehended," Levinas (1969, pp. 37–38) explains. Hence, the "primordial sphere" of the same is "the ground of being as the horizon on which every existent arises" (pp. 67–68). Further to this, Levinas sees that "sharing the same world" in being-with, means that other people are "understood precisely in terms of work and around the instrumental order of those things of the world, and thus," he states, quoting Heidegger, "'they are what they do'" (2000, p. 212). Heidegger notes that "the 'subject character' of one's own Dasein and of the others is to be defined … in terms of certain *ways to be*"; hence "the others are encountered as what they are," and "they *are* what they do" (2010, p. 122).

However, Heidegger also stipulates in his division one analysis of *Sein und Zeit*, that "beings are a *who* (existence) or else a *what* (objective presence in the broadest sense)" (2010, p. 44). Heidegger is here speaking of beings (noun), in their being (verb). A being has the being of existence, as a who, if it is Da-sein, there-being, whereas a being has the being of objective presence, as a what, if it is a thing. This ontological complexity highlights how other people can be considered, ontologically, as who or what, as Da-sein or thing, a distinction having significant implications for understanding the ontological categorization of people, where they can be positioned as what, as thing, not as who.

Levinas and Heidegger Asking "Who?": A Question of Ontology and Ethics

For both Levinas and Heidegger the positioning of others in terms of certain ways to be, as what they do, highlights the question of who, which Heidegger asks ontologically as: "*Who* is it that Dasein is in everydayness?" (2010, p. 111). In Levinas's consideration of this question of who, he recognizes that "most of the time the *who* is a *what*," interpreted in an ontic way: "We ask 'Who is Mr. X?' and we answer: 'He is the President of the State Council,' or 'He is Mr. So-and-so,'" where "the answer presents itself as a quiddity" (1969, p. 177), or whatness, the occupational label interpreted as describing what someone is. Heidegger is also aware of this ontic interpretation, highlighting a broad sense of "occupation" wherein "what someone undertakes" informs "how we determine *what* someone is and *what* [emphasis added] we ourselves in each case are" (2014, p. 54).

> The person makes shoes and thus *is* a shoemaker. That person is involved with instructing and educating and, in keeping with what he does, *is* a teacher. This one practices the art of weaponry and thus *is* a soldier. That one busies himself producing books that appear in public catalogues of booksellers under the "category" of "philosophy," and is therefore a philosopher. (Heidegger, 2014, pp. 54–55)

"Whatever one participates in continually, *what* he does, determines *what* he *is*," Heidegger (2014, p. 55) further emphasizes. Heidegger does not go beyond the simple occupational examples presented above, but the notion of occupation can be broadened to draw in nationality, class, gender, race, religion, age: the person *is* German, *is* old, *is* a female, *is* Jewish; or somewhat narrowed to everyday undertakings such as parenting, commuting, eating, cleaning, playing: the person *is* a mother, *is* a train traveler on the way to work, *is* a homemaker, *is* a sports player. These occupations, for Heidegger, are what one is in a referential totality, not who one is; they thus remain fragmentary for Heidegger.

Via his developing phenomenological analytic and continuing methodological quest for Da-sein as whole, Heidegger pursued the who question through the 1930s, beyond *Sein und Zeit*, aiming to disclose "not 'What is the human being?' and not 'Who is the human being?', but 'Who [not what] are we ourselves?'" (Heidegger, 2009b, p. 33). Ensconced in the reflexivity of his analytic, with the individualization of mineness now expressed as we, and critically informed by his interpretation of the poet Hölderlin whom he declared as the founder of German being (2014, p. 201), Heidegger eventually arrived at a response to this questioning. His response: that who we are ourselves is the being "of the fatherland …

that is, of the historical Dasein of a people," which "is experienced as the authentic and singular" being, "from which the fundamental orientation toward beings as a whole arises and attains its configuration" (p. 109). Here "the fatherland" described "the innermost and most far-reaching historical vocation of the people" (p. 123), the German people.

This was Heidegger's response to reflexive phenomenological questioning seeking there-being as whole, as who we are ourselves, authentic Da-sein. This continues the problem of reflexivity Levinas identified in division two of *Sein und Zeit*. For Heidegger, the wholeness of reflexive Da-sein was achievable in this dawning German Dasein, which he strove to bring the German people to, methodologically, philosophically; a hope he had envisaged proceeding with support of National Socialism. Heidegger supported efforts of the National Socialists to "guide the awakening actuality of German Dasein to its greatness for the first time" (Heidegger, 2016, p. 80). And while this path eventually left Heidegger frustrated, with National Socialism entrenched in "metaphysics" and "machination" (Heidegger, 2017, p. 33), herein lies a philosophical connection between the way Heidegger pursued his methodological project and what Levinas described as "Heidegger's sympathy toward National Socialism" (1989, p. 485).

Returning to Levinas's focus on Heidegger's earlier analysis in *Sein und Zeit*, Levinas understood the ethical challenges presented by Heidegger's ontology and the question of who, which positions the other person as being-with, and therefore "conditioned by being-in-the-world; an approach to the other person certainly, but in terms of occupations and works in the world, without encountering faces" (Levinas, 2000, pp. 214–215). For Levinas, relating ethically with the other as who rather than what requires more than knowing them, comprehending them, as what they are occupationally, in truth. And Levinas conveys this relation via reference to the face: "The face is present in its refusal to be contained. In this sense it cannot be *comprehended* [emphasis added], that is, encompassed" (1969, p. 194). "The relation with the face is not an object-cognition" (p. 75) encompassed within a particular referential totality, as a specific what; rather, "the question *who?* envisages a face" (p. 177). This is a response to the who question aimed at others, and very different to Heidegger's historical Da-sein of a people, which seeks the whole as the same.

The Face to Face as the Basis for Justice

For Levinas, the face signals the possibility of a face to face relation. This differs significantly from the side by side of being-with, for the "'face to face' position is not a modification of the 'along side of …'" (1969, p. 80). This difference indicates to Levinas that "for Heidegger intersubjectivity is a coexistence, a we prior to the I and the other, a neutral intersubjectivity," whereas, in distinction, "the face to face both announces a society, and permits the maintaining of a separated I" (p. 68). This separated I is the face of the other who "is incomparable to me and unique" (2000, p. 165). And for Levinas it is this face to face relation, "produced in multiple singularities" (1969, p. 251), that forms the basis of any larger social organization via "the revelation of the third party" (p. 305), by which he means the introduction of a third person beyond the two involved face to face.

Levinas's recognition of the third party leads to his considerations of justice. The third party "is also my other," but with the third party "I must judge, where before [face to face] I was to assume responsibilities" (2000, p. 104). Thus, with the third party "the concern for justice is born, which is the basis of the theoretical," Levinas (p. 104) acknowledges. But importantly, "it is always starting out from the face, from the responsibility for the other, that justice appears" (p. 104). This requires "judgment and comparison, a comparison of what is in principle incomparable, for every being is unique. Every other is unique" (p. 104), thereby raising the idea of equity.

Justice should always start with the face to face, building on those instances of little goodness that Levinas noted in Grossman's book *Life and Fate* – such as the example Levinas shares of the Russian woman giving her last piece of bread to the German officer. "But would ethics disappear in the justice that it requires and in the politics that justice requires?" he (2001d, p. 116) asks. This remains "a permanent danger which threatens goodness and the originary compassion of responsibility for the other" (p. 116). Importantly for Levinas, ethics arises in the relation to the other and "not straightaway by a reference to the universality of a law (p. 114).

The Face to Face as the Basis for Responsibility

The uniqueness and incomparability of the other in the face to face positions the other as exterior to a totality: "The unique is the other in an eminent way: he doesn't belong to a genus [a category] or doesn't remain within his genus" (Levinas, 2000, p. 205). The other is "emptied of all 'social role,'" or occupation, and thus embraced "in his nudity" outside a totality, in his "destitution, his mortality," all of which "straightaway imposes himself upon my responsibility" (Levinas, 2001d, pp. 114–115). This responsibility for the incomparable other can again be seen expressed in that little goodness or kindness of one for another of which Grossman had written; "a goodness without witnesses," a goodness that "escapes all ideology" (1999, p. 108). This is because "responsibility for the other is the experience of the good, the very meaning of the good, goodness," Levinas (2001c, p. 135) declares; an experience burdensome, or "heavy," for "that is what goodness is" (1999, p. 106).

Levinas's insights regarding responsibility are drawn from the problems he sees with Heidegger's phenomenological analysis of death, which, in striving for methodological wholeness, reflexively excludes other people. In contrast, Levinas considers the death of the other to constitute a central experience and "the significance of that event is infinite, its emotion ethical through and through" (1999, p. 162). This ethical significance is attributable to the "concerning-me-of-your-death," which provides "the *éclatement*, the shattering of being" (2001c, p. 136), the escape from totality. Therefore, "to approach the face of the other is to worry directly about his death," Levinas (p. 135) shares, "and this means to regard him straightaway as mortal, finite," as someone doomed to die, where death is the impossibility of possibility (rather than Heidegger's possibility of impossibility). Thus, "infinity is produced in the relationship of the same with the other," Levinas (1969, p. 26) explains; "the infinite in the finite, the more in the less" (p. 50), such that "a calling into question of the same … is brought about by the other"; and "we name this calling into question … by the Other ethics" (p. 43).

The Face to Face as the Basis for the Good

For Levinas, the face to face holds within it experience of the death of the other person, and thus the other, nude of occupation and mortal, is unique and incomparable; very unlike Heidegger's they of being-with, which never dies. This positions the other, for Levinas, as "beyond being" (1978, p. 19) in a particular totality, as more than being in this particular way, which Levinas "expressed as infinity" (p. 19), because infinity is *"a surplus always exterior to the totality"* (1969, p. 22). Levinas is clear that "infinity" is "not the 'object' of a cognition," because this positions it as comprehended within a totality, but rather "the desirable, that which arouses Desire" (p. 62). This is "Desire for the Infinite" (p. 50) beyond totality, beyond being, and thus desire for the good, and as such, "a desire that can not be satisfied" (p. 34); a desire sustained, because never wholly satiable.

Levinas's emphasis on desire for what is beyond being, on "desire for the Good" (Levinas, 1998, p. 67), can be juxtaposed with his interpretation of Heidegger's notion of care. Da-sein's care for its own there-being, ensconced in totality around a truth, is drawn from the reflexive claim that *"Dasein* is a being for whom, in its very being, being is an issue" (Levinas, 2001b, p. 136); whereas Levinas's desire for the infinite, for the good, is responsibility for the other, because "to be for the Other is to be good" (1969, p. 261). And to be for the other, "is no longer just a question of going toward the other when he is dying, but of answering with one's presence the mortality of the living. That is the whole of ethical conduct," Levinas (1999, p. 164) proclaims. Hence, in our responsibility, "we are answerable not only for the death of the other but for his life as well," because "it is in being answerable for his life that we are already with him in his death" (pp. 167–168).

In this responsibility for the death and thus the life of the other – emanating from the face to face – desire for the good, for infinity, is "stronger than murder" (1969, p. 199). For the idea of infinity, an idea "concretely produced in the form of a relation with the face" (p. 196), "already resists us in his face, is his face, is the primordial *expression*, is the first word: 'you shall not commit murder'" (p. 199). So, while the face offers the "possibility of murder" due to its nudity and mortality, the face is at the same time the "authority that commands me, 'Thou shalt not kill'" (1999, p. 104), because the face ruptures the totality which encompasses ontological categorization, revealing infinity and raising questions of morality, of the good.

The Face to Face as the Basis for Nonindifference

In his earlier work Levinas attempts to describe the other for whom one is responsible, in the face to face, as "the Stranger who disturbs the being at home with oneself" (1969, p. 39), believing that "the strangeness of the Other, his irreducibility to the I [in the same], to my thoughts and my possessions" (p. 43), will fulfil the sense of uniqueness and incomparability – the externality – required to instigate a disturbance or breach of being, of the totality. However, Levinas later recognizes that the other must, at the same time, have proximity in order to be significant enough to have such an impact, where proximity is contact with the other as "fraternity in proximity" (1978, p. 82). He stipulates that "it is in the *personal relationship* [emphasis added], from me to the other, that the ethical 'event,' charity and mercy, generosity and obedience, lead beyond or rise above being" (2000, p. 202), and to the good.

Consequently, Levinas envisages the other for whom one is responsible as neighbor, not stranger, where the neighbor is both exterior and proximal. "The face of a neighbor signifies for me an unexceptionable responsibility," Levinas (1978, p. 88) asserts. This responsibility for my neighbor is, for Levinas, "the harsh name for what we call love of one's neighbor" (2000, p. 103). Importantly, he specifies that this love of one's neighbor "is to be distinguished from everything that is erotic and concupiscence" (1999, p. 164). This is "not love as amusement," but rather "the extreme importance of the other as unique, uniqueness by which the neighbor is to me precisely an other, that is to say … torn up from the common genus [category or totality] that unites us" (2001b, p. 65). Hence, "the responsibility for the other is precisely not a simple kinship" (p. 65), and "not of the attitude toward the death of a being already chosen and dear, but of the death of the first-one-to-come-along" (2000, p. 167), face to face.

This highlights the "paradoxical relation of love," which Levinas (2001b, p. 58) refers to as "nonindifference" in order to play on the "double negation" expressed in this word. Nonindifference can "be thought of as difference, as alterity" (p. 58), as exteriority, whilst also maintaining proximity, "a proximity that counts as sociality" (1978, p. 16). This paradoxical relation of love, of responsibility, is "the sociality irreducible to knowledge" (2001b, p. 58), for love "is not simply the fact that I know someone – it is not a knowing," a comprehending, a grasping – as this occurs within a totality. Love is beyond totality, beyond being, because "love is an excellence, that is to say, the good itself" (p. 58). In practical terms then, "this goodness, this nonindifference to the death of the other, this kindness, is precisely the very perfection of love" (p. 58).

EDUCATING THE OTHER

The Other as Student: Education and Ontological Categorization

Can education work against categorial murder? Yes, it can. But in order to do so educators must first raise awareness of the ways in which education itself works with ontological categorization. The other is generally categorized by educators as the student, the pupil, the learner: they are what they do. These occupational labels are so ubiquitous in educational discourse that they are accepted and applied, seemingly without question, to capture what these young people are expected to do and who or what they are occupationally; and as a consequence a broader awareness of who they are is neglected. Even efforts at pedagogical differentiation tend to categorize young people in terms of what they know and can do, not who they are more broadly. Educators, while having a rich and descriptive language to express the nuance of curricula and pedagogies, possess only limited ways via which to embrace and share the there-being of young people as infinite.

A study conducted of the experiences of young people in secondary schooling (Quay, 2015) illuminates a limited range of ways of being expected of young people in school, with the generic being-a-student dominating all. In a more nuanced way, young people are expected to take on being-a-math-student, being-a-science-student, being-a-history student; indeed each school subject brought with it occupational expectations that subtly or not so subtly varied with different teachers, different year levels. In addition, each co-curricular activity asserts its own occupational, ontological expectations: for example, being-a-band-member, being-a-debating-team-member, being-a-basketball-team-member, being-a-school-production-cast-member.

For education to advance in an ethical sense, educators must come to recognize that ontological categorization is a central feature of the referential totality that is the organizational structure of schooling. Teachers too, of course, are encompassed in such organization via ontological categorization, as teachers of particular subjects, of particular grades or levels. Yet few educators consider schooling in this ontological sense. And without this ontological awareness, the ethical awareness that Levinas argues for remains at least partially obscured. Just as Levinas develops his ethical understanding and position through undertaking a critical analysis of Heidegger's phenomenological ontology, so educators must develop ontological understanding of education (see Quay, 2013) to further inform their engagement with the ethics of education. Going beyond being to the good, beyond totality to infinity, requires ontological awareness, and a discourse enabling shared expression of such awareness.

Beyond Being-a-Student: Teaching from Totality to Infinity

When Levinas discusses teaching, he often problematizes the maieutic understanding applied pedagogically by Socrates, where teaching and learning are believed to involve an awakening of latent understanding already present in a pupil (1969, p. 69). For Levinas, this maieutic pedagogy suggests that teaching and learning are unable to breach totality, instead simply drawing on the same, "to receive nothing of the Other but what is in me" (p. 43). Levinas is clear, however, that "teaching does not simply transmit an abstract and general content already common to me and the Other. It does not merely assume an after all subsidiary function of being midwife to a mind already pregnant with its fruit" (p. 99). Therefore, "teaching is not reducible to maieutics; it comes from the exterior and brings me more than I contain" (p. 51); it "continues the placing in me of the idea of infinity" (p. 180). And it can do this because, "in its non-violent transitivity the very epiphany of the face is produced" (p. 51).

Teaching and learning, for Levinas, are only achievable when premised on the face to face relation. The face to face enables rupturing of the totality, and revealing of infinity. A "being receiving the idea of Infinity, receiving since it cannot derive it from itself, is a being taught in a non-maieutic fashion," Levinas (1969, p. 204) asserts. And "the presence of a being not entering into, but overflowing, the sphere of the same determines its 'status' as infinite" (p. 195).

Teaching affords the possibility of rupturing totality, revealing the other as much more than student, pupil, learner; for "the Other cannot be contained by me: he is unthinkable – he is infinite and recognized as such" (Levinas, 1969, p. 230). Such awareness places significant ethical responsibility on the teacher and expands the intentions inherent to teaching and learning beyond a quest for truth to embrace desire for the good. Teaching that recognizes the other as infinite is, therefore, "not produced ... as a thought," where thought is ensconced in attempts to know, to grasp, within a totality, "but is produced as morality," Levinas (p. 230) declares. "The breach of totality is not an operation of thought," he insists; rather, it is the face to face, for the breach "can be maintained against an inevitably totalizing and synoptic thought only if thought finds itself *faced* with an other refractory to categories" (p. 40).

Teaching, via Levinas, is a moral endeavor because it does not settle for ontological categorization within a totality, but is instead premised on the face to face, rupturing totality and revealing the other as infinite. In this teaching, the other is resistant to categories. Yet education, especially as enacted through schooling, is commonly practiced within an organizational totality where ontological categorization is entrenched. This raises questions of justice, and of how education can be organized so that it is faithful to the face to face upon which it can be premised. If such questions of justice are not adequately addressed, then there exists a permanent danger, threatening goodness and the originary compassion of responsibility for the other (Levinas, 2001d, p. 116). Important to remember in this regard is that ethics arises in the relation to the other and not straightaway by a reference to the universality of a law (p. 114). Policy should not be the beginning of any consideration of justice.

For some teachers, ontological categorization of young people as students is deemed necessary, justifiable, in order to enable preparation of young people for futures beyond schooling, where, in Levinas's terms, their status as infinite can perhaps gain more adequate expression. Such preparation is considered to be a principal purpose of schooling, an ideological purpose that prioritizes acquisition of knowledge, including skills, which can be utilized unproblematically in the future. Being-a-student is the ontological category designed for this knowledge and skill acquisition, with preparation, via knowing, used to justify the need for ontological categorization. And yet this justification, it can be argued, is not premised on the face to face relation. As a consequence, it does not offer a rupturing of totality and reveal the young person as infinite, but instead strengthens the "association of side by side, around something, around a common term and, more precisely, for Heidegger, around the truth" (Levinas, 1987, p. 41), the truth that is schooling. Dewey recognizes this problem with preparation and labels it "a treacherous idea" (1938, p. 47).

> In a certain sense every experience should do something to prepare a person for later experiences of a deeper and more expansive quality. That is the very meaning of growth, continuity, reconstruction of experience. But it is a mistake to suppose that the mere acquisition of a certain amount of arithmetic, geography, history, etc., which is taught and studied because it may be useful at some time in the future, has this effect. And it is a mistake to suppose that acquisition of skills in reading and figuring will automatically constitute preparation for their right and effective use under conditions very unlike those in which they were acquired. (Dewey, 1938, p. 47)

This version of education is not premised on the face to face. In this version of education, even morality is taught as knowledge and skill to be acquired as theory within the totality that is schooling, for the purpose of preparation. Consequently, this version of education does not engage the idea of the good beyond being, where questions of morality emerge from the face to face, but retains an emphasis on ontological categorization within an organizational totality. And while little goodness or kindness does persist in such circumstances, every attempt to organize the human fails, Levinas (1999, p. 107) maintains, channeling Grossman's narrative. In this way ontological categorization becomes an entrenched way of relating with others, to the extent that others are what they do, not who they are with infinite possibility.

Educating for the Good Beyond Being: Teaching from Infinity to Totality

Can education work against ontological categorization so that it is working against categorial murder? To do so, it is not simply a matter of preparing students for their post-school future via knowledge and skill acquisition, for this version of education is itself premised on ontological categorization. Instead, education must embrace the face to face, to acknowledge the other as infinite, beyond the totality in which they are encountered side by side as being-with. In this regard, Levinas describes the relation with the other, face to face, as one of "nonindifference" (2001b, p. 58). The double negation expressed in this word conveys responsibility for the other as neighbor, as one loved but still other. This is not indifference, but neither is it knowing someone by grasping or comprehending them. This face to face other is not someone specifically known, but someone unique and of infinite possibility, not only in the future, but here and now, in this relation, demanding "infinite responsibility" (1969, p. 244).

Levinas's sense of nonindifference is, interestingly, visible in Heidegger's account of being-with as a possible mode of concern or care. In his account of being-with in *Sein und Zeit*, Heidegger acknowledges that "Dasein initially and, for the most part, lives in the deficient modes of concern" which includes "passing-one-another-by" and "not-mattering-to-one-another"; and that such "modes of deficiency and indifference characterize the everyday and average being-with-one-another" (2010, p. 118). These are modes, expressions, of care, recalling that, for Heidegger, care is the totality of the structural whole of the constitution of being of Dasein. Care is not a particular act or disposition, but the being of Da-sein as fragmentary, unfinished, as described by Heidegger via his phenomenological analysis in division one of *Sein und Zeit*, but problematized via his analysis of death in division two.

Levinas is well aware of this "Section 26 of *Sein und Zeit*" that "isolates the modalities of … *being-with*" (2000, p. 212). He reflects that this section "concerns *others* whose mode of existence … is the mode of human being-there, sharing the same world," and which is "understood precisely in terms of work and around the instrumental order of those things of the world, and thus in which 'they are what they do'" (p. 212), occupationally.

Importantly, beyond the indifferent modes of being-with, Heidegger also identifies in this section "positive modes" (2010, p. 118) of concern or care that can characterize being-with. These positive modes are not indifferent to the other person, indeed in Levinas's lexicon these modes may be described as nonindifferent. Amongst these positive modes Heidegger recognizes two extreme possibilities. At one extreme are modes of concern that "can, so to speak, take the other's 'care' away from him and put itself in his place in taking care" (p. 118), and in this sense "can *leap in* for him" by taking over care, which for Heidegger means taking over that concrete expression of care as there-being by displacing it, and in effect replacing it with another concrete expression of care as there-being.

Heidegger mentioned "welfare work" (2010, p. 118) as an example of this positive mode of concern which takes away the other's care. Here the welfare worker takes over what the other does, thereby changing what and who they are, replacing their care with some other way of there-being, as someone dependent and perhaps dominated, even if not fully aware that this is happening.

In contrast, at the other extreme, Heidegger acknowledges a mode of positive concern, "which does not so much leap in for the other as *leap ahead* of him ..., not in order to take 'care' away from him, but rather to authentically give it back as such" (2010, p. 119). Heidegger describes this positive mode of concern as pertaining to "authentic care" which means "the existence of the other" as who, as Da-sein, "and not to a *what* which it takes care of" (p. 119). This leaping ahead of the other requires comprehending the there-being of the other in the future orientation of care Heidegger calls project. Project is a characterization of occupation – they are what they do – but with acknowledgement that "something is always still *outstanding* in Dasein"; "a *constant unfinished quality*"; a "lack of wholeness" (p. 227), which Heidegger describes as the unwholeness in Dasein. Da-sein, as unwhole whole, is the focus for leaping ahead of the other by working with the other's project, their care; this is not leaping in to displace the other's project and to replace it.

Heidegger's leaping ahead of the other as a positive mode of concern is close in meaning to Levinas's nonindifference. Yet Heidegger is describing a mode of concern as being-with, in totality, whereas Levinas is referring to the face to face relation, as infinity. Both, brought together, offer a bridge between totality and infinity which, significantly, can inform teaching. Being-with and the face to face are not separate from each other but are two forms of relation. One offers being, and the totality, the world, the truth, that circumscribes it; the other offers infinity, and the idea of the good beyond being affording morality.

In this regard, Levinas notes that "the relationship with the Other is not produced outside of the world, but puts in question the world possessed" (1969, p. 173). Leaping ahead of the other is a relation of nonindifference that puts in question the world possessed, the totality in which the face to face occurs. This is a breaching, a rupturing of totality, premised on the face to face, that reveals the other as infinite. And this infinity, reflected back into being, is the source of an infinity of possible totalities which the teacher can call on in the crafting of educational situations, units of work, thereby impacting ways of being. The teacher does not have to exist in an educational totality that ontologically categorizes the other as student. Instead, the teacher can, via the face to face, breach this totality and engage with the infinity accessible, to masterfully craft units of work, totalities, that enact moral judgment by drawing on the idea of the good.

Levinas teaches that teaching and learning are about more than truth, they are about morality, which can only be accessed by moving beyond being to the good. But this then requires a reflecting of the good back into being in order to change it, drawing on the infinity revealed in the face to face, an infinity of possible totalities. Therefore, as Levinas put it, "teaching is a way for truth [totality] to be produced such that it is not my work, such that I could not derive it from my own interiority" (1969, p. 295), instead requiring the face to face relation.

This is how education can be premised on the face to face relation, drawing on infinity to inform totality, bearing in mind the third party, and justice. Justice involves change, which is a form of violence, Levinas acknowledges, "but one cannot say that there is no legitimate violence" (2000, p. 106). Such violence may include changes in ontological categorization. And because there is always some element of ontological categorization in any totality, in any being-with, education should be organized to require continual questioning and experimenting with ways of being, enabling development of a more detailed and subtle ontological educational language, so as to contend with questions of morality, always informed by the idea of the good, desire for the good. In this way, education can work against ontological categorization. And by working more carefully ontologically in a moral sense, there is opportunity to work against categorial murder.

The death of others teaches that education should be about more than truth, it must be about morality, holding truths up to scrutiny via the idea of the good. The face to face relation is crucial to awareness of the responsibility required, responsibility demanding an ontological educational response. Such a response must impact the educational situation being experienced, which involves planning and teaching, not just for knowledge acquisition, but for being (Quay et al., 2022). Educating in this way acknowledges both infinity and totality through the creation of worlds that intentionally harness the unwholeness of Dasein in the continuing moral ontological project that is education.

REFERENCES

Bauman, Z. (2004). Categorial murder, or: How to remember the Holocaust. In R. Lentin (Ed.), *Re-presenting the Shoah for the 21st century* (pp. 25–39). Berghahn Books.

Bielefeld, U. (2002). Conversation with Janina Bauman and Zygmunt Bauman (D. Roberts, Trans.). *Thesis Eleven, 70*(1), 113–117. https://doi.org/10.1177/0725513602070001010

Cohen, R. A. (1994). *Elevations: The height of the good in Rosenzweig and Levinas.* The University of Chicago Press.

Dewey, J. (1938). *Experience and education.* Collier Books.

Grossman, V. (1985). *Zhizn I Sudha* [Life and Fate] (R. Chandler, Trans.). William Collins Sons & Co Ltd.

Heidegger, M. (1982). *The basic problems of phenomenology* (Rev ed., A. Hofstadter, Trans.). Indiana University Press.

Heidegger, M. (1996). *Being and time: A translation of* Sein und Zeit (J. Stambaugh, Trans.). State University of New York Press.

Heidegger, M. (2003). Seminar in Le Thor 1969. In *Four seminars* (A. Mitchell and F. Raffoul, Trans.) (pp. 35–63). Indiana University Press.

Heidegger, M. (2009a). *Basic concepts of Aristotelian philosophy* (R. D. Metcalf and M. B. Tanzer, Trans.). Indiana University Press.

Heidegger, M. (2009b). *Logic as the question concerning the essence of language* (W. Torres Gregory & Y. Unna, Trans.). State University of New York Press.

Heidegger, M. (2010). *Being and time* (Rev. ed., J. Stambaugh, Trans.). State University of New York Press.

Heidegger, M. (2014). *Hölderlin's hymns "Germania" and "The Rhine"* (W. McNeill & J. Ireland, Trans.). Indiana University Press.

Heidegger, M. (2016). *Ponderings II–VI: Black Notebooks 1931–1938* (R. Rojcewicz, Trans.). Indiana University Press.

Heidegger, M. (2017). *Ponderings XII–XV: Black Notebooks 1939–1941* (R. Rojcewicz, Trans.). Indiana University Press.

Katsiyannis, A., Whitford, D. K., & Ennis, R. P. (2018). Historical examination of United States intentional mass school shootings in the 20th and 21st centuries: Implications for students, schools, and society. *Journal of Child and Family Studies, 27*(8), 2562–2573.

Levinas, E. (1969). *Totality and infinity: An essay on exteriority* (A. Lingis, Trans.). Duquesne University Press.

Levinas, E. (1978). *Existence and existents* (A. Lingis, Trans.). Duquesne University Press.

Levinas, E. (1978). *Otherwise than being or beyond essence* (A. Lingis, Trans.). Duquesne University Press.

Levinas, E. (1985). *Ethics and infinity: Conversations with Philippe Nemo* (R. A. Cohen, Trans.). Duquesne University Press.

Levinas, E. (1987). *Time and the other* (R. A. Cohen, Trans.). Duquesne University Press.

Levinas, E. (1989). *As if consenting to horror* (P. Wissing, Trans.). *Critical Inquiry, 15*(2), 485–488.

Levinas, E. (1990). *Difficult freedom: Essays on Judaism* (S. Hand, Trans.). The Johns Hopkins University Press.

Levinas, E. (1996). Martin Heidegger and ontology (Committee of Public Safety, Trans.). *Diacritics, 26*(1), 11–32.

Levinas, E. (1998). *Of God who comes to mind* (B. Bergo, Trans.). Stanford University Press.

Levinas, E. (1999). *Alterity and transcendence* (B. Smith, Trans.). The Athlone Press.
Levinas, E. (2000). *Entre nous: On thinking-of-the-other* (M. B. Smith & B. Harshav, Trans.). Columbia University Press.
Levinas, E. (2001a). Interview with Myriam Anissimov (J. Robbins & T. Loebel, Trans.). In J. Robbins (Ed.), *Is it righteous to be? Interviews with Emmanuel Levinas* (pp. 84–92). Stanford University Press.
Levinas, E. (2001b). Interview with François Poirié (J. Robbins & M. Coelen with T. Loebel, Trans.). In J. Robbins (Ed.), *Is it righteous to be? Interviews with Emmanuel Levinas* (pp. 23–83). Stanford University Press.
Levinas, E. (2001c). Being toward death and "thou shalt not kill" (A. Schmitz, Trans.). In J. Robbins (Ed.), *Is it righteous to be? Interviews with Emmanuel Levinas* (pp. 130–139). Stanford University Press.
Levinas, E. (2001d). Being-for-the-other (J. Robbins, Trans.). In J. Robbins (Ed.), *Is it righteous to be? Interviews with Emmanuel Levinas* (pp. 114–120). Stanford University Press.
Levinas, E. (2003). *On escape* (B. Bergo, Trans.). Stanford University Press.
Quay, J. (2013). *Education, experience and existence: Engaging Dewey, Peirce and Heidegger*. Routledge.
Quay, J. (2015). *Understanding life in school: From academic classroom to outdoor education*. Palgrave Macmillan.
Quay, J., Miller, L., Browning, D., & Brodie-McKenzie, A. (2022). Dewey's education through occupations as being-doing-knowing: An introduction to teacher planning with creative learning units. *Journal of Curriculum Studies, 54*(5), 632–646. https://doi.org/10.1080/00220272.2022.2070716
Robbins, J. (Ed.). (2001). *Is it righteous to be? Interviews with Emmanuel Levinas*. Stanford University Press.

COMPLICATED

A BOOK SERIES OF CURRICULUM STUDIES

Reframing the curricular challenge educators face after a decade of school deform, the books published in Peter Lang's Complicated Conversation Series testify to the ethical demands of our time, our place, our profession. What does it mean for us to teach now, in an era structured by political polarization, economic destabilization, and the prospect of climate catastrophe? Each of the books in the Complicated Conversation Series provides provocative paths, theoretical and practical, to a very different future. In this resounding series of scholarly and pedagogical interventions into the nightmare that is the present, we hear once again the sound of silence breaking, supporting us to rearticulate our pedagogical convictions in this time of terrorism, reframing curriculum as committed to the complicated conversation that is intercultural communication, self-understanding, and global justice.

The series editor is

>Dr. William F. Pinar
>Department of Curriculum Studies
>2125 Main Mall
>Faculty of Education
>University of British Columbia
>Vancouver, British Columbia V6T 1Z4
>CANADA

To order other books in this series, please contact our Customer Service Department:

>peterlang@presswarehouse.com (within the U.S.)
>orders@peterlang.com (outside the U.S.)

Or browse online by series:

>www.peterlang.com

www.ingramcontent.com/pod-product-compliance
Ingram Content Group UK Ltd.
Pitfield, Milton Keynes, MK11 3LW, UK
UKHW021849210426
5322IPUK00022B/557